John Hazlitt, William Carew Hazlitt

Four Generations of a Literary Family - the Hazlitts in England, Ireland, and America

Vol. II

John Hazlitt, William Carew Hazlitt

Four Generations of a Literary Family - the Hazlitts in England, Ireland, and America
Vol. II

ISBN/EAN: 9783337267599

Printed in Europe, USA, Canada, Australia, Japan

Cover: Foto ©ninafisch / pixelio.de

More available books at **www.hansebooks.com**

John Hazlitt.

FOUR GENERATIONS OF A
LITERARY FAMILY

*THE HAZLITTS IN ENGLAND, IRELAND, AND
AMERICA*

THEIR FRIENDS AND THEIR FORTUNES

1725—1896

BY

W. CAREW HAZLITT

*WITH PORTRAITS REPRODUCED FROM MINIATURES BY
JOHN HAZLITT*

IN TWO VOLUMES
VOL. II.

LONDON AND NEW YORK
GEORGE REDWAY
1897

GENERATIONS OF A LITERARY FAMILY

THE THIRD GENERATION

(CONTINUED)

CHAPTER V.

The Court of Bankruptcy—My father's legal experiences and friends—Baron Grant—Vice-Chancellor Bacon—Mr. Commissioner Goulburn—Hazlitt Road, West Kensington—Lord Kenyon—Lord Brougham—Lord Chancellor Westbury—Lord Coleridge—Mr. Justice Hawkins—Serjeant Wilkins—Street and the Law Courts—Baxter and the Tichborne case—Sir Charles Lewis, M.P.—Illiteracy of lawyers—My father and George Henry Lewes—John Payne Collier—The Second Shakespear Folio.

WHEN my father first went to the Court of Bankruptcy in 1854, his knowledge of his work was, I fear, very rudimentary. But by application and through a receptive mind he gradually became one of the most efficient officers in the building. Of his successor I hear on all sides a very poor account. His Honour seems, so far, to know as little as my father did, and to be unable or unwilling to learn.

The late Chief Registrar, when I spoke to him of the editor and proprietor of a society paper now departed, mentioning his apparently flourishing state, observed that he thought the time had come for him to pay his creditors the remaining 19s. 6d. in the pound.

My father has ere now consulted the present writer on cases before him, and he occasionally instanced remarkable courage on the part of solicitors in the direction of charges. I remember that he reduced one claim from £192 to £12, and then deemed the amount allowed to the honest practitioner too high. He had a good deal of trouble with some eminent firms, whose representatives came to the Court with an equally imperfect knowledge of their business and of the law. Baron Grant, while he was still in evidence, called at the Court, and laid before the Registrar, in connection with some pending arrangement, securities valued by him at £200,000. My father had to signify to the Baron that commercially they were worth precisely nothing.

Vice-Chancellor Bacon was of a very placid *laisser aller* temperament, and seldom allowed himself to be perturbed by any untoward incident or turn. He more than once said to my father, when the latter seemed excited about some case before the Court :

Point de zèle, my dear fellow—point de zèle.'

At the time that Mr. Kay, afterward judge, practised before Bacon, it used to be said that the latter spelled *equity* with a *k* because he was ruled by the counsel's views, and so long as suitors might choose the V.C. before whom they would appear, the plan in a doubtful case was to retain Kay, and have the matter tried by Bacon.

I could never exactly understand why Bacon was promoted to the Bench. He certainly disappointed the expectations which had been formed of him while he wore silk, and no man's judgments were more frequently reversed on appeal. To succeed in the discharge of judicial functions, as in other things, demands unwearied industry, even though one possess greater talent than Bacon had; but I do not think that Bacon was what the copy-books call *appliqué*—he took matters too easily, as the anecdote which I have given above may imply.

My father had a much wider experience of practice in bankruptcy, and would have been better qualified than either Bacon or Cave for the place of Chief Judge. His decisions, when he has sat vicariously on the Bench, have been almost invariably upheld; but

> 'Non cuivis homini contingit adire Corinthum.'

I suppose that there never was a man so extravagantly estimated as Bacon.

It is not generally known that one of the two persons to whom the Turk appeals in the cartoon in

Punch, July 31, 1880, is my father—the other, of course, is Gladstone.

I was talking to my father at the Bankruptcy Court about some one whom we both thought to be not overwise. 'Well,' said Mr. Registrar dryly, 'he *was* a fool, and as much of a rogue with it *as his incapacity would permit.*'

The Registrar, on his way home by train from the Court to Richmond, observed that one of his fellow-passengers had let something in her hand drop, and he said to the fellow with her : 'I think the young woman has let her parcel fall.' The party referred to looked daggers, but made no remark till she left the carriage just after, and, turning to the venerable Registrar, relieved her pent-up resentment by the crushing retort, delivered with an immense air : 'Thank you, young man.'

Mr. Commissioner Goulburn, who had been a Cornet in the army, in answer to some one who had asked him if he was not once a Welsh judge, said : 'Yes ; I was one with an understanding '—meaning, on certain conditions. 'Oh,' returned his friend, 'I never heard before of a Welsh judge who possessed such a thing.'

Goulburn told my father, when the law permitting personal petitions in bankruptcy was passed, that he knew a Cornet Goulburn who would have been very glad of such a facility.

Though I think that I have seen the same joke related of some one else, I perfectly remember, when Goulburn once fell on his head out of his carriage on the pavement, an inquiry was made as to the damage done to the latter.

It was Mr. Commissioner Fonblanque, of the Bankruptcy Court, who, when a suitable motto for the Serjeants' rings was mooted, suggested *Scilicet*.

When Hazlitt Road, West Kensington, was so christened, some one asked the builder why he gave it that name, and whether it was after the author of *Table-Talk* (Maclise Road being immediately adjacent). 'Oh no!' he replied; 'after dear old Mr. Registrar Hazlitt!' That gentleman, perhaps, in his official capacity had let him off more easily than he expected or deserved.

Lord Kenyon spoke of Julian the Apostate as Julian the Apostle. But perhaps one appellation is as sensible and fit as the other. The Emperor provoked the enmity of the clergy or priesthood by his advanced opinions, and since the Church formerly influenced so much the making of history, all who incurred its displeasure have naturally come down to us with tarnished characters.

Of the old school of lawyers Brougham was perhaps the last, if he was not the greatest. He was a man of varied attainments, and spared no labour to render himself conversant with every subject which happened to be coming before him as a judge or as a legislator, and which he had not studied, no matter how mean or trivial it might appear. He did not account it sufficient for a lawyer to be read only in the statute-book, the rules of the turf, the daily paper, and Joe Miller, or deem that the demands of culture were satisfied by the possession of a library. He was my father's steadfast friend, and the intimate associate from college days of my great-uncle Stoddart.

Brougham's physical constitution was as perfect a marvel as his intellectual activity and versatility. His power of endurance must have been enormous, and he was far from abstemious in any sense. The fatigue and strain which, in his earlier professional career he constantly bore, would have killed nine men out of ten. Port and brandy, of which he so freely partook, instead of impairing his energy, served as invigorating and recuperative stimulants.

The great Chancellor was apparently led by the coincidence of the name to make his country seat

(Brougham Hall) near the ancient castle in Westmoreland where Queen Elizabeth stayed and was entertained in one of her numerous progresses.

Lord Chancellor Westbury once took part in a discussion on eternal punishment, of which he repudiated the existence, and, lawyer-like, he wound up his argument by saying : ' Hell is dismissed with costs !'

Westbury was remarkable for preserving the old pronunciation of certain words, such as *whole*, *hot*, which he pronounced *wole*, *wot*. When Mr. Registrar Hazlitt was at work with him on the Bankruptcy Bill, 1869, he once said to him : ' I am sick, Hazlitt, of the wole business.'

His lordship, like many other great men, had his foibles, and one of them was in the shape of an Italian Countess, whom he scandalized some of his guests at Hackwood Hall by placing at the head of his table. Yet he was not wanting in polite attentions to his wife, whose parcels, and even bonnet-boxes, he would often be seen carrying home. Many a time he borrowed sixpence of some one at hand to pay for his omnibus.

A bookseller assured me that he had been commissioned to make the catalogue of the late Lord Coleridge's private library, but that, owing to certain circumstances, the business was a rather delicate one. I believe that this was a thorough fiction, for Coleridge's books were sold in the ordinary way by Sotheby and Co., and the person who was employed by the auctioneers to go to the house to look at the collection informed me that he discovered no trace of anything of the sort beyond the presence of such generally recognised works as the *Arabian Nights* or Payne's version of Boccaccio.

As Lamb's friend and correspondent, Alsop, very truly pointed out, the man to whom his family owed any distinction which they acquired was neglected by them, and the anticlimax was reached in a noble and learned lord, who inherited the name and nothing else.

Mr. Justice Hawkins, whose partiality for the turf is very well known, had once a horse case before him. There had been some betting on a horse for the Derby, and at the last moment the animal was scratched. His lordship interrupted the speech of the learned counsel in order to inquire what he meant by *scratched*. 'My lord,' said the counsel, looking very significantly at Hawkins, 'I am not exactly in a position to tell your lordship off-hand, but I will consult'—eyeing the Bench all the time—'a very high judicial authority, and shall be prepared to give your lordship the information to-morrow morning.'

Serjeant Wilkins, who died in poverty, commenced his professional career at Liverpool, but afterward removed his practice to Durham. His first case there was the defence of a young woman committed for the murder of her illegitimate child, and it brought him at once into notoriety. When the case for the Crown had closed, leaving no doubt of the prisoner's guilt. Wilkins rose, looked at the judge, then at the prisoner, then at the jury. Then he seemed to be collecting himself; but a second and third time he did the same thing. The Court was in a state of astonishment; but after the third repetition Wilkins left his place, went up to the dock, tore off a piece from the wretched tatters in which the girl was dressed, and, holding it up, cried: 'This was the cause of all! Now, gentlemen, I consent to a verdict of Guilty.' The prisoner was convicted, but her sentence was commuted—at a time when commutations were less usual. At the next sessions thirty briefs awaited Wilkins.

Street, who took the superintendence and drew the plans of the new Courts of Justice in London, had travelled a good deal abroad, including Italy, and had seen many public buildings everywhere, erected at intervals piecemeal from pecuniary or other exigencies in various tastes or schools of architecture. He had the opportunity, with the fine area cleared for the purpose, of placing on the site a grand homogeneous structure there was no pretence for irregularity of design—and what did he do? He did just as a Chinese tailor would do, if you gave him a pair of breeches with a patch in them as a pattern. It was certainly a deplorable muddle, yet characteristic enough, no doubt, of all similar arrangements in this country. There was no adequate provision for light, air, or hearing, and solid mahogany doors had to be unhinged, that the panels might be cut out and glass squares substituted, when it was found by this person of genius that staircases or corridors were in almost complete darkness at mid-day.

Baxter, of the great firm of solicitors, Baxter, Rose and Norton, in Great Queen Street, Westminster, afterward in Victoria Street, was an Evangelical preacher, and used to go down to Aldershot to deliver discourses to the soldiers. This procured him the name of *Holy* Baxter. The business of his firm was at one time extraordinarily great; they had 130 clerks in 32 rooms. It might be said of them, as Horace does of Rome:

'Suis et ipsa Roma viribus ruit.'

Baxter himself was not considered a first-rate man of business; but he was an excellent lawyer, and much consulted in railway cases. He carried about an inch of pencil, and often amended a clause in a Bill by adding a few words, as when he outwitted Sir James Allport, of the Midland, in the 'running' question with the Wolverhampton and Walsall, by inserting the words 'and account,' which precluded the Midland from evading the liability to pay under certain contingencies.

The misfortune of Baxter was his support of the Tichborne Claimant; it led to a reconstruction of the firm, and he died a poor man. I have been told that there was little doubt as to the relationship of Orton to the family, and that the Colonel of the regiment to which Tichborne had belonged recognised the Claimant as the same man who had served under him, when he happened to see him coming out of Court, and mentioned the matter to Baxter casually, without knowing that the latter was concerned in the defence.

A late well-known jeweller in Richmond, Surrey, was saying that, while he was engaged in breaking up sovereigns for his professional purposes, Mr. Arnold, the police magistrate, came into the shop, and asked him what he was doing. He answered that he hoped he was doing no harm, but did not like being challenged by such an authority. There seems, however, no objection to utilizing the currency for jewellery, so long as it is not defaced and passed into other hands. You may destroy it, but you must not tamper with it.

In a case at a London police court, where two Jews were parties, the magistrate asked one of them whether he called himself *Montagu*. He replied in the affirmative. He asked him again if it had always been his name, and he said that he believed so. 'Had it ever been Moses?' 'Well, yes ; but Moses and Montagu were the same.' 'Oh, then,' said the magistrate, 'I suppose that the Moses in the Bible was also known as Montagu.' The race being so ancient, and its prospective advantages so exceptional, it seems strange that so many Jews should be anxious to disguise their nationality and nomenclature. The late Mr. Hyman Montagu, the numismatist, married a Miss Moses, who became Mrs. Montagu ; but she ought by right to have kept her maiden name. Montagu did not desire to pass as a Jew, but it was relevantly to him that some one expressed to me his regret that the extinction of the Hebrews had not been accomplished by King John.

My father told me the following anecdote about

Sir Charles Lewis, M.P. Lewis had had his full-length portrait presented to him by his constituents just before some one called to see him. 'I have something to shew you,' said Lewis, and took the other into the room where the likeness had been placed. 'What do you think of it?' he asked. 'Very good indeed,' replied the friend, 'except that the artist has painted you with your hands in your own pockets.'

A curious circumstance happened to an intimate friend. Several thousand pounds, which he had been entitled to expect, were left elsewhere, owing to offence taken by the lady-relative who had the money at her disposition. He came behind her chair at dinner one day as a boy, and pulled her cap or her wig. At the death of the party to whom she bequeathed it, he willed it away with other property, but this money could only pass by deed; my friend brought his action, and recovered it. I observed to him that in this instance the *will* was not as good as the *deed*.

A man, who had bought land at Brockley in Kent, when it was cheap, and boundaries were occasionally obscure, used to classify his property jocularly among his intimates as freehold, leasehold, and *catchhold*.

The general illiteracy of the legal profession is tolerably well known to such as have mixed in that kind of society, or even have taken the trouble to study the Law Reports in the daily press. The explanation is that lawyers are specialists, and have no leisure to devote to topics outside their vocation. Of the two, barristers are perhaps more open to this charge than solicitors; yet there is little enough to choose between them. An eminent Q.C., speaking on this subject to my father, observed that he was not at all so well versed as he could have desired in points of general culture, but that most men at the Bar were utterly ignorant of languages, even of Latin and French, and of literary history. Another learned counsel mentioned to myself his intention of writing a *monogram* on a subject in which he happened to feel an interest.

It is a painful business if you have to go into Court on any matter pertaining to literary copyright. It is vast odds if the judge, the counsel, and the solicitors are not absolute blanks, unless they have very greatly improved since I committed my father to an action in respect to his edition of Montaigne. I was never more frightened in my whole life, for it was not more than a sum of £10 that was at issue. I worked hard, however, to protect my father's pocket, and the result was that the defendant had to pay about £300 in costs on both sides. If the suit had concerned the Turf, the Stock Exchange, or the Prize Ring, there would have been less difficulty.

But the Lord Chief Baron Pollock was an honourable exception to the prevailing rule. He was a person of cultivated taste, and liked to gather round him men of letters and artists. Thackeray used to visit at the house. The Chief Baron expressed in a letter of 1868 to his friend Dr. Diamond, of Twickenham, a warm admiration of my grandfather, and he stated there that he always kept Hazlitt's volumes near him.

The late Lord Chief Justice Coleridge and Mr. Justice Day belong to the roll of book-collectors.

The last time that my father saw George Henry Lewes, husband of George Eliot (Miss Mary Evans), he was standing, like Collier, at Charing Cross, and presented a singular appearance, being dressed from top to toe in white, and the only thing about him that was not white was his red hair and beard.

There is always in printing even unpublished matter of comparatively modern date a feeling of uncertainty and indecision as to the wisdom of the proceeding. A letter which has the sanction of age does not require such high testimonials as one of perhaps superior interest, of which the subject-matter bears on persons either still among us or recently added to the appurtenances of the past. I hold a large number of notes, many curious in their way, from Leigh Hunt, Douglas Jerrold, William Jerdan, Bulwer, the Procters, Dickens, Harrison Ainsworth, Laman Blanchard, and others, on which the crust, I take it, will have to accumulate somewhat before they become publisher's game.

There are here and there a few which may possess a special interest, or which, though of recent origin, treat of questions which have acquired a tincture of historical character, and I may not be blamed for citing them in evidence, if I do not transcribe them at length.

But there is in my collection, independently of all these, a large assortment of communications on literary topics from several of my own more particular correspondents — Payne Collier, Halliwell-Phillipps, and so on — which must certainly await the time when they may have gained a sort of classic nosegay, and be read by some forthcoming generation in a longer perspective.

Some of these epistolary remains owe their

interest to bygone days, and incidentally illustrate points of biography and literature already beginning, like wine of the fifth year, to acquire a tone and a bouquet. I could fill volumes with such things; but let me select from a bundle of about sixty two or three letters from John Payne Collier, whose father was acquainted with the Lamb circle, and who was for some time a colleague of Hazlitt on the *Morning Chronicle*. The first and second are addressed to my father; the former was written in consequence of the scandal arising from the alleged Shakespear fabrications.

Collier often joined Hazlitt in his box at the theatre, and would ask his opinion about the piece in course of performance—what he thought of this or of that—and 'then the next morning,' said my grandfather, 'what I had told him appeared in the newspaper as his.' Peter Patmore did much the same thing.

Riverside,
Maidenhead,
March 22, 1860.

MY DEAR HAZLITT,

I am especially gratified by your note, because it so happens that you seem almost the only one of my old co-mates who remember me with any feeling of regard. I do not say that you are the only one, because there is one other who has expressed somewhat similar sentiments regarding me. You know that while you and I were fellow labourers in the same not very profitable, nor very agreeable field, if I did not do my best to make every man my friend, I did nothing to render any man my enemy. Yet I hear that the great body of those who were similarly employed are now, for some reason or other, opposed to me, and take pleasure in forwarding the views of my adversaries by such means as happen to be in their power.

This is rather hard upon a man who all his life exerted himself, as far as he could, to advance and elevate the position of journalists. God knows that I never was, and certainly am not now, in a position to excite the envy of my contemporaries.

Therefore I thank you the more heartily for coming forward in the unsolicited way you have done.

The discovery of that corrected folio, 1632, is to be made the bane of the latter part of my life, if my enemies can accomplish it.

I know that you have got on, and are getting on well, and I am most rejoiced at it. I trust, too, that all about you are prosperous and happy.

I am, as I have always been,
Yours most sincerely,
J. PAYNE COLLIER.

William Hazlitt, Esq.

What the true history of the Shakespear emendations in the folio of 1632 was and is, and whence they were derived. I am far from pretending to know. But Collier, like the majority of our commentators on old English literature, was essentially a dull man ; and it is incontestable that, while nearly all the proposed improvements were too clever for him to have originated, some of them were such as only an ear-witness could have handed down. My father was always of opinion that, whoever inserted the manuscript matter in the Devonshire second folio, it was not Collier, and I quoted to him in support of such a view that splendid correction of the passage where Mrs. Quickly narrates the end of Falstaff.

I am bound to confess that whenever I applied to Collier for information on literary facts within his presumed knowledge, I always found him anxious to parry inquiry. He usually sent evasive answers to my not unreasonable call for fuller particulars about a book or a statement, for which he was perhaps the sole authority.

In the second (1865), also to my father, the writer, after entering into some matters of unimportant detail, goes on to refer to his literary amusements, his personal affairs, and his mode of life.

This trifling diverts my old age (I am nearly 77), and keeps me from being devoured by ennui and selfishness. Men who have no employment at my time of life think a great deal too much about themselves.

You are prosperous, and your family, I am rejoiced to hear, sufficiently so. They say that it is bad for a family to be too well provided for. I should like to try the experiment, as I told the late Duke of Devonshire, when he asserted that I was richer and happier than he.

Both my sons and one of my daughters are married, and the two first have large families.

What a time it is since we met or rather parted - at Charing

Cross, when you told me that you hoped to obtain some office. You have a good one, and deserve it. I have none, and deserve none. I might have been a Police Magistrate or a Colonial Judge, but I refused the first, and my late wife would not let me take the last. She would rather have lived upon £300 a year here, than upon £3,000 a year in Ceylon or the West Indies. Now 3 or 400 a year is the extent of my income; but I live by the riverside in a charming part of the country, and my daughter keeps my house—never sparingly, but always economically.

I declare that I am writing almost as badly as you or your son Carew. The fact is that my old hand is rheumatic.

Good-bye. Health and happiness to you and yours!

The concluding specimen to myself was a reply to an application for assistance in the preparation of the *Memoirs*, and is dated June 2, 1867. The interesting portion, after all, is that which immediately concerns Hazlitt:

'The only remembrance I have of your Grandfather is the note-book I mentioned to you, and which he gave me. You will not be surprised, therefore, at my unwillingness to part with it. If I had any other relic, it should be yours. He was not in the habit of writing to me, and we, of course, often met at the *M[orning] C[hronicle]* Office and at the Fives Court, where I was fond of seeing him play. He was famous for what was called Volley.'

The manuscript volume here mentioned has been already described by me in the *Memoirs* as the one which was among Collier's books, and as containing the transcript of Coleridge's *Christabel*.

CHAPTER VI.

The Club founded by Jerrold and his friends—Its distinguished members and guests—Thackeray—The melodists and other entertainers—Charles Dickens the younger, my father, Holl, and Dillon Croker—Hazlitt's Wiltshire songs—'The Wiltshire Convict's Farewell'—A general favourite—Anecdotes of Jerrold—Sir B. W. Richardson—Dr. Diamond—Farther glimpses of John Hazlitt the painter—Sundays at Twickenham House—Account of the house, its contents and its visitors—Sir Frederick Pollock—Hepworth Dixon—Dr. Doran—The *Fasti* of Our Club—'Shakespear at Our Club,' 1860—Evans's.

BETWEEN forty and fifty years ago Douglas Jerrold and a few friends established a social club called the *Hooks and Eyes.* I believe that the number was very limited at first, but it was at all events made up to forty, when the name was changed to the *Forty Thieves.* The final nomenclature, *Our Club,* was adopted in or prior to 1860. My father was an original member, either a *Hook* or an *Eye.* He became in due course one of the Forty, and he continued with the set when it was rebaptized for the third time. One by one all have passed away.

During a long series of seasons a good evening might be fairly counted upon. Jerrold himself, his son Blanchard Jerrold, Shirley Brooks, the younger Dickens, Dillon Croker, Henry Holl, Dr. Diamond, Dr. Richardson, F. W. Cosens, Sir George Jessel, Charles Knight, Hepworth Dixon, Professor Masson, Joseph Durham and Richard Woolner the sculptors, Robert Keeley, Dr. Doran, my father, and others —all these I have seen round the dinner - table together or in succession, and besides the roll of members there were the guests, as each fellow had the privilege of introducing one or more friends.

I remember that Horace Mayhew once brought Thackeray. They came after dinner, and I recollect Thackeray's commanding figure as he entered the door. It was the only time I ever saw him. He paused on the threshold in a hesitating manner, as if uncertain of his reception, and his introducer had almost to push him forward.

The younger Dickens, my father, Holl, and Croker were the mainstay of the institution in one respect, for each of them, if present, was expected to favour the company with a song or recitation. Dickens generally sang 'Tom Bowling.' Holl and Croker furnished recollections of the old and living actors. Hazlitt contributed one of his West-Country songs. There was a fair gathering, as a rule, of men of mark and likelihood, and some good talk passed.

Chappell, in his *Popular Music of the Olden Time*, has printed one of Hazlitt's Wiltshire ditties, which I have so often heard my father give with all the gusto and raciness of the local twang, to the infinite enjoyment of the audience, and here is the remaining production from a copy in Mr. Registrar's autograph :

THE WILTSHIRE CONVICT'S FAREWELL.

Come, all you young fellaws, wherever that you be ;
Come, all you young m'idens, j'in choruus with me ;
'Tis of ten stout young fellaws as was tried the other d'y ;
And they are bound doon for Woolwich to set s'il for Botany B'y.
   With a right fol de riddle, fol de ray.

Then we went from the D'vizes bound doon in iron so strong ;
From D'vizes unto Fisherton they march'd us all along ;
As I was passing by I heard the people s'y :
'What a pity such foine fellaws should be gaain' to Botany B'y!'
   With a right fol, etc.

Then in comes the j'iler about six o'clock ;
Then in comes the j'iler our doors to unlock,
Saying : 'Come, my lads, make ready, for ye must haste aw'y,
For you're boun' doon for Woolwich to set s'il for Botany B'y.'
   With a right fol, etc.

Then in comes pretty Sally, with ten guineas in her han',
Saying: 'Take this, my laddies, I've brought ye all I can.'
So fill us up a glass, I will drink my love's adieu ;
'Tis ten thousan' to one I ever more sees you.
With a right fol, etc.

And when we gets to Botany B'y some letters we will write,
Unto our loving sweethearts and pretty girls in white ;
So kind heaven now protect us for ever and a d'y,
And God send every Wiltshire lad safe home fro' Botany B'y !'
With a right fol, etc.

This effusion was a wonderful favourite, and was invariably encored, a circumstance which made the singer a less frequent visitor of late years, as a call for Hazlitt was as much a part of the evening as the dinner itself. The Lord Chief Baron Pollock, whom I have already introduced, was greatly delighted with the performance when he heard it.

My father not only possessed a voice, which with proper training might have proved a fine one, but was a highly proficient whistler, and would accompany himself or another to the piano. He carried what is generally a nuisance to a pleasing accomplishment, as those who have heard him might testify. During the best years of his life, and chiefly in Brompton and Chelsea days, he was much in request at musical soirées. He once laboured under a not uncommon form of delicate embarrassment, in going in morning dress, and told me that he kept himself intrenched behind the piano to conceal the incorrectness of his nether habiliments.

It was an inexorable ordinance of the club that invited guests should, in response to the toast of their health, which was equally peremptory, deliver an oration. But if there was more than a single stranger, one spoke for the rest, whereas at the Noviomagian gatherings each individual had to rise in turn—a refinement of cruelty.

Professor Bain, of Aberdeen, told me, when I once met him out at dinner, two or three anecdotes of Jerrold which I had not heard before.

Jerrold was dining at some place where a salad was put on the table. Some one observed that it was unusually gritty. Jerrold calls the waiter, and says: 'What's this?' 'Salad, sir.' 'No,' says Jerrold, 'it's a gravel walk with a good many weeds in it.'

He was at a lecture on the races of men, and specimens of the various types were exhibited. When the Caucasian type was shown, 'Ah,' he says, 'that's the type I would go to press with.'

This reminded me of the story of the girl in an omnibus on a very cold day, who observed to a fellow-passenger that it was fine embracing weather.

In reference to a literary man, who was supposed to be dead, but who, though of great age, proved to be still extant, Jerrold said : ' He may be ever green, but he is never *red*.'

Holl and Croker, of whom the latter was never, I believe, a member, were excellent mimics. I used to prefer Holl. His impersonations of some of the characters of O'Smith, Keeley, Macready, Fechter, Charles Kean, Buckstone, and Webster were capital. He was always ready, when he was in fair cue, to favour us with a specimen at his own house *in camerâ*. My old friend, Henry James Byron, was also a very clever hand at hitting off Buckstone and other artists of his own day ; but some of those whom Holl had known were before his time.

One of the standard pleasantries at Our Club was at the expense of Dr. (now Sir B. W.) Richardson, an extremely pleasant and popular member, but a prominent advocate of teetotalism. A noble lord having bequeathed his fine cellar of wines to Richardson, the latter found himself in possession of a white elephant of very unusual dimensions. Of course, the doctor could not dream of drinking the wine himself, still less of offering it to his friends. Nor could he sell it, nor could he present it to a public institution. What would he do? One suggestion was that he should run it down the sewer, where it would destroy the rats; but this was deliberate cruelty to animals, and the doctor was a kind-hearted man. The liquor was ultimately wasted, I believe.

Dr. Diamond, of Our Club, and Dr. Powell, were the two earliest amateur photographers in England. The latter dined with my father at Brompton when he was last in England on a visit from the Mauritius. He had become acquainted there with the only son of John Hazlitt the miniature-painter, who, after settling at Demerara, removed to Mauritius, and died there. He possessed a few miniatures executed by his father, but I never heard what became of them. He had at one time accumulated a tolerable fortune, and lived to lose it, to make a second, and lose a great part of that, too, in a commercial paper. We corresponded together during many years, and his letters to me contain many interesting particulars relating to the island. He once forwarded to me some representations as to political parties there, with the desire that I should get them printed. I submitted them (unread, I confess) to an editor, who returned them with the observation that their appearance in his columns would have probably involved the paper in several lawsuits.

The Sundays at Twickenham House, while Diamond resided there, and so long as the establishment and its excellent host were in their palmier state, were remarkably enjoyable and instructive. The circle which collected round the Doctor during several years included a long catalogue of names illustrious in letters and art. Some of the same set which assembled at Our Club and at the Noviomagians formed also the habitual visitors at Twickenham, where there was a free entrée and a hearty welcome for every recognised comer. Three o'clock was the dinner-hour.

The house was filled with valuable curiosities of every description; but the speciality of Diamond was old china, about which his knowledge and fund of anecdote were inexhaustible. The room in which we all dined resembled a crockery shop : every available nook and corner was filled ; the cases were two or three deep, and the drawers of the cabinets, if opened, disclosed treasures which the owner himself had almost forgotten, but of which he soon recalled every particular—the place and date of purchase, the name and personal history of the former owner, and the circumstances under which he had secured this teapot or that jar.

It was not an unfrequent observation on his part

that his friend Lord Willoughby d'Eresby, who was
a connoisseur of old china, considered no thorough
judge ought to require to see the potter's mark, but
should be able to pronounce what the piece was
from the texture and the paste.

The Doctor had also a few coins, a few prints, and
a few books, and latterly he was bitten by the rat-
tailed spoon and Queen Anne plate crazes. I
remember him when he was extraordinarily tenacious
of his acquisitions, and would not have listened to
any proposal to part with his specimens. One day
he shewed me a very fine old Vincennes saucer, to
which I had the cup; but his piece was badly
broken, and I should not have valued it, yet
he anticipated me by saying that he never let
anything leave his hands.

Toward the end, however, his feeling in this
respect underwent a great change, and many of the
beautiful old bits of plate and other rarities mysteri-
ously disappeared; and the house with its circular
drawing - room, once the residence of Sir John
Hawkins, and the grounds, and our kind-hearted
entertainer, and nearly all who once met under that
hospitable roof, have disappeared, too. There was
an atmosphere enveloping the whole spot, and
seeming to raise it out of the dead level of common-

place every-day life; and of good fare there was no stint, nor of good talk.

May I be pardoned for perpetuating so trivial a trait as the way the good Doctor had, on a Sunday in spring or in summer, in the garden, of finding a worm, placing it on the open palm of one hand, and whistling, when a robin appeared, and, after circumspectly reconnoitring for a few moments, alighted on Diamond's hand, seized its prey, and flew off to a more convenient place for its meal. Our host used to relate that it was his practice to patronize the Maid of Honour shop at Richmond for his cheesecakes; but he had them made at home after detecting a hair of a maid in one of those acquired by purchase. A very similar confection was formerly, and may be yet, made at an old-fashioned depôt at Wokingham in Berkshire. The Doctor had an eccentric lady patient, who once engaged with him in a theological discussion on the teaching of St. Paul the Apostle. He entered a little into the views and doctrines of the latter on a certain point; but his listener interrupted him by observing: 'Ah, yes, I am aware of it; but that's just where Paul and I differ.'

Diamond unquestionably carried away with him much curious and unique information about those matters which interested him, and it was hard to say what had not done so at some period or other of his active and observant life. On china, books, engravings, birds' eggs, stuffed birds, medals, and coins, he could discourse largely and learnedly, and in conversation on any of these topics, he was peculiarly *supplemental*. He generally knew all that you did and a little more. If you mentioned a man who was tolerably in years in your youth, and narrated some trait of him, the Doctor would be very apt to chime in with, ' Ah, sir, I knew his father,' and so forth ; and he did so without improper assumption or any desire to give umbrage.

Diamond wrote little : I think that he occasionally contributed to *Notes and Queries*—an excellent miscellany at one time, notwithstanding that Thomas Wright assured me he never saw anyone read it except an old woman once in an omnibus. The Doctor's friends often pressed him to prepare a descriptive catalogue of his china, with all the valuable and attractive *minutiæ*, of which he was the sole repository. But he never did.

My late brother was his executor ; and I conclude that it was only in a Pickwickian sense that he once said of him, that he was the most trustworthy man he knew, for if he engaged to do anything, you might depend upon it that he would not. My brother had no literary taste, but was a reader, and possessed some sense of humour. He repeated to me what an omnibus-driver had once said to him, as he sat by him on the box : 'Ave 'eared say, sir, as there's countries where elephants burrows in the ground.'

Mr. Hepworth Dixon, at one time editor of the *Athenæum*, was, I have understood, the son of a Lancashire mill-hand. He was a clever but superficial person, and had no breeding. Jerrold used to call him 'Ha'porth Dixon.' I had a conversation with Dixon at the *Athenæum* office about the relative merits of two of our old poets, Herbert and Crashaw, and he said to me, paring his nails, when I had expressed my preference for Crashaw : 'Well, that's a matter of opinion.' I do not imagine he knew anything about either ; and when Henry Holl was once speaking at Our Club about our old writers, Dixon broke in with some critical remarks, and concluded with, 'Just the sort of thing, you know, that Jack Webster would have said,' without the faintest idea of Webster or his style of writing. He never did much after leaving the *Athenæum*. Dilke took him rather unexpectedly at his word when they differed on some principle, and he told

'Charlie' that he was ready to go if he could get another man to suit him better, which 'Charlie' did.

As an editor, Dixon was, on the whole, comparatively fair and moderate in the tone which he maintained, and which he prescribed to his staff of reviewers. He enjoined them, I understand, not only to be just, but to be generous, where a book possessed a reasonable share of merit and evidences of genuine work.

It was a trait perfectly in keeping with Dixon's utter want of sensibility and training, that one Sunday, at Diamond's, he took up his son, and threw him into the centre of a splendid box hedge on which the doctor especially prided himself—a hedge, so far as I recollect, some four feet across. It stood—alas! it stands no longer—close by a fence formed of old Culloden sword-blades.

Dixon utilized his vacations by visiting some locality likely to yield marketable stuff for a book against the next winter season. One year he went to Cyprus, and after a six weeks' stay appeared in due course as the historian of that island and ancient seat of arts and government. These literary manufactures can only be viewed in the same light as the artist's 'pot-boiler,' but in this particular case the question is whether the writer was capable of anything better and more durable.

The author of *Spiritual Wives* was gifted with the art of quick study. He came, saw, and conquered. The history of an ancient empire or the picture of a latter-day heresy, it mattered little. He had the knack of disguising his lack of knowledge and information under a specious and flippant style emphatically Dixonian, and his object was achieved. His work meant money, even if at present it means naught.

It was amusing to listen to him as he delivered a speech on some subject, such as Shakespear, with which his conversance was of the most deplorably limited and inaccurate nature ; and it was this facility for uttering a string of commonplaces in the absence of a competent knowledge of the topic under treatment which first led me to speculate on the title of Parliamentary and other orators to rank *ipso facto* as possessors of first-class gifts, or, in other words, whether fluency of speech is not, except in a few cases, the actual outcome of a deficiency of critical acquaintance with a subject.

The younger Dickens sang well, and Lawrence had his song, too, with the peculiarity of ignoring a certain letter of the alphabet. The last visit I paid with my father to the Club, there were only nine present—Cordy Jeaffreson, he and I, and six others (all knights).

Dr. Doran came to dine at my father's at Brompton about 1857. I was a very young man then, and heard Doran, in speaking of books, declare to my father that he never gave more than fourpence for any. I had at that time a very imperfect acquaintance with bibliography, but I remember that I formed a very unfavourable estimate of Doran's library. I do not think that it was ever publicly sold.

The last letter which Doran ever wrote was addressed to my father, and is inserted by Mr. Cordy Jeaffreson in the biographical notice which he wrote at the time of our common friend's death. Doran had been private physician at one period of his life to the Earl of Harewood. I once met him and Dixon at a private dinner given by F. W. Cosens, and I was infinitely disgusted by the coarseness of both in their conversation. I do not think that our kind host was either pleased or flattered by the gross vulgarity of the two distinguished *littérateurs*.

The Club passed some of its happiest and most prosperous times under the Piazza in Covent Garden, while it occupied a room at Clun's Hotel, next door to Evans's. It has since migrated from place to place, and at each removal has, I fear, left some of its old prestige behind. It bids fair to shrink into a *caput mortuum*. My father, ' the last of the Romans,' at length gave up attending ; and, as Lamb said of himself in reference to the *London Magazine* in its declining days, Cordy Jeaffreson and Macmillan (not the publisher) linger among the rafters of the sinking ship like the last rats.

Our Club long kept up its Shakespear night, when it became from season to season increasingly difficult to moot any fresh point, and to lend an original air to the gathering, of which the guests form a majority. There is also the annual meeting. Some years ago it was held at Richmond. My father invited me to join him, and Woolner was there. The chief thing which I recollect is that, as we were coming away to the train, Woolner's laugh could be heard from one end of the hill to the other.

What may be called the *Fasti* of the club were composed by Holl and Brooks at different times. The production of the former bears no note of date, and describes a representative evening in the earlier and brighter epoch, but after the loss of Jerrold. It is entitled, *The Retaliation Imitated.*

Shirley Brooks prepared his effusion, the only

other relic of the kind, for a special occasion—the Shakespear anniversary. It proceeds on the plan of making each of the company, members or guests, deliver a sentiment more or less appropriate to the circumstances or characteristic of the supposed speaker. It is sufficiently clever and interesting to warrant its insertion here, more particularly as it is probably almost unknown even to the present generation :

SHAKESPEAR AT OUR CLUB.

April 21, 1860.

R. FENTON.

Why, how now, what does Master Fenton here? Truly an honest gentleman.

O. DELEPIERRE.

He has done nobly, and cannot go without any honest man's voice ; therefore let him be *Consul*, and the Gods give him joy.

G. DUPLEX.

How he solicits Heaven
Himself best knows. But strangely visited people,
The mere despair of surgery, he cures.

P. CUNNINGHAM.

If you want drier logs,
Call Peter, he will tell you where they lie.

F. LAWRENCE.

Now, afore God, this reverend holy *Lawrence*,
All our whole city is much bound to him.

J. H. PARRY.

This is the Serjeant.

I charge you by the law,
Whereof you are a well-deserving pillar,
Proceed to [the bench of] Judgment.

G. JESSEL.

And you, his yoke fellow of Equity,
Bench by his side.

H. MAYHEW.

The Prince of Darkness is a gentleman,
Modo he's called, and *Mahu*.

C. DICKENS, JUNR.

Your mind is tossing on the ocean.   They are not *China* dishes,
but very good dishes.

G. CHESTERTON.

Not your Gaoler, then,
But your kind host.

W. HAZLITT.

Or Zummerset or York, all's one to him.

W. H. COOKE.

Yea, marry, William Cook, bid him come hither.   Any pretty
little tiny kickshaws tell William Cook.

J. C. O'DOWD.

The cloud-capped towers, the gorgeous palaces,
The solemn temples, the great *Globe* itself,
Yea, all which it inherit, shall dissolve.

ALLEN.

He sings several tunes, faster than you'll tell money.   He hath
songs for man or woman, and the prettiest love songs for maids,
without mischief, *which is strange*.

H. DIXON.

He gives you all the duties of a man,
Trims up your praises with a princely tongue,
Speaks your deservings like a chronicle,
And chides your truant youth with such a grace.

H. HOLL.

He shall taste of my bottle. *If he have never tasted wine before,*
it will go near to remove his fit. . . .
He's a Brave God, and bears Celestial Liquor.

F. JOYCE.

He is something stern,
But, if he vow a friendship, he'll perform it.

F. SIBSON.

He is a gentleman. One that indeed
Physics the subject.

W. A. MATTHEWS.

My man's as true as steel.

W. B. JERROLD.

Thou bearest thy father's face.

Thy father's moral part
Mayst thou inherit too.

D. MASSON.

Sir, we bless God for you. Your reasons at dinner (and else
where) have been sharp and sententious, pleasant without scurrility,
witty without affectation, audacious without impudency, learned
without opinion, and strange without heresy. . . . Well said,
Davy.

J. HANNAY.

He did ever fence the right,
Nor buckle falsehood with a *pedigree.*

J. B. Tomalin.

Now, what news on the Rialto?
What news among the Merchants?

F. M. Evans.

In faith, he is a worthy gentleman,
Exceedingly well read, and profited,
And wondrous affable, and bountiful.

C Knight.

(Shakespear *loq.*) He is a Knight, and will not any way dis-
honour *me*.

T. Reeks.

Shall we be thus afflicted in his *wreaks?*

J. W. Davison.

He hath the musician's melancholy, which is fantastical.

R. Orridge.

Sing, sir! You shall not *bob* us out of our melody. He gave
you such a masterly Report for art and exercise in your Defence.

J. Doran.

After my death I wish no other herald,
No other speaker of my living actions,
Than such a chronicler.

S. Brooks.

Such Brooks are welcome to me that overflow such liquor.

The Treasurer.

(F. Hamstede *loq.*) You owe me No Subscription.

I have entered into these details about Our
Club, because it has constituted since its commence-

ment a feature in the social life of my father—nay, in my own ; and it was the only institution of the kind with which either of us has ever been connected, save a concern in Arundel Street, of which my father* enjoyed an ephemeral membership ; this must have been the place to which, no liquor fit to touch being procurable on the premises, Frank Talfourd said that it was necessary to come drunk. I have, no doubt, kept unwisely aloof from literary fellowship, and my life has been disadvantageously secluded. A lady, when I once, in reply to an inquiry, told her that I had never joined any society, turned round on me, and rather unkindly observed : ' Perhaps you think that you are a society in yourself.'

I did not even join the Merchant Taylors' Old Boys Club, though I have been repeatedly honoured by an invitation to do so. I once attended a dinner as a guest, and all the faces were strange. There was no one there, save perhaps the Vicar of Upper Hackney, who had been with me in the forties in Suffolk Lane. I left the scene early, never to revisit it.

* My father died at Addlestone in Surrey, February 21, 1893, in his eighty-second year. His grandfather, the Rev. W. H., was living there in 1814. See i., 127.

A famous resort close by Clun's was Evans's. Evans, who started the Cider Cellars in Maiden Lane about 1831, was originally a singer, and had an engagement at one of the theatres at what was then accounted a heavy salary. But, losing his voice, he arranged to retire with a sum, and started the establishment so well identified with his name. The speciality in Maiden Lane was kidneys and stout ; there was no wine till just before the removal to the Piazza in Covent Garden ; and no women were admitted. There was music and singing, and for some time a man named Sloman was the pianist.

THE FOURTH GENERATION

PART I.

THE FOURTH GENERATION

PART I.

CHAPTER I.

Childhood of the writer—Merchant Taylors' School The old-
fashioned régime—What I learned there, and did not learn
—Anecdotes of the place and the masters - Remarks on
University education—The treatment of the classical writers
— Dr. Bellamy The Rev. John Bathurst Deane The
Merchant Taylors' Company The War Office in 1854—
Sir Robert Hamilton My intimacy with him and his family
—Abuses in the service and mismanagement of our military
affairs—Recollections of two years' stay in the War Office
My Irish programme— Hamilton's tale of second-sight My
Venetian studies— Macaulay and Ruskin—The librarian at
St. Mark's—A little incident on the Piazzetta—My maiden
literary publication—Murray's proposed *Dictionary of National
Biography*—My *Early Popular Poetry*.

THE narrative, as we proceed, has necessarily and
unavoidably become rather involved and irregular
by reason of the extent to which the later portions
overlap each other, and the writer plays the double
part of a showman and an actor in his own person.
I have done my best to obviate the admitted inconvenience and impropriety, so far as the circumstances
and my ability would permit.

Two of the earliest reminiscences which I have

are connected with our residence at Alfred Place ; the death of my younger brother Richard in a fit in 1839 he lies, poor little fellow! in Brompton churchyard ; and the visit of Lord Lansdowne to my father on horseback to deliver a copy of the catalogue of his pictures for a projected edition of Hazlitt's *Criticisms on Art*.

I also realize the almost opaque deafness of John Landseer, whom my father, when I was as a great treat in his company, met at one of the theatres, and with whom it amounted to an interruption of the performance to converse. The great painter, Sir Edwin, inherited, or at least acquired in later life, this unfortunate characteristic. The elder Landseer had known Hazlitt himself in the *London Magazine* days.

The principal part of my education was received at Merchant Taylors' School, in Suffolk Lane, to which I was nominated through my father's cousin, the Rev. William Welwood Stoddart, of St. John's College, Oxford, in 1842. The course of studies there at that time was very slightly varied, I apprehend, from what it had been a century before. The only subjects taught were Hebrew, Greek, Latin, writing, mathematics, and arithmetic. The school was held in an upper and a lower room, of which the latter was reserved for the writing and arithmetic classes in the afternoon. In the upper apartment during the mornings, the five forms, with the Monitors and Prompters, and sixth form, on a sort of raised platform at the top, followed their studies or repeated their lessons to four masters. In 1842, and for some time after, these were Dr. Bellamy, Mr. Bathurst Deane, Mr. Blunt, and Mr. Russell. In the afternoons this room was devoted to mathematics. There were about 200 boys altogether; but a small minority took the more difficult classics and mathematics, and a still smaller one Hebrew, although I understood that Bellamy was a fair Hebraist. Prayers were read every morning before school by one of the sixth form, who knelt in the centre of the room just below the Monitors' table, and held a printed sheet in front of him with the appointed ritual. It was long my duty to perform this ceremony.

Before I quitted this institution in 1850, it had undergone a remarkable development. Vigorous efforts were made to meet modern demands by enlarging the programme and extending the utility of the old foundation. One by one, French, drawing, music, and other sciences, were added to the meagre educational régime of my own earlier boyhood. I stayed long enough to join the French class, and one of my most agreeable associations is the delightful manner of Delille, who presided over it. What a contrast to the other instructors! He was before his time.

I never heard to what influence or agency the improvement of the school was due, but as it existed down to 1850 it was little better than a charity school of a high grade. There was once a year a strange piece of archaism in the shape of an Examination or Probation Day, when we had to put in an appearance at eight o'clock in the morning, and to have our breakfast on the premises. All the arrangements were of the meanest and most barbarous character. Except that the *menu* was differentiated by the modern introduction of sausage rolls, three-cornered-tarts, and Bath buns, the scene was perchance, in its general costume, not dissimilar from what it had been in the founder's life-time. Of course the Merchant Taylors' Company could not afford to find us our modest repast. For 200 boys it might have involved them in an outlay of £10.

It long used to be considered a good joke to lay hold of every newcomer to the establishment, and throw him into a large clothes-chest upstairs as an introductory ceremony; it was at any rate a dry christening; and if it did no good, it did little harm. It is curious how a mere accident gave me a peculiar ascendency over nearly the whole school. While I was in the fifth form, a schoolfellow (Fat Nelham) attacked me one day, and I went for him. I was very strong, and I thrashed him well. My reputation and prestige were placed on the most solid foundation from that hour till the day on which I left. I was honoured by the *sobriquet* of the ' Black Sheep,' not by reason of any misdemeanour of which I had to plead guilty, but on account of the awe which my exploit inspired.

Better books, better masters, more liberal ideas, have no doubt set Merchant Taylors' on a totally different footing from the place as I knew it nearly fifty years ago. I spent eight years of my life within the walls of the old mansion in Suffolk Lane, and I came out *grounded*.

I believe that I possessed a slight knowledge of figures, of Latin, of Greek, and of French. I had mastered a few of the problems of Euclid, and quadratic equations. Writing was an art which I never acquired either then or since, although many of the printers of Great Britain, and a very large number of correspondents all over the world, have made the best of a sort of substitute for the English written character in vogue with me.

I shall never forget the mingled despair and contempt which his futile endeavours to educate me in this direction inspired in the breast of an eminent calligrapher, commissioned by my father in afteryears to qualify me for clerical duties. My chief at the War Office declared that, if he had not had absolute ocular testimony to the contrary, he should have thought that I held my pen with my left foot.

They employed Lemprière, Anthon, and Bos, among other class-books in my day. The information imparted by these works was, according to present notions, meagre and imperfect enough ; but they marked an advance on the yet older material. Lemprière's *Classical Dictionary* was, in particular, a highly creditable commencement on modern lines. The first edition was in 1792, but Hazlitt, as a boy, met the author at Liverpool two years before, and tells his father in a letter that he paid him (L.) great attention.

The Lemprières are Jersey people, and the lexicographer's grandson is now living at Roselle. The late Sir John Millais was a countryman of theirs, and is made by an interviewer to offer very high testimony to their character and breeding. By the way, the said interviewer misunderstood the President of the Academy where he refers to his knowledge of *Hazlitt*—he meant my father. Sir John was not born till 1829.

In the main, whatever I have acquired may be regarded not unfairly or very disrespectfully as self-taught. I have in nearly the whole intervening period occupied my time in reading and writing books by way of supplementing compulsorily my shortcomings ; and here I must not be understood to imply that the deficiency would or could have been made good by a longer course at the school and a translation to the University, for on that topic I hold my own special convictions, which gain strength as I grow older ; an academical career may be socially beneficial ; but it warps and narrows the intellect, and as the colleges of Oxford and Cambridge are constituted, they do not form the best training for a man who aspires to independent thought, although I quite see and grant that they are excellent nurseries for clergymen, schoolmasters, and mathematicians. I never met with any Merchant Taylor who had attained distinction beyond that possibly latent in a colonial bishopric or a silk gown ; and all the University men with whom I have associated have struck me as wanting in originality of ideas.

Even in those isolated instances, where distinguished persons have belonged to one of our ancient seminaries of learning, I am tempted to ask myself the question, how far greater they might have been, had they never graduated. There seems to be an atmosphere about those time-hallowed spots, to which the blood assimilates, and which renders the brain proof against external thought and progress. Time will alone modify this growth of centuries, and then everyone who is really great will be, from contact with the master-minds of antiquity, and from a power of collating ancient with modern philosophy, all the more eminent.

The spirit and temper in which the classical authors, as they are termed, were taught, were utterly deceptive and unprofitable. Poets and prose-writers, like Homer, Horace, Herodotus, Cæsar, instead of being introduced to our notice and rendered intelligible and tangible to us as writers, of whom the best part still lived, were made to appear impersonal abstractions. There was no attempt to bring these masters before us in their relationship to their own times and to ours.

I was usually considered a rather proficient scholar. My name repeatedly, almost habitually, stands at the head of the respective forms in the printed school-lists, and I preserve five volumes purchased at the cost of the Gild of Merchant Taylors, and handed to me as prizes between 1845 and 1850; they are of the usual type and quality.

But I declare that it was not till long after I had bidden farewell to Suffolk Lane that I acquired anything resembling a correct estimate of the great authors of antiquity, and learned that they were men of flesh and blood, actual realities, as much as Chaucer and Spenser, or as Shakespear and Milton.

Progress has been made since that day in this salutary direction. There is Sir Theodore Martin's charming monograph on Horace, and the present writer printed long since a paper having a similar aim on a particular aspect of Homer's *Odyssey*.

When I entered Merchant Taylors' I was eight years old, and I continued for some time after, while I was an occupant of the Petty Form, to wear a tunic or frock with clocked stockings. I believe that I was rather proud of a very smart red velvet dress which my mother had made me; but Dr. Bellamy beckoned me up to him one memorable day, and made a deep impression on my mind by saying, though good-humouredly enough, that if my parents did not find me a pair of trousers, he thought he should have to try and see what he could do to make a man of me.

It was a very long journey for a little boy in those days from Old Brompton to Suffolk Lane. We were due at nine in the morning. The founders of the charity had not provided for scholars residing beyond the precincts of the City. Not merely were there no trains, but the omnibus service was very imperfect, and with my parents' humble means cabs were out of the question. There were small omnibuses, holding ten inside, plying between London and Hounslow, Brentford, and Richmond, and a few others which accommodated twelve. On the Brompton and Chelsea roads I do not retain in my memory the first experiments. I walked to and from Sloane Street, and from or to that point a Hounslow omnibus conveyed me to my destination : my place was reserved. All these vehicles were in the hands of private proprietors. There were no fares below sixpence when I began to ride to and fro. The Richmond hackney carriages had drivers and conductors in livery, but their terminus was in St. Paul's Churchyard, and the charge for the entire distance was a shilling. I jot down these trivial facts for the sake of comparison.

Deane, who was master of the fourth and fifth forms in my time, was author of the first work in English on *Serpent-worship* and of a biography of his ancestor, General Deane. He was a rather irascible and foolish person, addicted to giving extravagant tasks and personal chastisement, and to Bath buns, of which the undevoured remainder often distended his cheek on entering the school-room after lunch, awakening a titter which, if the culprit was detected, brought down on him an order (usually rescinded) to write out the *Iliad* or the *Æneid*. But these vagaries indicate to us a little in how untrue and unfortunate a light the classics were viewed by the teachers of a generation or so back, and made to appear to their pupils.

I once fell under the displeasure of Deane when he was giving our form some English dictation to turn into Latin by rendering ' the soil of Rhodes ' *solum viarum ;* and I also incurred his censure by making *virtuosus* the Latin equivalent of ' virtuous.'

Mr. Barlow, who presided over the junior afternoon classes in arithmetic and writing, was, of course, baptized Billy Barlow. An unlucky wight was overheard by him using this irreverent *sobriquet*, and summoned to his desk. Taking him by one ear, he said to him : ' My name, small boy, is not Mr. Wil-li-am Barlow, but Mr. Sam-u-el Barlow,' spelling out the words, and giving at each syllable a lug at the offender's auricular pendant. Barlow was rather short-sighted. A boy played him a practical joke one day by spitting on the floor just where the old fellow used to patrol up and down before the tables, and poor Barlow stooped down, mistaking the white object for a shilling.

Of the seminary where I acquired my alphabet I have given some further particulars in *Schools, School-books, and Schoolmasters*, 1888.

I witnessed one morning on Ludgate Hill, as I passed to school in the omnibus, a not unusual spectacle in those days. At the turning to the Old Bailey a man who had been hanged that morning was still suspended in the air, preparatory to being cut down. It was not then quite nine o'clock, and an hour was always allowed to intervene. This was about 1845.

In the printed account of the Merchant Taylors' Company there is some difficulty about a piece of land which was left to the Gild in trust, and I mentioned to Mr. Nash, the clerk, one day, in much later life, that I thought I knew where it was.

'Where?' he asked. 'Why,' said I, 'your hall stands upon it.'

I confess that I look back without pleasure at the two years which I passed during the Crimean campaign in the War Office about 1854, and a few years after quitting school.

The late Sir Robert Hamilton and I were both supernumeraries, and both failed to pass the examination for the permanent staff. All our colleagues, high and low, temporary or otherwise, were men, as a rule, of inferior type. I believe that Hamilton and myself are the only two who succeeded in our several ways in emerging from that slough, or rising above the ordinary dead-level of official routine.

Hamilton, whose family belonged to Shetland, was always considered a remarkably able accountant and man of business. He constantly came down to my father's house at Brompton to dinner ' when we were clerks together,' but I lost sight of him when, by the assiduous support of Sir Charles Trevelyan (his father's distant connection by marriage), he succeeded in outstripping me, so far as official status went.

He was a son of the Rev. Zachary Macaulay Hamilton, a relative of the historian, and incumbent of a parish in Shetland not far from Lerwick, where part of his income was derived from a tithe of herring. It was through Macaulay and his sister, who married Trevelyan, that my fellow-clerk was enabled to profit by his natural intelligence and industry.

An extremely intimate friend of Hamilton was Charles Ogilvy of Lerwick, who is, however, not otherwise memorable than as the victim of a strange corruption of his name by a correspondent into Huckleford. An old acquaintance of my uncle Reynell, a Mr. Hicks, was transformed in a similar way into *Lx*.

The Crimean War thus found Hamilton and myself a little behind the scenes. I had acted during a short time before as editor of the evening edition of the *Daily News*, where my successor was the present Sir John Robinson. It was certainly not a very creditable campaign from beginning to end, whatever the general reader or critic, looking back after forty years, may think of it. I was in two or three departments, and Hamilton visited the Crimea, as did my own brother: and we all heard more than enough of the shameful abuses and blunders in the commissariat, clothing, medical, and other services, of the shoddy arms and accoutrements, the brown-paper boots, the useless swords and bayonets, and the surgeons sent in one direction, and their drugs and appliances in another. Then, when we had everything in order, because the French could not proceed, we abandoned the business, and let Russia restore Sebastopol. What we did achieve was by pluck and muscle; our Generals were deplorable. The part played by His Royal Highness the late Commander-in-Chief is familiar.

If we had to do the same kind of thing over again, should we not perpetrate the same blunders and incur enormous outlay before we were thoroughly in working order? We want plenty of time to look round. If we were as great as a Government as we are as a people, we should be strong, and we might be proud, indeed. But there is no School of Statesmanship, and we are ruled by a succession of gentlemen-adventurers of ancient family and their plutocratic allies, who spend our money and amerce us in credit without remorse. See, at the present moment have we not at the helm the old firm of Derby, Disraeli, and Cecil reconstructed, with the junior partner at the head? The new members of the house are as dear to the latter as holy-water is said to be to H.M. the Devil; but, you perceive, Salisbury is where he is through them; they hold him up; and in his riper life he has grown so that he requires a good deal of that. It comes to this, with our make-shift political system, that our rulers are periodically, whenever there is any real difficulty or peril, falling back on the nation, and the 'Humble and Obliged' has to pay the double bill in honour and cash. Luckily, our foreign friends know pretty well that, when it comes to the point, they have to reckon with the people, and not with the Government.

The only gain I derived from my two years' stay at the War Office was the information with which my colleague, Mr. Leslie, furnished me about my grandfather's second wife, whom he had known as a girl of about nineteen in her parents' home in Scotland before she married Colonel Bridgewater. But, curiously enough, he had not retained her maiden name.

I am not, however, without some curious reminiscences of my association with that establishment. One of the most genial and conciliatory personages with whom I was brought into contact was Gleig, the Chaplain-General, who was at Waterloo, and who lived to a patriarchal age (ninety-four, I believe); and one of the most distasteful, the Right Honourable Sir Frederic Peel, about whom I committed to writing an official minute, for which, looking back, I feel surprised that I was not cashiered, inasmuch

as I gave the Under-Secretary of State the lie direct.
I remember the late Marquis of Clanricarde coming
to Whitehall Place in the summer season in a pair
of trousers which I took it that his lordship had purchased from a necessitous Ethiopian minstrel ; and I
had a very agreeable chat one day with the Marquis
of Westminster, father of the present Duke, a man
concerning whom all sorts of odd contradictory
stories used to circulate.

Of course, my colleagues were individuals infinitely
various in their ideas and qualifications, and the
majority struck me as having little enough of one
or the other. Many were grossly ignorant ; hardly
one possessed a considerable degree of gentlemanly
culture, save Mr. Wheeler, who published the book
on Herodotus. The reply to a letter from a noble
Duke was addressed by one of these luminaries to
' Messrs. Buckingham and Chandos,' but it was
luckily intercepted.

If I had pursued my official career, I might be at
present a richer and more dignified member of
society, but I should not be writing these Memorials.

When Hamilton was Under-Secretary for Ireland,
I roughly formulated a scheme for the settlement of
that unhappy country, and it may be known to a
few that in 1886, in a pamphlet, which was mainly

a criticism on Mr. Gladstone's policy at home and abroad. I pointed out what had struck me as being the weak points in his management of Irish affairs.

But in my plan I entered a little further into detail, and set forth what appeared to me at that time the only method of vindicating public order, and protecting the peaceable portion of the community in that part of the Empire. I scarcely see ground for hoping that without a stronger element of militarism any plans for the gradual social and moral amelioration of the country are likely to succeed, and I should be one for giving Mr. Balfour, or anyone else who is willing to accept such a thankless commission, even a freer hand than at present against a factious and selfish minority.

Hamilton told me this curious little story of second-sight. A party of fishermen started one day from Lerwick ; the weather was pretty fair, and their friends were there to see them off. After their departure, a storm arose, and great anxiety was felt for the absent boat. The relatives came down to the shore to make inquiries and to watch, but nothing was heard of it, till one of the look-out group (so ran the tale) descried the craft nearing land, saw it touch the ground, and the inmates file out, one by one, and proceed to their homes in the town. But the boat had really been wrecked, and all hands lost, and some of the bodies were subsequently washed ashore.

I see no objection to state that a version of *The Months* from the French of Garcin de Tassy, printed in *Chambers's Journal* for December 10, 1853, was, so far as my memory goes, my first independent literary effort, and brought me the apparently extravagant sum of fifty shillings. I certainly did not look for so much money, but it was a form of surprise and *oppression* of which in later life I have not been troubled by too frequent experience.

Before Smith and Elder started their *Dictionary of National Biography*, John Murray projected a similar undertaking under the inevitable William Smith, with Thompson Cooper as sub-editor. The latter was a capable man. He set me to compile certain lives, and the manuscript was duly delivered. After a lapse of time, I wrote to Smith (the late Sir William), and suggested a settlement. He asked me to wait till the book was printed. I might have waited till the proverbial Greek Calends. The work was abandoned. Of course Albemarle Street paid the score.

F. spoke favourably of my *Early Popular Poetry*,

published over thirty years ago in the 'Library of Old Authors,' and remarked that it was the best twenty shilling's worth he knew. 'But,' said he, 'of course you did not write all the notes yourself.' He meant to flatter me, perhaps. There are various ways of doing that. I know full well that the work cost me a vast amount of labour, and brought me a very small return.

It is comparatively immaterial at the present juncture under what circumstances my career shaped itself after War Office days to what it has been and is.

My interest in the historical antiquities of Venice arose, I remember, from reading Smedley's *Sketches from Venetian History*, and I flattered myself that something more worthy of the subject might be the result of my own labours, more especially when I was apprised that the large French work by Count Daru was far from satisfactory. This was in 1853, when I was a youth of nineteen; my opportunities of consulting books were rather limited, and my father's circumstances rendered it at that time out of the question to purchase any. I succeeded, however, in procuring a reading ticket for the British Museum, and we had a subscription to the London Library. At a distance of forty-four years from that date, when we were residing in Chelsea, I am still keenly looking out for every fresh point illustrative of that subject ; I have already printed separate papers from time to time illustrative of Venetian Architecture, Trade, Coinage, Prison Discipline, and other points, and some day I shall reproduce the book in a different form from the edition of 1860, in four volumes, which was only too indulgently received. But it was the work of a young man of five-and-twenty.

While I was planning my history, I wrote a polite letter to Mr. Ruskin, soliciting his advice regarding method and authorities, and that philanthropist did me the honour to leave my appeal unanswered. When the first crude edition appeared in 1858 (I was only twenty-three), my father sent a copy to Macaulay, who replied in a most kind note, saying all that he could say—that the work did credit to so young a writer.

I have always thought that in Mr. Ruskin's literary vein was to be detected a trace of his physical conditions, which so influentially operated on his life.

When I was at Venice in 1883, I visited the Library of St. Mark, and asked the custodian whether he could shew me any interesting manuscripts or other archives relating to the old Republic. He went away, and when he returned he bore in his hands a copy of my own book on the subject. I suppose that he thought it the only one which I was likely to understand.

A friend and myself were one day strolling about the Piazzetta, and we noticed a couple of women, who might have stepped out of some *cinquecento* canvas, and presently a gondolier (perhaps in league with them) made signs to us, and called out: 'Comandàre, signori?' He saw that we were not keen upon his boat, and he added, as an inducement, in another tongue: 'Avec mesdames?'

CHAPTER II.

The *Letters* of Charles Lamb —The two concurrent editions by Canon Ainger and the writer—Observations on the Canon's treatment of the subject, and attitude toward me —Mischief arising from imperfect and unfaithful texts—The Canon's lost opportunity—His want of care, knowledge, and experience — Talfourd and the *Letters* · My other literary efforts — Bibliographical labours—Samples of my correspondents.

Two essays of recent years in the direction of presenting the singular and extensive correspondence of Charles Lamb in a better and more complete shape appear to have been undertaken about the same time, independently of each other, by the present writer and Canon Ainger. Both had before them the antecedent labours of Talfourd, Fitzgerald, Babson, Cowden Clarke, Kegan Paul, Procter, and one or two more, not to mention that I enjoyed the advantage of having already launched an edition of the works in 1868 and a monograph on Charles and Mary Lamb six years later, while Canon Ainger had in addition an opportunity of consulting and using the Hazlitt book, which preceded his own in order of publication by two years.

The Ainger and Hazlitt collections of the *Letters* constitute, as I have said, the two latest attempts to serve the English-speaking community in this particular direction. But than the treatment and temper manifest in the books of the layman and the Canon nothing can well be imagined more thoroughly distinct and unsympathetic. The evident object of the latter has been to draw together as many specimens as he, in council with a few trusted advisers, deemed sufficient to convey to the reader an idea of the subject, and to eliminate without comment all passages calculated to shock the delicacy of prudish perusers, however characteristic they might be of the author and the age, and however important for a full comprehension of the subject-matter. The writings of Lamb are to be administered to us in elegant or genteel extracts, like spoon-meat. On this principle, nothing in time would be sacred from these meddling Philistines. All our classics nay, the Bible would have their turn.

It may be a moot point whether the Church is entitled to lay a veto on the exercise of private judgment in religious questions; but an ecclesiastic who devotes his leisure to the *belles lettres* ought surely to permit some latitude to his readers in a purely literary question affecting, comparatively speaking, a very limited and a very liberal constituency.

The committal by God-fearing publishers of the letters and other writings of Lamb to the editorial supervision and censorship of reverend personages must strike thousands on both sides of the Atlantic and among English-speaking communities in general as a grotesque anticlimax. We recall to our memory somehow the passage in the Elian paper on the "Old and New Schoolmaster," where Lamb describes the pedagogue who offered to instruct him in the science of literary composition. Because the sensitive imagination of a lawyer or a Churchman descries indelicacy where none was intended, and at the time none was perceived, are the writings of an English classic to be emasculated?

And if English publishers insist on employing gentlemen of dignified position and squeamish temper to edit their books, and there arises a natural reaction against this sort of abuse, the porcess, instead of being, as now, openly avowed, will be carried out under the rose, so that by degrees ordinary readers will scarcely know what

the older writers committed to paper, but will be
helped to just as much as is considered good and
safe for them to receive. This is the clerical
element under new colours.

The Master of the Temple is entitled to the
honour of having given for the first time much
valuable matter, and in numerous instances of
having restored missing or corrupt passages; but
his undertaking is far from satisfactory, nor could
it well be expected to be otherwise. It was due
to the co-operation of others, who were more
familiar with the ground than himself, that the
Canon's labours proved even so fruitful as they
actually are, for he was a comparatively new
worker in the field.

Nevertheless, the opportunity was before him,
with the prestige and reputation which his professional rank conferred, of rendering a signal
service to the Lambs and to us by bringing within
reach of everyone such a body and sequence
of epistolary matter as it had never fallen to the
lot of any preceding editor to accumulate. Yet
he did nothing of the sort, but laid before the
public—professedly not as an exhaustive assemblage
of letters, but as one embracing everything of
importance and interest (in his opinion)—an arbitrary

selection—arbitrary in two ways: in the rejection of entire documents, and in the castration without reason of many of those actually printed; and I maintain that an irreparable wrong has been done to literature by this *mauvaise honte* and this counterfeit gentility.

The Works of Lamb, if we take out of the account *Mrs. Leicester's School* and the rest of that little group, can never be widely popular reading. By the younger student they will, as time goes on, be less and less appreciated, with the exception of a few of the lighter articles in *Elia*; and now that all personal motives for suppression have ceased to operate, what useful end is attained by the continuance of Bowdler in office?

Canon Ainger was, in 1887, as I have said, a rather new hand at this sort of work, and was indebted to friends all round for help and guidance, not merely in the editorship of the *Letters*, but in that of the *Essays*. I feel bound in self-defence to state that he consulted me, among many others, on questions of authorship, and in particular he asked whether two papers in the *London Magazine* by Procter and Allan Cunningham were by Lamb — a circumstance which I should not have mentioned, had not the Canon, after adopting so much of my plan and text, improved the occasion by a disingenuous and improper disparagement of my enterprize. There comes into one's head a passage in a great dramatist about a man's purse and his good name.

As for the Talfourd text of his friend's epistolary writings, one can never tell whether one is reading Lamb or his executor. Even in 1848, however, Talfourd was hampered by the survival of many who might be naturally supposed to take umbrage at certain allusions in the correspondence, and he held it to be necessary, as perhaps it was, to refuse admittance into his select garland of much which there is no longer any adequate justification for keeping back. The judge was to Lamb what Southey might have been to his own offspring if he had yielded to the temporary clamour, and brought into the world the ' Family' *Doctor*.

Canon Ainger was quite differently situated in 1808. His hands were free.

The Canon's volumes constitute a disappointing an-Elia-like medley of texts good, bad, and indifferent and of letters often deficient of beginning, middle, or end. Instead of being, as they might have been, and as we were entitled to expect that they would have been, a marked step in advance of the 1886 book, they are actually retrogressive and reactionary, a backsliding Talfourdward.

' Incidit in *Ainger*, cupiens vitare *Talfourdum*.'

The worst feature about the Canon's book, next to his insufficient recognition of previous labours, is his exasperating revelation in his prefatory remarks, that there were, and are, certain letters to Manning, Procter, and so forth, which he has not given. He tantalizes us with extracts which only render us desirous of the whole, nor does he plead any valid reason for the exclusion. Again, it is surely bad enough to find that some of the letters were not received or admitted till it became necessary to throw them into the notes at the end. But, with portions of the correspondence under his eyes by the favour of the owners, to help us, and that out of due chronological order, only to extracts, is heinous.

It has not been without the deepest regret that I have offered the comment which precedes on the book of the Master of the Temple—a gentleman of whose learning and amiability one hears equally good accounts.

Of my own I have only a few more words to

say. Although I was indefatigable in hunting on the last occasion for unpublished letters of Lamb, as well as for the means of collating those already in type with the original manuscripts, I was by no means so successful as I could have desired in either of these respects. Not merely the appearance at intervals of letters unknown to Talfourd in the publications of others, but my own systematic appropriation of every autograph scrap which came into the market or into the hands of friends, has gradually, however, produced a result which, still imperfect as I know it to be, even those (including myself) who were aware that a considerable unprinted residue was in existence, could scarcely have hoped to realize.

My Elian Recoveries, rather than Discoveries, are divisible into four epochs or stages: 1868, when I added very notably to the correspondence in Moxon and Co.'s edition; 1874, when I brought out my *Mary and Charles Lamb*, on which the late Mrs. Gilchrist based much of her volume; 1886, when I completed Bell and Sons' edition, already specified; and 1896, when I have just recently gathered into a small book the biographical and epistolary gleanings of the last decade, including sixty-four new or uncollected notes and letters.

The aggregate effect has been, and is, to cast a vast amount of new and unexpected light on the personal and literary history of the brother and sister, and to widen very importantly and interestingly their already fairly large circle of friends and admirers.

My other literary publications extend over an exceptionally large area from the self-educational motive, which has partly underlain them throughout; they embrace Early and Modern History and Biography, Poetry and the Drama, and other departments of the *belles lettres*. But they are before the section of the reading community which cares for such topics as I have happened to treat, and I shall say no more about that point. My bibliographical researches, stretching over thirty-six years (1860 to 1896), have, I hope, been of value to some, as I am sure that they have been a source of pleasure to myself.

This is the only civilized country in the world in which an undertaking of national magnitude would have been permitted to devolve on an individual of slender means, and where he would have found himself reduced to the necessity of printing his Collections at a pecuniary sacrifice. I have at last six volumes in type, and I add to my manuscript accumulations day by day; it is my ambition to consolidate the whole in one alphabet, and to enable Great Britain to point to such a work of reference and authority as no other European literature can boast of possessing. This is a part of my habitual employment, yet only a part—a small one.

An acquaintance flattered me by saying that he thought I was the most indolent person whom he had ever known, and my brother would declare that he never saw me doing any work. Only to think, what a plague I should have been to society had I been even moderately industrious! I once disconcerted O. by observing to him mischievously that I had laid myself across the age. '*Laid yourself across the age?*' he repeated after me with his eyes fully expanded. He did not quite perceive my drift. What I meant was that I had produced certain books which would in all probability perforce remain works of reference and keep my name before a portion, at least, of the public during, if not after, my life. O. did not pursue the subject, nor did I open my mind to him; but he left me, considerably to my amusement, with the impression that I was a deuced conceited fellow.

From my personal point of view, gentlemen, during the last thirty and odd years, seem to have

gathered together, regardless of time and cost, all
the most curious and rare books of former periods
in order to send them, when the result in each case
justified them in giving me so much trouble, to the
auction-rooms for my use. It is so infinitely more
comfortable, you perceive, to work in this sort of
piecemeal fashion—a library or so at a time—and
the process can always be going on. Other parties
do their share, and I mine. They beat the bush,
and I catch the bird.

There still remain a few collections which I have
not yet had the means of examining, particularly
those at Ham House, and in the possession of the
representative of Mr. Cunliffe of the Albany. The
former library, when I applied for leave to take a
note of a certain volume, was declared to be 'in a
state of chaos'—rather a good hearing for an
opportunist !

It is, I venture to conclude, superfluous to mention
that I could readily fill more than a single volume
with details of my literary correspondence and bibliographical experiences. Probably no one has an
adequate idea of the extraordinary variety of the
written demands or representations which have
been addressed to me since I began to assume the
form of a distinct individuality on certain branches

of knowledge and inquiry. My special bent might lead some to augur that my views were almost exclusively sought on matters connected with old books ; but such is by no means the case.

I have in my mind's eye about a ream of paper covered with extracts from Burns by a clerk in the service of the Great Western Railway, soliciting my opinion, and a long letter from an operative at Newcastle-on-Tyne, wishing to know if I deemed it expedient for him to emigrate with his family. Some of those who honoured me with these and other questions were occasional in their appeals ; others, till I had in self-defence to expostulate, interviewed me through the post two or three times a week. Now and then my help was recognised ; more frequently it was not.

But the worst luck was, where one had furnished the most important material to a Reverend Doctor for his edition of an early poet, and he disparaged its value in acknowledging its arrival, was absolutely silent as to the source whence he derived the manuscripts, and cited them throughout as the basis and backbone of his volumes. He was not merely a Doctor, but a Reverend one. Think of that, Master Brook !

CHAPTER III.

The western suburbs of London— Their aspect half a century since
The made ground in Knightsbridge, Battersea, Westminster,
and elsewhere—Delahaye Street and the chief pastrycook of
Charles II.—Long Ditch— Gradual formation of highways
and growth of buildings—The ancient waterways in Knightsbridge and Old Brompton— Carriers' carts, waggons, and
coaches Some account of the system and its incidence—
Suggestion as to Shakespear —The primitive omnibus—That
which ran to Edmonton in Charles Lamb's time —Loneliness
and insecurity of the suburban roads—Anecdote of Hazlitt—
Precautions against highwaymen and footpads—Notting or
Nutting Hill Waggon houses at Knightsbridge, and on the
Oxford and Uxbridge Roads—Changes on the northern side
of the Metropolis The scattered markets Their value—
That at Knightsbridge – Snipe in Tuthill Fields and at Mill-
bank—Partridges, snipe, and rabbits on Barnes Common—
The turnpikes Those at Hyde Park Corner and Tyburn, etc.
The Farmer of the Gates.

I NOW propose to devote some space to a description
of the suburban districts in which we as a family,
and I as the founder of an independent home in the
usual course of events, resided and moved between
1838 and the present time, taking occasion to inter-
sperse the topographical sketch with particulars of

such friends and acquaintances as we were fortunate enough to acquire within this radius, and especially in Old Brompton from time to time, and of others of whom our knowledge was more indirect, yet sufficiently considerable to justify a passing mention.

The westward route from Sloane Street—as at one time, indeed, from Hyde Park Corner—lay fifty years since between garden-houses, only broken occasionally by stretches of dead wall appertaining to the Park or some ancient mansion, by lines of fencing where a nursery abutted on the road, or by the boundary hedge of a market-garden. The undulating and uneven surface betrayed the absence of a Highway Board for the parish; and the variations in the elevation and width of the footpaths were traceable to changes in the character of the buildings adjoining.

If there were such a thing as a plan of Old Brompton and the environs as they appeared many hundreds of years ago, it would present to our view an open and probably uncultivated tract, abounding in wood and morass, and intersected by streams flowing from the northern heights of Hampstead, Highgate, and Holloway. Within living memory a few of these water-courses still existed, while others had dwindled into ditches or, as in the case of the

Efra, which flowed into the Thames at Vauxhall, and was navigable by small craft up to Brixton or further, had been converted into an underground sewer, except where a portion may be yet seen dammed up at the Lawn. Queen Elizabeth is said to have ascended the Efra in her barge, possibly on a visit to one of her court at Streatham or Brixton.

There are probably many who have not taken into account the vast changes produced in the course of ages by the creation or improvement of thoroughfares. Modern Paris is said to be eight feet higher than it was in the days of Philip Augustus. Modern London stands twenty feet above the Roman city. The bulk of the superficial area of all great centres of population and building is *made ground*, which, as immense bodies of soil or *muck* are frequently transported from a distance to supply a *vacuum* where the gravel or sand has been removed, as well as for the purpose of raising the level, is apt to do violence to geological harmony.

Thus, in the decline of a district from its early speciality of aspect, and its adaptation to a general standard suitable to the requirements of the builder, we find a variety of contributing factors. Some of the details are bound to vary according to the level; but the reforming hand of the enterprising owner or speculator is equal to all emergencies. In low lands the causeway and the shoot play a leading part. They did so in Battersea, where they are even now emptying the mud-carts day by day, and in Pimlico, where, between Knightsbridge and the river, lay a desolate waste, dotted with ponds, the wreckage of Ebury Farm and the contiguous fields. I used to think that Battersea Fields, with the Red House and other amenities, were not all that could be desired ; yet I would joyfully vote for their restoration instead of the actual scene which they present, with their honeycomb of railway-line and doleful blocks of poverty-stricken houses.

The hedge, the park-pale, or the buttress wall, gives way to the railing before a terrace or a row of detached or semi-detached houses, and these are subsequently degraded into places of business, of which the front-gardens make a part. So it has been in Brompton on the West, and in Whitechapel on the East—exactly the same law and same process.

In parts of Westminster, built on the ancient Thorny Island, they have come, in laying foundations, on submerged and buried willows, formerly flourishing on the banks of the water-courses, which branched from the Thames inland, and of which the sole modern vestige is the Long Water in St. James's Park. One of these channels passed through the existing Delahaye Street, a thoroughfare named after Pierre de la Haye, Chief Confectioner to Charles II., who died in 1684, and is buried at Mickleham. He had two houses here, of which one went to the St. Aubyns with his coheiress; the other belongs to a personal friend of the writer, and it was in rebuilding the premises about fifty years since that the original nature of the soil, and the strangely altered conditions of the scene, were brought to light.

The site of the southern extremity of Delahaye Street, where Royal Charles's head-pastrycook lived, was once designated Long Ditch, the original stream having degenerated in the usual manner. But the levels hereabout must have suffered a remarkable change, and nearly the whole of the ground, as it now stands, is doubtless artificial. It was two centuries ago several feet lower—in a line with the Stuart willow-beds.

Then, again, in the City proper, look at the Wallbrook, which once flowed through the moor, now only known by tradition, but originally stretching at least as far as the site of the Bank of England. On removing an old house in Coleman Street in

1896, the peaty bottom was reached, with its Roman remains.

The brook degenerates into a ditch, the latter into a sewer, as civilization advances or as the builder spreads his ravages. The old maps do not assist us much in tracing the waterways of this particular tract. There were at least two, of which one, the most westerly, flowed through Brompton Vale across the fields and the Fulham Road, before it was constructed as a highway, and so through Chelsea to the Thames. A second traversed Hyde Park and Knightsbridge, as I have elsewhere noted.

Of the rivulet which crossed the Western Road at Knightsbridge, mention occurs in the literature of the Tudor era, and my uncle Reynell remembers it before it was transformed into a covered drain. Some of the portion which flowed through Hyde Park has been filled up within my time.

The environs of London on all sides were formerly rich in roadside inns, of which the custom was derived in principal measure from the waggoners, carriers, and stage-coaches which plied between the Metropolis and the provinces. The carriers and coaches had regular days for going and returning to London, Westminster, and Southwark, and small penny and twopenny handbooks were published from time to time to enable travellers, or persons desirous of transmitting parcels and messages, to keep themselves informed of the times of arrival and departure on the various routes.

It once took my own family a week to reach Wales or Cornwall.

Anterior to omnibuses and railways, the transport service was, in fact, performed by coaches, waggons, and carts; the two latter were employed not only by the lower, but by the middle class, and such a man as Shakespear, when even the coach was unknown, must have journeyed to and from Stratford in a waggoner's or carrier's conveyance. The supply of fish to inland towns within a measurable time was by cart or van from the nearest port. The local dealer kept a vehicle constantly on the road, and had to arrange for relays of horses.

Folks whose traditions happen to be associated with the West End may not have heard, as a rule, of any halting-stages or starting-points less central than the White Horse Cellar (whence my grandfather set out for Winterslow Hut, and on a special occasion on his way to see the Fight), or the houses in Coventry Street and Holborn, where the Old Bell yet survives. But about Bishopsgate and in the Borough this feature in everyday life, prior to railways and other modern appliances, was seen in its fullest vigour and picturesqueness, and the attendant costliness and loss of time would under present mercantile and social conditions be out of the question. A late City Chamberlain (Scott), who died at eighty-nine, and had known personally sixty Lord Mayors, paid half a crown, when he became rich enough to afford it, for his fare part of the journey from Hampstead to the City, in what he described as 'a blue-bellied' coach.

Piccadilly, Westminster, Holborn, Bishopsgate, Islington, and the Borough, we see, were the points of departure and arrival for the mails, and a little later on came the long-distance omnibus, starting from some of these centres. Judging from the number of coaches (about sixteen) which left Piccadilly and the Angel at Islington daily, there must have been a large complement altogether; and there were also the mail-carts and post-chaises, the latter with the boy-outrider. This illustrates Dunton's periodical, 1698 to 1700, entitled *The Post-boy robbed of his Mail*. One prime feature in the coach was the guard, with his blunderbuss and pistols, which were so carefully wrapped up against the weather that a highwayman might have scuttled the conveyance before they could be disengaged.

The Piccadilly coaches chiefly took the Great Western Road on their way to Oxford, Worcester, Salisbury, Devizes, and elsewhere; but one crossed Putney Bridge *en route* for Portsmouth. The northern, eastern, and southern counties were served from Islington, Bishopsgate, Westminster, and Southwark. In my earlier days, the omnibus which used to take Charles Lamb and his friends to and from Edmonton still started regularly from the Flower-Pot at Bishopsgate. I never went by it further than Tottenham. A second ran between the Bell, in Holborn, and Wendover, and a tedious journey it was. You had earned more than the fare when you alighted, if it was in the winter, after nightfall.

Places which now constitute part of our great city were till a comparatively recent date completely isolated from it, and distinct hamlets or townships. Hounslow, Turnham Green, Brentford, and even Kensington and Old Brompton, were rendered independent of the capital by wide stretches of open ground and impracticable roads— the latter such as are pictured by Macaulay in his *History of England* and by many travellers and diarists of the eighteenth century. Yet within my time and recollection many of these outskirts were delightful retreats, and to a modern eye fabulously rural and solitary. Those who have only known the western approach to London since 1850 must be strangers to what it was when I was a boy. My mother, who was born in 1804, remembers that when she was a child, and lived in her father's house in Black Lion Lane, Bayswater, there were no buildings between them and Harrow. The Oxford Road, as it was called, was so desolate in Hazlitt's day that he was afraid to traverse it by night.

My grandfather, when he walked to the Reynells', became at last so alarmed by the reports which reached his ears that he purchased a brace of pistols, which his son used to carry, till, growing more afraid of the weapons than of the footpads, he discarded them.

Within comparatively recent years what is Lancaster Gate was a meadow with a hedge to the highway. Between this meadow and Porchester Terrace was a tea-garden. The property hereabout included the Bread and Cheese land left to Paddington parish by maiden ladies for the periodical distribution of relief from the church-steeple. It was after my settlement in Addison Road, Kensington, in 1862, that those sweeping changes occurred,

which thoroughly demoralized the neighbourhood
and drove me to Barnes. Like old General Boone,
who hunted up to ninety, I retreat before *civilization*.

Notting Hill, properly *Nutting Hill*, is at present
beyond redemption. I recollect it a very pleasant
countrified locality, surrounded on the north and
west by fields. I have walked from Clarendon
Road, even after that was built, the whole way to
Hampstead with very few houses, and those
scattered about, between. Notting Barns, which
was a farm lying between Notting Hill and Camp-
den Hill, still survives in a small patch of open
ground near Bute House and in Farm Street,
which is just where the old turnpike gate stood.
You go down from the main thoroughfare in entering Farm Street, probably because the highroad has
been much raised.

I have mentioned that the environs of London
on this side were down even to 1850 very lonely
and insecure, and that both the highwayman and
footpad formerly infested the whole tract of country
now almost completely covered by houses and protected by well-lighted thoroughfares and police.
In the Kensington highroad, near Knightsbridge
Barracks, stood a queer old hostelry with the back
looking to the Park, and I have always understood

that this was a regular haunt of the knights of the
post, who, if pursued into the premises, escaped at
the rear into the large open space behind, and so
got away from the not very dexterous or alert
guardians of public safety and order who preceded
our modern constable. A second lay at the junction
of the Fulham Road and Bell and Horns Lane,
and a third formed part of a short row of very
antique shops on the northern side of the Fulham
Road, opposite Stewart's Grove. In the Fulham
Fields there was a very quaint halting-place of this
kind; it was on the right-hand going toward Hammersmith Broadway. It was known as the Grey-
hound, and was a noted haunt of highwaymen; and
the site of Holcrofts in the village itself was originally occupied by a similar establishment before it
was transformed into a private mansion—the usual
process inverted.

The oldest house at Walham Green was the
King's Head, previously known as the Hare and
Hounds, and dating from 1680; and at Putney the
Fox and Hounds, of Henry VIII.'s time, once
famous for its bowling-green.

There were waggon-houses of a similar type, no
doubt, on those sides of the city with which I was
less familiar. Three yet lingered in modern times:

two on the Uxbridge and one on the Oxford Road. Of the former, one lay at the corner of Wood Lane, facing Shepherd's Bush; the other, not far from Kew Bridge, was a halting-place for George III. on his way to Windsor. Many must call to mind how recently at Bayswater, opposite the Park, survived an ancient structure seeming to have no relationship to the scene around it.

The changes in the route from the Metropolis to the north have been, even since the present century, equally immense. The road to Barnet used to be straight down Gray's Inn Lane, till it was diverted through the Bishop of London's park at Paddington. The gate which gave its name to Highgate was placed to collect the Bishop's tolls. I personally spoke at the Holborn end of Gray's Inn Lane to a well-known artist about forty years since, who remembered a haystack where the St. Pancras station now is.

The scattered markets, which formerly lay at intervals over all this area, possess greater significance than may at first sight appear. They were the sole depots for the convenience of the householder when all the small neighbourhoods about the west and other parts of the Metropolis were yet detached hamlets, with oases of meadow or demesne between them. I may mention Oxford Market, Newport Market, Clare Market, Carnaby Market, Shepherd's Market (at the foot of Down Street, Piccadilly), Chelsea Market, and the one which, ever since I can remember, has been at Knightsbridge, or rather on the western side of Sloane Street, near the remains of Knightsbridge Green.

My maternal grandfather Reynell, who was born in 1777, remembered Sloane Street partly in carcase, and his son (my uncle) has fished for sticklebacks in the ponds about the Five Fields, Pimlico—the area between Sloane Square and St. Peter's Church. Cattle used to graze on the site of Belgrave Square within living memory, and my informant recollected the erection of the Square railing.

We have all heard of the sport enjoyed by General Oglethorpe in the time of Queen Anne, where Regent Street now is, and snipe were also shot within living memory in Tuthill Fields behind Bird Cage Walk. The old door belonging to the barracks, from which some of the officers sallied in pursuit of their game, was till lately preserved *in situ ;* but snipe were also to be found in the osier-beds and the Willow Walk at Pimlico, near the present Warwick Square and Street.

It is curious how many changes of this kind have been accomplished by the builder. Partridges were occasionally seen, not many years ago, in the immediate neighbourhood of Barnes Common, in the eight-acre field adjoining Mill Lodge – they may have been strays from Richmond Park and I have been credibly informed that on the common itself snipe were to be got. There are still rabbit-burrows there, but the population will soon drive away the makers and occupants. The cuckoo and the nightingale are yet habitual visitors; but they become year by year rarer and shyer.

London, in allusion to its numerous turnpikes, gained the Theban *sobriquet* of the *Hundred-gated*. There was a parallel series on all the main roads. From the Piccadilly side, the first was at Hyde Park Corner, with the weighing apparatus a little lower down for the heavier traffic. This bar was successively set back to Sloane Street and the Queen's Elm, before which within living memory the actual tree spread its branches and its shadow, lending its name equally to the terrace opposite, which dates from about 1822, when Mayers the baker built his premises at the corner of what was long known as Elm Terrace. The general structure on the northern side from the church to the end of Brompton Row has not yet undergone vital alteration, except the removal of the gardens and the enlargement of frontages; but opposite the entire aspect is changed for better or for worse, as people may think. These suburban gates were long farmed by Jonas Levi, whose name was to be found upon them, and who is recollected by old inhabitants coming periodically down to inspect his property. The speculation must have succeeded, for Levi lived in good style at Kingsgate Castle, near Broadstairs. He was a large shareholder in the Brighton Railway.

I take it that the King's and Queen's Roads were originally out of the category of public thoroughfares, and had consequently no toll-gates. The latter was a virtual *cul-de-sac* at both ends till it was opened up by the modern builder and the removal of the barrier at Chelsea Hospital, and even now it is not a main artery.

The gate at Hyde Park Corner was exactly parallel with the one at Tyburn, near the Marble Arch. The latter was removed in 1829. On a blue earthenware cheese-plate belonging to the commencement of the present century is painted a view of Tyburn turnpike, with all the country toward Bayswater and Edgeware open.

CHAPTER IV.

Knightsbridge—Original levels and boundaries—Traces of it in 1371 and 1526—Knightsbridge Green—The old watch-house—Old Brompton—Brompton Row—Some of its early inhabitants—Count Rumford—Anecdote of the Duchess of Kent—Mrs. Lloyd of Crown Court—Grove House—William Wilberforce—Elliot's Pine Pits—John Hunt—Some account of Faulkner the historian—Bell and Horns Lane—Pollard's School—Gore Lane—Charles Mathews—Robert Cruikshank—Sir John Fleming's daughters—Cromwell House—Brompton Vale—Chelsea Pound—Curious discovery there—Vestiges of Chelsea Common—Brompton nurseries—Walnut-tree Walk—The Bull—Gunter the pastrycook—Brompton Heath—Thistle Grove—Little Chelsea—Purser's Cross.

IN 1840 there were very few shops in the Brompton Road between Sloane Street and the Bell and Horns, and again between that and the Queen's Elm.

The original village of Knightsbridge extended in a broken and irregular manner or form from the western corner of Sloane Street (then unknown) to the end of Queen's Buildings. There were at the outset no houses on the southern side till you passed Sloane Street, nor on the northern till you reached the village of Brompton. Even now the peculiar levels shew that the primitive road (including the pathway) has undergone repeated alterations. Of the mediaeval Knightsbridge mentioned in records of the fourteenth, fifteenth, and sixteenth centuries, probably not a vestige remains; and the made ground here, as well as at Brompton Row, was found necessary to lift the residences, which were gradually erected, above the uncared-for and sometimes almost impassable coach and cart track. The place derived its name from the bridge which (above the modern Albert Gate) spanned the stream running from the North of London across Hyde Park and Pimlico to its outlet into the Thames opposite Vauxhall. This structure in some shape was of very great antiquity. It was the theatre of an adventure narrated in the *Hundred Merry Tales*, 1526, but one by no means merry in its *dénouement*.

We hear in 1371—525 years ago—of Knightsbridge as a hamlet, to which the Butchers' Gild was permitted to send cattle for slaughtering purposes. A second principal *abattoir* was Stratford-le-Bow.

Plantagenet Knightsbridge presumably consisted of a single row of tenements, first on the northern side by the old bridge, and then (after an interval) of others on the southern side, where Queen's Buildings at present stand, the former facing the fields toward the river, where Ebury Farm subsequently extended, and having at the back an enormous sandy area, now partly represented by Hyde Park, the latter facing an open heath, successively reduced to a green and a triangular grass-plot, and looking behind, till the eighteenth century was far advanced, on a wide expanse of waste. I have understood that there was no regular grass-land in the Park till George III. caused parts to be sown with seed as a relief to his eyes when he began to suffer from ophthalmia. There used to lie in the rear toward Sloane Street a nest of curious antique hovels, which might have been part, in their first state, of the primæval hamlet. They were reached by a court, possibly once a lane.

On the once waste plot between the present Knightsbridge Green and Sloane Street stood the watch-house for the district, and a friend remembers peeping in at the window one day when he was a boy, and seeing the body of a woman just recovered from the Serpentine lying for identification. The ordinary use of these places was as a lock-up for pickpockets and other nocturnal offenders till they were taken before the magistrate.

Knightsbridge Green must have been in its second state, so to speak—that is, subsequently to the creation of Brompton Row and Queen's Buildings—of much greater extent than I can recollect it. It appears to have fallen a gradual prey to encroachment by private persons and the Highway Board; but it is easy to recognise that the whole tract was at the outset waste of the Manor of Kensington, and came down in a fork to the point where Sloane Street at present opens into Knightsbridge.

Queen's Buildings, which face the Green, were originally private residences, with small plots of pleasure-ground divided from them by the footway exactly as the case was in Brompton Row; and these spaces were gradually absorbed into the thoroughfare, one or two at the western extremity being the last to disappear. At the opposite corner, where the ground began to recover the natural level, you formerly descended a short flight of steps to the first shop. Here, in fact, the country at one time recommenced, and all was open in the rear. There is in a story-book of 1526 an account of a thief making his escape across the fields just at this point. There were down to my time only a few primitive places of business on the southern side, facing Brompton Row, and then private houses standing back in long gardens. That was doubtless the second state of the locality, when it had ceased to be meadow or arable land protected by hedges.

Many of us recall the cavalry barracks in Kensington Gardens, near the turnpike at Gloucester Road; but there were also barracks for the footguards on the site of St. Paul's, Knightsbridge, the church standing where the old barrack-yard once was.

The scene is as different as if we were looking back on occurrences of two centuries ago. The exigencies of traffic, the feverish competition of trade, the seething population springing up around us and choking many healthy forms of the earlier English life, have accomplished the metamorphosis :

> ' In nova fert animus mutatas dicere formas
>   Corpora.'

The region now incorporated in *South Kensington,* but formerly known as *Old Brompton,* was once and long a country village, or little more. The scenes amid which I spent much of my youth now survive only in the mind's eye. The ancient mansions which abounded there, the historical sites or records, the delightful residences in grounds, the market gardens, and, best of all, the quaint Old Vale, have vanished like a dream.

Brompton Row, which connected the place itself on the northern side of the road with Knightsbridge Green (in its far greater amplitude) at an epoch long posterior to the existence of Old Brompton as an independent name and locality, I take to have a topographical affinity with Chigwell Row, Channor Row, and Forest Row, a block of buildings erected on the skirt of a hamlet or a waste. The first houses which occupied the site were of low elevation and humble pretensions; they lay back some forty or fifty feet from the main road, and the boundary-line of their front-gardens, with the projection on the opposite side, where Grove House stood, left a narrow passage for vehicles of all kinds, yet enough to meet the demand of that day. During a protracted period the dwellings just here enjoyed an uninterrupted view of the open area behind, so far as the eye could scan.

The Row about 1840 presented altogether a sufficiently picturesque aspect; it was quiet, green, and rural ; and the grape vines trained over one or two of the exteriors, with the clusters hanging unmolested in the season, may give some idea of the thorough transition which the locality has undergone since my early years.

Faulkner, in speaking of the villages which bounded the town of Kensington proper on the southern side, mentions *Old* and *New* Brompton ; but he omits to delimit them, and to do so would now involve greater trouble than it would have done seventy years ago, when Faulkner wrote his account of Kensington.

Still, I think it probable that New Brompton was the name applied to the eastern end, including Brompton Row, and that Old Brompton centred round Cromwell or Hale House, Cromwell Lane, and the lower end of Bell and Horns Lane toward Brompton Hall and Cowper House. The Row was plainly, as I have suggested, an aftergrowth, and originally abutted on the waste of Kensington Manor, without any other buildings between it and the Manor of Hyde. Like Queen's Buildings opposite, its level was probably raised to what we now see it, when at a later date private residences of a superior character were erected there.

Two celebrities who resided in Brompton Row

were Sir Benjamin Thompson, better known as Count Rumford, who was there quite in the beginning of the century, and Leach, a boatswain who had served on the *Victory*, and had lost an arm. He was full of all sorts of yarns, and his conversation was eagerly sought by the frequenters of the Crown and Sceptre at the corner of Rauston Street, going toward Montpelier Square, where Trafalgar was fought over again almost nightly in a recital accompanied by copious potations of malt liquor. Leach had an adroit way of ordering a half-pint of beer in a quart measure, and his tankard was constantly replenished for him by his admiring audience. He it was who used to give an account of the Duchess of Kent, the Queen's mother, tripping on some occasion and saving herself by catching at the stump of Leach's arm, on which occasion Her Royal Highness, according to the narrator, expressed her satisfaction at being able to lean on the buttocks (bulwarks) of England. This may have been while the Duke and his wife resided at Kent House, Kensington Gore.

Count Rumford did not probably reside long at Old Brompton. I have seen a letter from him written there in 1801, and in the following year he settled in France. He was one of the earliest improvers of our domestic stove. John Reeve I notice elsewhere.

I must not omit to record Mrs. Cooper, who in my boyhood kept the confectioner's shop in the Row, and made a speciality of the Brompton Bun, of which I was a munificent patron.

A notability of a different character in the Row was denoted by a brass plate with the name *Lloyd* on it, attached to one of the doors. Mrs. Lloyd resided here, and was a person of some means. She had a son, an officer in one of the line regiments. Mrs. Lloyd was, in fact, in business—what business was not exactly known, not even to her son. Her headquarters, however, as a matter of fact, were in Crown Court, St. James's, where she could shew a cheval-glass in a silver mounting, given to her by H.R.H. the Prince Regent; I dare say that she was very proud of it.

A very sad story was connected with this woman and this house. One day a lady brought a gentleman there, and the door was opened by Mrs. Lloyd. The gentleman was her son—he had discovered the secret; and he never recovered from the shock. The poor fellow's commission had been bought out of Crown Court.

Facing Brompton Row lay Grove House and

other private residences in grounds. Grove House had been the abode of William Wilberforce, but in 1840 was converted into a dame-school, kept by Mrs. Warne, a connection of Colonel Maceroni, aide-de-camp to Murat, the brother-in-law of Napoléon. Mrs. Warne did her best to initiate the writer into some of the rudiments of learning. Her governess, Miss Foster, who married Osborn the nurseryman, tried to make me an advanced scholar by teaching me a few words of French, and one day it came to the turn of the word *oui*. 'Say *oui*, Willy,' quoth the lady. 'I won't say *oui*, Miss Foster,' was my hardy, Loftus-like reply.

A portion of the extensive gardens once attached to these old buildings survives in the small oblong enclosure of Ovington Square.

At the back of Grove Place, Elliot's Pine Pits occupied ten acres, extending nearly to the western side of Hans Place, formerly a delightful spot where Sir Charles Shuckborough had a mansion in grounds. Elliot afterward removed to Fulham, but he naturally found pine-growing unremunerative when a better specimen than he could produce for a guinea was obtained from abroad for half a crown.

In one of the small houses in Grove Place, Mr. John Hunt, Leigh Hunt's elder brother, spent his last days and died. I recall visits which we paid to him there. His wife, like old Mrs. Hazlitt, was addicted to distinguishing him as '*my* Mr. Hunt.' She might have had good reasons for this.

In Alexander Place was a magazine for the sale, among other sundries, of short basket-hilted iron swords and wooden broadswords. My brother and I fought *à l'outrance* with the former, and exhausted many a pair, regardless of the outlay, which was fourpence each; but the broadsword was a shilling, and was only for ceremonial use. The reports which came to us from our elders of the sanguinary conflicts in transpontine melodramas led to this playing at soldiers or brigands; but I think that the shilling weapon associated itself in my mind with a commission in the Household Cavalry. How many foster such illusions and mental cobwebs, varying only in character as time goes on!

Faulkner, who wrote the local histories of Chelsea and other places, was a second-hand bookseller at the corner of Smith Street, Chelsea, nearly opposite Gough House. He was a little man, and had a brother as small as himself, who lately (1895) died in Paulton Square. Faulkner brought out his *Brentford and Ealing* in 1843, and proposed to my father, then living in Church Street, Chelsea, to exchange a copy for some book of my father's doing. I recollect—it was about 1847—Faulkner left his own book, the equivalent not being ready, and called nearly every day, till my father told him, I think, he might have his volume back again.

I have the most distinct impression of Bell and Horns Lane, commencing with the old-fashioned unpretending hostelry at the corner, with its yard, in which a cobbler had his stall.

A hedge bounded the lane right down the south side, where Thurloe Place and Square were subsequently erected, and the ditch was a good hunting-ground for the rat-catcher. On the north side of the lane beyond Brompton Church lay Pollard's School, a nursery ground, Ingestrie House, and a number of other detached residences in their own grounds. Webster and Harley the actors lived there. The high massive wall enclosing the nursery and Ingestrie House was supported by buttresses, which formed a source of alarm in those days to women and children who were passing after dusk, from fear of attacks by thieves or footpads. Leigh Hunt said that these buttresses reminded him of the legs of the Knave of Clubs. At the other end of the lane was the Hoop and Toy public-house, originally a very primitive establishment, with trees in front of it. Nearly opposite on the north was Gore Lane, leading to Kensington Govor or Gore, and down there, on the right hand, was a house once tenanted by Charles Mathews the younger.

I accompanied my father as a child to the sale of the effects at Ingestrie House prior to its demolition. The only private residence of all those once standing hereabout which still remains is that formerly rented by Sir John Fleming, who had two handsome daughters. These ladies long kept their maiden condition, but had their love affairs. Their father used to say that they were very good girls, and never did him any discredit.

Prospect Place owed its once more appropriate designation to the complete absence of any buildings between the lane at that point and the Fulham Road, till the first wing of the Consumption Hospital was begun, and Sumner Terrace was erected.

On some of the ground nearly opposite the Toxophilite Society held its meetings. Robert Cruikshank, the brother of George, was one of the members.

Pursuing the course of the lane, one had Cowper House on the left and Brompton Hall, a house with eagles over the entrance, on the right, and turning sharply round by the latter, the pedestrian found himself in another and narrower lane, which led to Brompton Vale, the Almshouses, two or three nurseries, and then either to Gloucester Road through a turning to the left or to Kensington across the fields. By taking the right-hand instead of the left, which brought you to Gloucester Road, you reached, down a short *cul-de-sac*, the entrance to Cromwell House, otherwise called Hale House, one of the many reputed residences of the Protector Cromwell, and of which my uncle Reynell was the latest occupier. One of the mantels from this ancient edifice, which stood in four acres of ground, is now in the South Kensington Museum, but it has been unskilfully repaired.

The Vale, of which no trace now remains, lay on the right-hand side of Cromwell Lane, turning down from Brompton Hall toward Gloucester Road and Kensington. It was approached through a doorway, and consisted of a group of cottages on either side of a sinuous footpath. There was no carriage-road. Each residence stood in about half an acre of garden ground, and was enclosed by a high black fence. The Vale, which partly abutted on Cromwell Lane, had been originally formed by the enclosure of some of the demesne of Cromwell House, and the waste plots along the lane were gradually occupied by houses of various styles, including one where the Gunnings formerly lived. On the left-hand side once stood Bute House, and beyond it the Almshouses.

When I knew the Vale, three of the residents were the Reynells, the Spagnolettis, and the Edward Wrights. The ditch which traversed it and skirted the Reynells' garden on the southern side (one of its slopes was their strawberry-bed) came out at the Admiral Keppel inn, where the Chelsea Pound stood, and where there was a meeting of cross-roads. When they were draining this ground about sixty years since, the skeleton of a man who had been buried in lime a suicide or a murderer—was discovered.

On the site of Pelham Crescent was Colville's Nursery, or, rather, one of them. A path, flanked by a ditch on one side and a hedge on the other, led right across to that portion of Bell and Horns Lane, by Brompton Hall. The Crescent was built about 1837 by Bonnin. Old people recollect the fields there, and the stile over which you had to climb to the path which led to Brompton Hall. Pelham Place was a much later creation, *teste meipso*. Our relatives, Sir John and Lady Stoddart, on their return from Malta, were among

the earliest residents there. This was about
1845.

I am reminded that opposite Pelham Crescent
there was in my early time a considerable open
space immediately at the back of Pond Place, and
I went with H. J. Byron, when we were quite lads,
to see a fair held there. This space may have been
the last vestige of Chelsea Common, which, according to Lysons, consisted of thirty-seven acres, and
lay between the Fulham and King's Roads. I
believe that St. Luke's Church and churchyard
occupy part of the area, for it is observable that an
unusually large piece of ground was assigned to this
purpose, bespeaking the relatively small value of
land at the time.

Onslow Square covers the old grounds of several
mansions, including Cowper House. It is the
mutilated avenue of the last which is seen in the
centre and in a passage leading from the Fulham
Road. Many years since a gentleman in this
square had a large collection of papers on Old
Brompton, but who he was, and what became of
them, I never heard.

Bell and Horns Lane practically extended to
Earl's Court, and was bounded on both sides the
whole way down to about 1850 by private mansions

or other houses, market-gardens, and nurseries, among which I may mention those of Gray, Siggers, Colville, Conway (by the turnpike, where the Bolton estate was laid out), Rigby, and Kirke. My mother bought her morello cherries for preserving at Conway's.

The lane eventually debouched near what is now the Brompton Cemetery and the Redcliffe estate, and on the left was Walnut-tree Walk, leading to the Fulham Road (a not very safe place for pedestrians, as I have known ladies robbed at mid-day), while on the right the road wound round to Kensington, and brought one out opposite Holland House.

On the right and left of Walnut-tree Walk, and between that and the cemetery, there was nothing but market-grounds and orchards, except a field on the right, where, years after the presence of any actual danger, a board was to be seen, warning the public 'to beware of the bull.'

On the other side of the cemetery toward the Fulham Fields was a country road, where one of my godfathers, Sir Goldsworthy Gurney, inventor of the Bude Light and of the Steam Tram, was the first, I believe, to put up houses. I accompanied him as a youth on his visits to his property, and have the flavour of the red currants yet on my palate, which I gathered in the remains of the old dismantled orchard.

An amusing experience befell my father while he was in his early married life a visitor at Gurney's in Cornwall. He was rather addicted to woodmanship, and sallied out one day with an axe, wherewith he lopped a number of trees on somebody else's estate. The owner applied to Gurney, who was on the commission of the peace, for a warrant for his guest's apprehension, and that document I possess. But I believe that the matter occasioned some merriment, and was amicably settled.

The ground now occupied by the Brompton Cemetery was a market - garden down to 1836, when, or in 1837, it was surveyed, enclosed, and laid out. The whole area between it and Walnut-tree Walk, and between the Earl's Court and Fulham Roads, was also cultivated, and principally orchards. The grounds of Mr. Toogood's house at the Earl's Court end of the Walk, and Mr. Popart's at the other, nearly met. This was a thoroughly rural bit.

Gunter the pastrycook lived at Earl's Court, while it was still a retired and rustic neighbour-hood. Of course, he had had the opportunity of buying up all the parcels of land outside the Harrington and other estates on both sides of the Fulham Road, and he eventually employed George Godwin the architect, one of the first occupiers of the houses in Pelham Crescent, to lay out the property for him in what is known as Bolton's, Tregunter Road, where Halliwell-Phillipps resided many years, and (on the opposite side) in Gunter's Grove, on the borders of Chelsea and Fulham.

A friend of mine, who was articled to Godwin, recollects Pollard the schoolmaster, next door to Brompton Church, coming in every week to see the *Builder*, which was then a comparatively new undertaking, at Pelham Crescent. Pollard sold his school-site to the Oratory.

Opposite Chelsea Park, or Wharton Park, as it was originally named, in Little Chelsea, lay Brompton Heath, an open space which must have originally extended from the village of Little Chelsea to Swan Lane on the east side, and have abutted on the Earl's Court Road, or continuation of Bell and Horns Lane. This has all utterly vanished. Thistle Grove preserves in its name an indication of the former condition of the site.

Thistle Grove appears to have been parcelled out into building allotments about 1816, and was a *cul-*

de-sac at the northern end, the extension known as Drayton Grove being under cultivation, and the sole approach from the Fulham Road at this point to Earl's Court and Kensington being through the narrow lane at the back of the Grove.

Beyond Little Chelsea lay Walham Green and Fulham, and to the south Sand's End and Parson's Green, all detached hamlets separated from London and each other by wide stretches of open land or garden, now consolidated into one huge continuous street, as it were, resonant with some of the least attractive forms of modern life. Scarcely anything but Peterborough House and Fulham Palace remain to shew what this side of the Metropolis originally was. Fulham Palace possesses a unique interest as the only moated house within the Metropolitan area.

Between Walham Green and Fulham, on the left-hand side, after turning the angle in the road by the modern fire-engine house, lay Purser's Cross, which is lost in the so-called Percy Cross House opposite.

CHAPTER V.

Anecdotes of the Duke of York and Duke of Wellington—Thomas Wright, F.S.A., and Madame Wright—The Carter Halls at the Rosery—Anecdote about Tennyson—Guizot at Old Brompton—An original letter from him to my father—Gloucester Lodge—George Canning—Don Carlos—Braham the singer—Brompton 'parliament'—A mysterious resident in Brompton Vale—The Spagnolettis—The Holls—Henry Holl the actor—His circle—G. V. Brooke—Holl as a mimic and story-teller—Dickens and Forster—Some account of the latter—Frank Holl, R.A.—Dr. Duplex.

FIFTY years ago, Siggers the market-gardener had a large piece of the ground on the Earl's Court side, opposite Conway's Nursery, and contiguous to the turnpike. I met Siggers by chance many years since, and entered into conversation with him about the old place. He narrated a curious anecdote of the Duke of York. He had instructed all his children never to accept gratuities from strangers; it was a very secluded and thinly-populated part, and the precaution was necessary enough. His daughters came home one day, and told him that a gentleman on horseback had stopped them, asked them their names, and, pulling a shilling out of his pocket, stooped to offer it to them. They declined to receive it, and the gentleman asked their reason. They said that their father had ordered them not to take money from anyone. From their description Siggers guessed who their interviewer had been.

This account probably referred to the time when the Duke kept Mrs. Carey at Fulham or another lady at the White House, Putney. His Royal Highness had children by the former, who passed under the name of Gibbs, and strongly resembled the Georges. They went to Roy's school, at Burlington House, Fulham, and were afterward drafted into the War Office.

The public service at that period was the ordinary destination of the offshoots or superannuated servants of the nobility and of Royalty. Indeed, so late as the time of the Crimean War such was still the case. While I was at the War Office, a son of Sidney Herbert was on the staff under an assumed name; he was well nursed.

Siggers told me some queer and unproducible stories of the old Duke of Wellington in connection with Brompton, where he favoured a resort partaking of the character of a casino and something else. His Grace was a regular Orlando Inamorato or Don Juan, and not always of a very high type.

He had the habit of keeping at Apsley House a considerable amount in bank-notes, and on one occasion, when he was paying for a heavy purchase, the vendor respectfully suggested a cheque. But the Duke told him that he liked to settle such matters in cash, as he did not wish Coutts's to know what a fool he was sometimes.

In Sydney Street, Fulham Road, during the last years of his life resided Thomas Wright, the distinguished antiquary and man of letters, the intimate associate of Halliwell-Phillipps. Wright married a discarded mistress of Francisque Michel. I saw her once or twice—a lady of imposing appearance, but, from what Halliwell gave me to understand, and from what I learned otherwise, by no means a crown to her husband, unless it was one of thorns. A credulous relative of mine described her to me on one occasion as a scion of the ancient French *noblesse*. Very possible; and this *noblesse* yielded an abundant crop of such phenomena.

She was poor Wright's evil genius. He was a man of vast industry and erudition, and deserved a better fortune. Halliwell allowed him a pension supplemental to the munificent one of £65 with which the discerning and impartial British Government requited thirty years of archæological scholarship and research.

The royal housekeeper at Kew Palace, her nephew informs me, has £350 a year, with lodging and perquisites. How equitable and how consistent!

Wright was not a journalist, nor a Liverpool man, nor a Scot, or Mr. Gladstone and his *alter ego* might have made him a grant out of the public funds, followed at a decent interval by a pension for life, as they did in the case of a very young man who had written a few copies of verses, and who will, it is to be feared, be a charge on the taxpayers during the next forty or fifty years, thanks to these two eminent Liberal statesmen.

One of the small detached houses along the Earl's Court Road, before you came to Jenny Lind's, was the *Rosery*, or, as Jerrold called it, the *Roguery*. I recollect being taken here as a boy to see the Carter Halls, and being struck by their wall-plums, the bloom on which yet lives in my mind's eye. My companion (or, rather, I suppose I ought to say, escort) was Lily Blanchard, afterward Mrs. Blanchard Jerrold.

Mrs. Carter Hall was generally allowed to be a

very accomplished and able woman; I have always heard that the gray mare was the better horse in this case, and 'Cairter,' as she used to call him, was little better than a book-maker. Yet he continued during a long series of years to earn a handsome income out of journalism and letters, and to secure a pension. He never failed from lack of courage. He asked Moxon and Co. £600 for the right to reprint in book-form his *Memories of Writers*, which he had communicated to some periodical.

This was toward the close of his career. I happened to be the next client whom the firm was to see, and Hall went out as I went in. His aspect was truly venerable, and I noted the amplitude of his shirt-collar, to which he was indebted for the *sobriquet* of *Shirt-Collar Hall*.

The personage who received us both in succession was the manager engaged to look after Moxon's business after his death for the benefit of the widow, Lamb's Emma Isola. He did not do much to promote the interests of his unlucky employer. One of his exploits, I was informed, was to signify his disapprobation of the late Poet Laureate by surmounting his portrait in Moxon's parlour with ass's ears. Because the present deponent objected to certain commercial irregularities in connection with an edition of Charles Lamb's works in 1868, the same individual launched through the hospitable columns of the *Athenæum* some amenities not worth remembering about 'the tribe of Hazlitt,' which yet survives.

A temporary resident in Brompton about this time was the ex-Minister Guizot, whose works on *Civilization* and the *English Revolution of* 1640 my father translated. He sent the books to Guizot, and received the following acknowledgment:

SIR,

Je vous remercie beaucoup des quatre volumes que vous avez voulu m'envoyer. Je suis heureux que mes ouvrages aient rencontré un traducteur tel que vous, et si je rencontre en lisant votre traduction quelques inexactitudes qui meritent d'être remarquées, je m'impresserai de vous les signaler.

Recevez, je vous prie, l'assurance de ma consideration très distingueé.

GUIZOT.

Brompton, Juillet, 1848.

The father of Guizot had perished on the scaffold in the first Revolution, and as, next to his master, he was the best hated man in France in 1848, he naturally lost no time in placing the Channel between himself and his countrymen. Those who were in Paris at the acute crisis must remember the ominous cries of '*A bas Guizot!*'

One of the famous old houses in Brompton was Gloucester Lodge, built for the Duke of Gloucester, one of the sons of George III. It stood on the right-hand side of the Gloucester Road on the way to Kensington. George Canning afterward lived there, and at a later period Don Carlos, whose sudden disappearance one morning in July, 1834, was soon explained by his arrival as the head of an insurrectionary movement in Spain. The building, which occupied with its grounds a considerable area, surrounded by a very high fence, remained unoccupied for a long time, and was at last pulled down. Just before its demolition I went over it with my boyish and almost life-long acquaintance, Henry James Byron, whose name will recur.

Although Michael's Place and Grove and Brompton Crescent, now no more, are in the parish of Chelsea, they were in such immediate contiguity to Old Brompton that I may be excused for mentioning the residence of Braham the singer—Lamb's 'Jew, gentleman, and angel'—in the house at the end of Michael's Grove. The singer's daughter became Lady Waldegrave. My father, who had a very promising voice, was, as we have heard, very nearly becoming his pupil.

Leading up to Braham's house, on the left hand,

and not far from the highroad, was Hume the baker's, a depot for white and brown *parliament,* oblong cakes of farinaceous material slightly sweetened, and cruciformly divided on the face into four smaller squares. The brown variety is still in commerce ; but the other is forgotten, and the cruciformity has been discontinued. A curious book might be written on the origin and archæology of sweets.

Within the limits of Chelsea lay also York Place, adjoining the Jewish Burial Ground, and opposite the Consumption Hospital. I merely refer to it because there was in my nonage a preparatory establishment kept in one of the houses by Dr. Frampton, who, when I was among his pupils, freely applied the ruler to our knuckles, and also employed the old-fashioned *abacus* for arithmetical purposes. I was of the day-scholars, and Frampton rather uncommercially took us out for a walk before dinner, which put a serious edge on our appetites. We had pudding twice a week plum-pudding on Tuesdays and baked rice on Thursdays. The former was always the day when my step on the homeward route was most elastic.

From the preference shown by many of the musical and theatrical professions for this delightful retreat, we are led to infer that the soft air of the locality recommended itself to the bronchial requirements of these gentlemen and ladies, as well as the attraction of the rural scenery and quiet.

I judge it to have been one of the truest pleasures of my life, if not one of its greatest privileges, to contemplate with my own eyes the beautiful hamlet of Old Brompton, as it appeared prior to the Exhibition of 1851, which virtually destroyed it— and not it alone. When I was a child this outskirt of London was much in its primitive condition as it had been in the days of the early Georges, if not of the Stuarts. Fragments of it yet remain to shew what it has been, just about Alexander Place and Square, the old Church, the Queen's Elm, and a few other points.

A mysterious personage preceded my uncle as tenant of the premises in the Vale. It was a forger or utterer, or both, of flash bank-notes; and an old gardener, who afterward worked for Mr. Reynell, gave this account of him, that he rode out every morning on horseback, and returned in the evening, both his beast and himself presenting the appearance of having ridden far and hard. It was conjectured that his practice was to change the notes at different points, and at as considerable a distance as possible from headquarters. What became of the fellow the narrator did not know; if he was apprehended, the 'three-legged mare' was his infallible destiny, and the mere fact that his proceedings were capable of explanation seems to shew that the fraud was discovered, if it was not punished.

Through the Reynells we knew the Spagnolettis, through the latter the Farrens, and through these the Holls, and so on. This was in the early forties. The Byrons became acquainted with us through my father's engagement in the reporting gallery.

Spagnoletti, father of my old friend Charles Spagnoletti, was not only the son of the famous leader of the Italian Opera, and one of the immortal triumvirate in the ballad of *Old King Cole*, but he married the daughter of Stowasser, leader of the Horse Guards Band. My friend's father was a first-rate musical teacher, and might have done very well in his profession. But he was not very methodical, and was greatly addicted to the gentle, but not remunerative, science of angling. Many a time, when his pupils were expecting him, Spagnoletti absented himself on the plea of indisposition, while he had really set off on a pleasant little excursion with his rod and bag. He was another of the worthies of the Vale.

Charles Spagnoletti narrated to me the following naughty little story :

A lad, whose mother had bought some lamb, and had forgotten to ask her husband, who was the leader of the church choir, how she was to dress it, was sent after his father to make the inquiry, and reached the place when the service had already commenced. He went up into the organ-loft, and affected to join in the anthem, chanting :

> ' Mother has bought a quarter of lamb, and how shall she do it ?'

To which the parent, responding, said :

> ' Roast the leg, boil the loin, and make a pudding of the suet.'

It is well known that the boys in the choir frequently mimic the choral intonation in talking to each other, when they have cast their white clerical bed-gowns.

I also owe to him a second anecdote :

Mr. James Forbes and Sir Edward Watkin, long the two leading spirits on the Chatham and Dover and South-Eastern Railways, conferring together on some arrangements propounded by the former to be for mutual advantage, Watkin allowed his friend to go on for some time, but, at last interrupting, said very quietly: ' And where do I come in, James?'

When we first knew the Holls, they resided in a small cottage in Stewart's Grove, a turning out of the Fulham Road. He was a handsome man, and had married a very pretty woman. So far back as I can remember, Henry Holl had an engagement at the Haymarket under Webster's management, but latterly he joined Gustavus Vasa Brooke at the Olympic, and eventually gave up the stage. He was the author of a few dramatic trifles and two or three novels, of which the best, the *King's Mail*, was founded on an incident connected with the Haslemere district - his wife's native place.

We often saw Brooke at Chelsea. He was one of those lost in the *London* in 1866. Holl played second to him in Shakespear and melodrama. As a boy I was most impressed by the American tragedian's *Othello*, *Richard III.*, and *Sir Giles Overreach*. I presumed to set him before Charles Kean all round ; he had a better presence and voice. Alike in Kean and in his wife the voice failed, but he (Kean) was fairly good in such pieces as the *Corsican Brothers* and *Pizarro*.

Holl had known a very wide circle of educated

and intelligent people ; his family had been always associated with art ; and his own ties were principally dramatic and literary. He was fond of books, and sought the acquaintance of bookish men. There were few of the prominent authors of his day whom he had not met, and with some of them he was on intimate terms. He was a man of excellent address, but I always looked upon him as rather artificial.

I mention elsewhere his entertaining imitations of his leading theatrical contemporaries—Keeley, Buckstone, Macready, Webster, and others. When Holl was in the right cue, an evening spent at his house in Brompton over talk about the old poets and playwrights, or, as an alternative, a taste of our host's quality as a remembrancer of other men's styles, was an enrichment of the experience and the thought. To his great annoyance, people often confounded the late Henry Howe and him, both at one time members of the Haymarket establishment ; and I believe that the displeasure was reciprocal.

Holl used to say that when Dickens and Forster took a long walk together, the latter, being somewhat pursy, had to pause occasionally to get breath, and would try to make Dickens relax his pace by drawing his attention to the beauty of the scenery, especially if the route was uphill. Holl's mode of telling the story was very funny—the way that Forster puffed and blew, and held his sides with, ' My dear Dickens, just observe that bit——' He was an excellent *raconteur* as well as mimic.

I pointed out long ago that the Bill Stumps pleasantry in *Pickwick* was borrowed from the *School for Wits*, a jest-book published in 1813. I have heard that the notion of the Golden Dustman in *Our Mutual Friend* was derived from the immense pile of dust which remained for many years untouched at the back of Gray's Inn Lane, somewhere between Coldbath Fields and Mount Pleasant, and that a large sum was eventually cleared by the owner, who sold it to the Russian Government in 1812, after the destruction of Moscow, to mix with the lime for cement. I give this *dit* for what it is worth.

John Forster—Lady Bulwer's Butcher's Boy— was a self-made man, very agreeable to those who could keep him at a distance, but highly unpleasant when he chose. A cabman once described him idiomatically as 'an arbitrary cove.' There was a small *jeu d'esprit* about him related in connection with some wine at the dinner-table, of which Forster, on being asked, characteristically affected to know nothing.

'What's this wine, John?' he says to his man.

'Three-and-six,' says John.

The artificial condescension of Forster was a thing never to be forgotten. This manner arose from his poor training, and was a kind of self-protection. He did not know how you were going to approach him, and he put out his elbow first. His letters to me were polite enough, but he was unpleasantly overbearing to those who did not hold their ground. He was a thorough beggar on horseback.

Frank Holl, the Academician, a nephew of our old acquaintance, was most unassuming and agreeable, but very irritable, partly owing, perhaps, to his always indifferent health, for he was a chronic sufferer from *angina pectoris*, and I was surprised at his lasting even so long as he did.

One day, when a right reverend prelate was sitting for his portrait, everything seemed to go wrong. Holl could not find his colours, and when he found them he missed something else. Then something slipped down; Holl began to mutter curses on Fortune, and at last he swore audibly, till the Bishop got up and, taking his hat, wished the painter good-morning, observing, 'You are the most ungentlemanly man, Mr. Holl, I ever met.'

A common acquaintance of the Holls and ourselves was Dr. Duplex, M.D., to whom I have understood that the Duplex lamp owed its origin. The name always haunts me as a felicitous one for a novel, where the central character was some medical Janus.

CHAPTER VI.

The Byrons—H. J. Byron and his family—Early development of a dramatic taste—As a medical student—My peculiar intimacy with him—Our evenings together—People I met at his house—Story of him and Arthur Sketchley—Byron's earliest love affair—The Bancrofts—Mary Wilton at the Strand—Robertson—Anecdotes of Byron—One of his last sayings—*Robinson Crusoe* and Miss Larkin—*Cupid and Psyche*.

THE Byrons were a second family with whom we met in those days. Henry Byron, father of Henry James Byron the dramatist, was on the *Morning Post*, and secretary of the Conservative Association. He had married Josephine Bradley, daughter of a medical man at Buxton, and an extremely attractive woman; and young Byron, when he left school, was intended to take up his grandfather's profession. I, of course, knew him when we were lads together, and his father lived in a small house near Eaton Square. Henry Byron, who was related to the poet, had been a College man, and had squandered a fortune. He obtained a consular appointment in later life.

The elder Byron was a most genial fellow, and a thorough gentleman by breeding and instinct; but he was deplorably insincere, and that defect was doubtless aggravated by his straitened circumstances and his fondness for little dinners and other sweet impoverishments. I remember that we generally knew when the Byrons of Pimlico were expecting friends to dinner, as an application for a loan of wine, if not of other accessories, was at the last almost a matter of course. When he obtained his appointment, he proposed to requite my father's manifold kindness by an early consignment of choice cigars and preserved ortolans, which never presented themselves. Nor did we expect them.

The dramatic bias of young Byron betrayed itself at a very precocious age. He used, almost as a schoolboy at St. Peter's, to compose scenes, and, like a second Molière, recite them before his father's cook when Mr. and Mrs. Byron were out. From the date of his father's departure for Hayti till his marriage and settlement in Brompton, I saw nothing of him. The last glimpse which I had had was as a medical student with a practitioner near Westbourne Grove.

It was of the latter individual that he quoted

the joke about the boiled rice on two successive
days for dinner, and his principal's exclamation :
'What! boiled rice again! How we do live!' It
was to Hepworth Dixon that they used to ascribe
the impatient rejection of ice-pudding at a dinner,
because he understood the waiter to offer a more
familiar dish.

Subsequently to Henry James Byron and myself
resuming our intercourse, in direct consequence of
our accidental meeting one day in 1858 near the
Queen's Elm, I probably saw more of him than
anyone till within a few years of his death, when
certain private circumstances produced an estrange-
ment. But during a long succession of years I
had the good fortune to enjoy his society and
conversation, and I affirm that, while I knew Byron,
I owed to him some of the pleasantest days of
my life, and that in losing him I lost that which
it was out of my power to replace.

The evenings which he and myself had
together at Brompton and in Doughty Street
proved to me his inexhaustible store of humour
and fun, and that his productions for the stage
and the press were very inferior to his real powers
of talk and aptitude for repartee. His remarks
and his anecdotes, unlike those of duller men, were

diverting and racy without being coarse; and I believe that if his training had been better, and his mind more balanced, he might have shone in the most brilliant society. The lax and corrupt school into which he was brought by his choice of a dramatic and theatrical career exercised the most pernicious influence on a not-very staunch character. The environments of the theatres and the seductions of the green-room sapped his morals and his health.

At Doughty Street I met Sothern and his wife, Mrs. Charles Mathews, Edward and Albert Levi, Arthur Sketchley, Tom Robertson, Marie Wilton, Bancroft, and many others. It was the house associated with Byron's most prosperous period and with his unhappy downfall through the Liverpool speculation. The Levis were the sons of J. M. Levi, who was at one time a printer in Fleet Street. He published a sixpenny series of Tales, including *Joan of Naples*, for which he paid my father as the translator £7 10s. I recollect Mr. Levi handing me the sum on my father's account, and I likewise call to mind a small trait of the same gentleman when he was proprietor of the *Daily Telegraph*, namely, his aversion to tautology. He must have emphasized this sentiment to lead Byron to mention it to me. The Levis were long on the most cordial terms with my friend.

While Byron, Arthur Sketchley, and myself were once at early dinner, an area sneak found his way to the kitchen window, and made off with the silver teapot and some spoons. It was very droll to watch Byron, with his tall, slim figure, and George Rose (Sketchley's real name), a very Falstaff, pursuing the thief into the neighbouring square, and picking up the spoons, which the fellow dropped one by one, to enable him to secure the teapot, at all events. But he was overtaken.

Byron's earliest acknowledged theatrical flame was the accomplished lady once known far and wide as Miss Woolgar. It was a lad's fancy for a woman considerably his senior, and the passion, such as it was, was quenched by the mortifying discovery that his goddess was in reality a married person playing under her maiden name—in fact, that she was the wife of Alfred Mellon.

Mr. and Mrs. Bancroft were architects of their own fortune. He was a provincial actor, whom Byron took up, and brought from Liverpool to the Prince of Wales's Theatre, formerly the *Queen's*

Dusthole, when it was first opened under the joint management of Byron and Marie Wilton. Bancroft, although barely tolerable in private life as I saw him on his first settlement in London, made a very gentlemanly and careful performer on the boards.

Marie Wilton, I heard from Byron, who was very intimate with her through their theatrical companionship, and called her indifferently *Marie* and *Wilton*, was the daughter of strolling players. I knew nothing of her till through his association with the Strand Theatre I saw her in his burlesques, where she was very much applauded for her success in the *breakdowns*. I recollect her *retroussé* nose, her very curtailed petticoats, and her saucy carriage. *Quantum mutata!* They tell me she is now a *grande dame* living in a fashionable square, and plays now and then 'to oblige.'

Robertson, author of several well-known Society pieces, attracted notice as a playwright at last ; but his fortunes had been sadly checkered, and his success came too late to be of much service to him. When his comedy of *Ours* was in course of performance at the Prince of Wales's Theatre, the name was posted up all over the neighbourhood, and some Frenchmen went, thinking it was an exhibition of bears.

When Byron and I have been together talking over things, putting matters in queer lights, or doing a little quiet scandal about common acquaintance, we have sometimes become so convulsed with laughter that we have been scarcely able to keep our feet. It was a favourite trick to pace up and down the room while we talked, and often he took one side and I the other. He was thoroughly honourable, though extravagant and unbusinesslike. When his affairs were on the drift, and he was short of money, I offered to lend him a considerable sum ; but he declined to take it, not being certain whether he should have it in his power to repay me.

He proposed as a motto for the booking-office at the Prince of Wales's, ' So much for Booking 'm.'

My old friend was a lover of good things in a convivial sense as well as otherwise, and keenly enjoyed his meals when there was anything to his liking on the table. I once impudently suggested that the family motto, instead of *Crede Byron*, should be *Greedy Byron*.

Byron amused me by his description of his interviews with old Mr. Swanborough, who was stone deaf. The two sat at opposite sides of a table, and Byron, having provided himself with a series of small slips of paper, had to do his part of the conversation by writing down what he had to say, and passing the memorandum over to the manager. Swanborough read it, and replied orally; but sometimes, when the topic under discussion involved a serious divergence of opinion, the singular medley of written and verbal dialogue became more and more animated, till the dramatist exhausted his stock of material and his companion grew breathless with excitement and indignant gesticulation. Byron, however, maintained his amicable relations with the Strand during many years, and it was the scene of some of his earliest successes.

He was mentioning one day at dinner that he had met the manager of the Surrey Theatre. This was when his pieces were commanding high figures, or bringing him in a splendid royalty. The manager said that he should be very happy to arrange for something. *B.*: 'Well, it's only a question of price. How much do you give?' 'Well,' replied Manager, 'I have given £5.' *B.*: 'Oh, don't let me rob you of all that money, my boy.'

I was told a story about a barn-stormer who used to make the round of the out-of-the-way Scotish towns and play the regular pieces, not forgetting *Hamlet*. He and his company were so successful that they ventured at last to raise the tariff from threepence to sixpence, when the *Prince of Denmark* was put upon the stage. The audience was, of course, rather dissatisfied and mutinous, and after the performance, says Sandy to Jock : ' Wall, an' what did ye think of it?' 'Wall,' says Jock, 'it war pratty well, but war not a saxpenny *Hamlet.*'

Someone having been sent up into the gallery of a theatre where Nelly Farren was playing in *Cupid and Psyche,* to test the acoustic properties of the building for her voice, heard two men debating the signification of the title of the piece and the proper mode of pronouncing the name : one said to the other : ' It's Cupid and Zych, you know ; you must pronounce it like *z* in zinc.'

As in the case of Henry Holl and so many others, the special characteristics of Byron were purely personal. He was in a certain sense the first and the last of his family. He had a daughter, however, who married Major Seton. She was telling me one day that the present Lord Byron called at Colonel Byron's while she was staying there to ask the Colonel or one of his sisters what relation he was to the poet of the same name, in case he should be questioned.

Byron and myself happened to bring out a novel concurrently. I forget the title of his, and that of mine is not worth preserving. It was in 1865. We both knew the editor of the —— very well, and I applied to that gentleman for leave to review my friend's book, and he to review mine. We were mutually encomiastic—too much so, I fear. Gentle reader, if you have not yet printed anything, be sure, before you do, that you engage your critics, and see that they are perfect in their parts. Of course, they must all be friendly, but their friendliness has to be adroitly varied, and even to be thinly sprinkled with guarded qualification, for that evinces a discriminating vein and the hand of a man whom money will not buy. I am rather proud to be able to say that this was the sole occasion on which I thus compromised myself

When Byron brought out his *Robinson Crusoe*, he had a little difficulty with one of the lady *artistes*, Miss Sophia Larkin, because the latter had a part assigned to her (that of the mariner of York himself) which required her investiture in tights, and the fair performer was not too slight in figure. There was some fun over the matter at the time, but Miss Larkin pulled through—the tights and the part. The author was immensely tickled, however, when his buxom Crusoe presented herself for approval.

The remarkable *gaucheries* about persons who

were till yesterday, so to speak, among us, only become amusing from their preposterous character. The son of a publisher in Fleet Street, who had something to do with Byron's literary productions, when I asked him whether he had not frequently seen him at his father's place of business, promptly replied : ' Yes ; he wrote the *School for Scandal.*'

One of the last sayings recorded of him was when Hollingshead and one or two others were with him at the last, and John Colman the actor asked him if he was not the first Hamlet he ever saw. ' No,' replied Byron, leaning on his arm in bed, ' you mistook me, John ; I said you were the *worst.*'

I used now and then to venture at Byron's table to edge in something of my own. When the advertisements of a now wellnigh forgotten public character were placarded everywhere in the London thoroughfares, I remarked that those were the *Woodin* walls of old England. Woodin was for some time the rage. He was to be seen at the Hall in King William Street, Strand, where the Christy Minstrels once performed, and where Toole's Theatre now stands.

Neighbours of the Byrons—that is, of H. J. Byron's parents—in the region bordering on Sloane Square, and equally a family which my father knew through his association with the press, were the McCabes. They were Irish folks and Romanists, and had literary evenings, at which my father was occasionally present. He would say that if he got McCabe on a theological point, and fancied that he had him in a corner, his opponent would always slip somehow between his legs. He used to speak of this gentleman as *Father McCabe* or as the *Patriarch of Pimlico*. Many years after McCabe's retirement to Ireland, he wrote to me personally to solicit my aid in obtaining a publisher for a monograph which he had written on the Romano-British Emperor Carausius The work was scholarly enough, but the topic was not judged to be saleable.

Two names intimately identified with our Brompton, and indeed Chelsea, life are those of Blanchard and Keymer, families connected by marriage. I have, I find, mentioned both elsewhere,* and incidentally I refer in these pages to Blanchard and his daughter, wife of Blanchard Jerrold. Keymer lived at Kennington, opposite the Common, and subsequently at Peckham Rye, and under his hospitable roof assembled Kenny Meadows, James Hannay, F. G. Stephens, whom I so vividly remember in his studio at Lupus

* *Letters of Charles Lamb*, 1886, ii. 290, 433.

Street, Pimlico, and many other literary men and artists.

Our host's eldest daughter is best known as the late Mrs. Charles Heaton, and as Editor of Cunningham's *Lives of the Painters*.

Meadows was a desperate stay-maker. He liked his glass perhaps a little too well, and he had no notion of hours. The Keymers often went to bed, and left their guest to finish the bottle and find his way out. Meadows was a fair designer, but had a very poor idea of drawing.

There are many who look upon *Rowland's Odonto* and *Macassar Oil* as mere trade terms, but Rowland and his wife lived somewhere about Forest Hill, and were, at any rate, acquainted with the Keymers. He was a small man and she a large lady. One night there was an alarm of thieves, and the two got out of bed and proceeded downstairs to reconnoitre, she leading the way, and little Rowland bringing up the rear with the hem of her night-dress in his hand. So the scene was described to me at the time, and it must have been one calculated to disconcert the apprehended invaders.

One of Charles Lamb's latest contributions to a particular class of literature was written in Keymer's album.

At that time, what a neighbourhood it was! All the environs were rural ; they had not been socialized ; Dulwich Wood had not been desecrated. Halliwell-Phillipps lived at Brixton Rise, Ruskin at Denmark Hill. City merchants chose these southern suburbs for their residences, as they had the northern a generation earlier.

CHAPTER VII.

The old actors at Brompton—John Reeve—Liston—The Keeleys—Mrs. Chatterton—Some account of Mr. and Mrs. Keeley—The Farrens—Characters played by old Mr. Farren—*Contretemps* at a dinner-party at Thurloe Place—Durrant Cooper, F.S.A.—His *canards*—One about the Queen and Prince Albert—William Farren the younger—Sir Henry Irving—Webster and Harley—Anecdotes of both—Buckstone—As an actor—The short-petticoat movement—Madame Vestris and Miss Priscilla Horton—Menken's Mazeppa—Mrs. Fitzwilliam—The Spanish Dancers—Behind the scenes at Jerrold's benefit—Charles Mathews and his second wife—Edward Wright—Paul Bedford—The Adelphi melodrama—The more modern pantomime—A daily incident at Old Brompton—The French Plays and Ethiopian Serenaders at the St. James's—The Kenneys—The Baron de Merger—His father and Napoléon I.—My visit to the Château of Plessis-Barbe, near Tours—De Merger and the Third Empire—My first acquaintance with the illustrated French literature—Dumas—Henri Mürger's *Scènes de la Vie Bohème*—Compared with Du Maurier's *Trilby*—Saxe Bannister—His Life of Paterson, founder of the Bank of England—Mrs. Astor at Old Brompton—Her relationship to the Reynells—John Jacob Astor—Origin of his fortune.

AMONG the actors who formerly made Old Brompton their home from its rural attractions, which recommended it to them, or otherwise, was John Reeve, who lived in Brompton Row, and whom a few still surviving may remember at the Adelphi in the *Commissariat*; Liston, who had one of the smaller houses, afterward for years in Chancery, in St. George's Terrace, opposite Hyde Park; Mr. and Mrs. Keeley, the Buckstones, the Farrens, Mathews the younger, who had a place in large grounds in Gore Lane, and Edward Wright. Reeve, who died in 1838, lies in Brompton churchyard. I have noted above the connection of Mrs. Chatterton with Brompton Square after her marriage to Place, the literary tailor.

The Earl of Carlisle, whose name is associated with the Russell, Grey, and Minto set, is said to have resembled Liston; they were both remarkable for their plainness.

The Keeleys were familiar figures in Brompton in my boyhood, and Mrs. Keeley still survives. The last time I met them was in Brompton Row, and my impression was that they were even then— it is fifty years ago—pretty old. But young people have that sort of notion about their seniors, where the difference is sometimes not so very considerable. This distinguished couple belonged to an epoch which can never return or be so much as realized by those who did not form part of it either personally or by direct tradition. Such as had the privilege of intimacy with Keeley or his wife might listen to their account of the stage as they found it—as it was *when Hazlitt wrote*. What have we now but a shrunk volume of capacity spread over an infinitely ampler superficies?

I have personally known three generations of Farren. The original William Farren lived, when I first remember him, in Brompton Square. He was a man of the most gentlemanly appearance and address, and his wife was a handsome and showy woman. My father, when he lived at Thurloe Place, got into trouble by asking some rather starchy people to meet them at dinner. Farren excelled in old men's parts. I saw him in Grandfather Whitehead, the character he was playing at the Strand when he was seized with a fit.

His son Henry, who died young, took the same sort of business, when he was hardly more than twenty. His other son William, who cut a sorry figure when he first came on the boards, became eventually a finished and delightful artist.

My uncle Reynell told me that the elder Farren was considered very fine as Dr. Primrose in the *Vicar of Wakefield*.

It was Durrant Cooper, the Sussex antiquary,

and his amiable sister, who met the Farrens on the occasion just alluded to, and the former was scandalized at having to sit down at table, or at his sister having to do so, with -well, it was a case, as rumour went, of Bonaparte and Josephine, according to Talleyrand's *mot*, over again, and perhaps with no better foundation. Farren and his wife were a remarkably majestic couple. It is more than fifty years since, yet I retain their appearance distinctly. Child as I was, I thought the Coopers too squeamish ; perhaps it was because my parents did so.

Cooper had been solicitor to the Reform Club, but proved too porous. He was a lamentable chatterbox, and some of his *canards* were excruciating, but a thoroughly good-hearted fellow and an excellent local archaeologist. One of Cooper's tales for the Marines was about the late Prince Consort. He made out that the Queen, when Her Majesty found her husband stopping out late rather frequently, put her royal foot down, and declared that she would not permit him to go so often to that Mr. Cooper's in Bloomsbury.

William Farren the younger, as we used to call him, succeeded in keeping or recovering some of the property left by his father, and latterly performed only very occasionally, or for benefits. He formed a plan one autumn for revisiting Italy, when an offer or proposal arrived from one of the theatres, inviting him to take his favourite part in Holcroft's *Road to Ruin.* He wrote back, asking, as his daughter told me, exorbitant terms, in the hope that the manager might decline, and he might go abroad. But I believe that he was disappointed.

Farren resembled, in the extraordinary change which occurred in the public estimation of his power and value as an actor, a second distinguished theatrical character of our time, Sir Henry Irving, than whom any one more desperately hopeless at the outset probably never trod the stage. But the comparison ends with the broad circumstances ; for Farren has risen to his present position by unassisted ability and genius, while Irving seems to have owed his triumph to collateral auspices and the happy (not new) idea of making his pieces spectacularly attractive and accurate—accurate, so far as his knowledge permits. Sir H. Irving does not seem to be very well advised in his presentments, which are, of course, useful to make out any shortcomings in strict dramatic art. The popular ideas, or want of ideas, on certain theatrical subjects may answer for a Covent Garden or Drury Lane pantomime ;

but when a manager aspires to classical propriety, we expect something rather better.

Benjamin Webster and John Harley were both inhabitants of Bell and Horns Lane. The former had a house in that portion which was demolished to widen the thoroughfare opposite the Kensington Museum. Harley lived in one lower down on the same side of the way, facing the site of Thurloe Square. He had quitted the stage before my time, but I recollect Webster both at the Adelphi and Haymarket. He was in his true element in melodrama, and might have done infinitely better if he had never deserted his old quarters in the Strand. I retain in my mind a trivial incident about Harley, which must be half a century old. Some street musicians played before his house, to his infinite annoyance, and when they asked the servant for a *douceur*, Harley desired to see them personally. They were not pleased when he, in response to their appeal, explained his idea that they had come to apologize.

When Webster brought out *Monte Cristo* at the Adelphi, it was thought, as his daughter had married Mr. Edward Levi, son of the proprietor of the *Daily Telegraph*, that a good lift might be fairly looked for in that quarter. Sala was sent to notice it, and the *critique* was anxiously expected. The next morning a most elaborate and characteristic account of Dumas, *père et fils*, their various works, their careers, and so forth, running to two or three columns, appeared in the *Telegraph*, and at the very end there was a casual announcement that Mr. Webster had recently produced a drama on the romance of *Monte Cristo*.

Webster was a liberal, kind-hearted man. When Dion Boucicault was once on the eve of starting for America, he went to him, and asked him to advance him £100 on a manuscript play he brought with him. Webster did so, and did not discover, till his good friend had gone, that only the title-leaf was filled in.

This reminds me once more of Byron, who, being very behindhand with some piece he had undertaken to write for one of the theatres, was waited on by the lessee. The latter complaining of delay, H. J. B. assured him that he had begun the production, and shewed him a sheet of paper on which was written *Act I., Scene* 1.

Webster died poor, yet it used to be averred that at more than one period of his career he might have retired with an ample fortune.

In a note from Buckstone to my father he mentions the *Crimson Hermit* as a piece which the latter had recommended to his notice. The title is suggestive of the Coburg or the Surrey, or even of the meridian of Shoreditch. It was beyond doubt abundantly sensational and sanguinary – perhaps rather too much so for the Theatre Royal, Haymarket.

It must have struck many besides myself that the parts in which Buckstone appeared were mere *noms de théâtre*. His acting was essentially personal. He performed under a variety of designations, but it was always Buckstone under an *alias:* the same voice, the same gestures, the same mannerism. He never threw himself into a part, or realized to the spectators any character but his own; and if he is remembered as having excelled in anything, I take it to be the case that it was a creation which fairly suited his style, and in which he could not perpetrate any serious impropriety.

The short-skirt movement in the ballet and extravaganza under the auspices of Vestris at the Lyceum, and during Buckstone's management at the Haymarket in Miss Priscilla Horton's palmy days, made considerable progress just before the period when the burlesque came so much into vogue, with its supremely offensive and silly impersonations of female characters by men. The abridged petticoats of the ladies proceeded, no doubt, to an intolerable pitch; and they tried, as Byron said, to outstrip one another. Speaking of Menken, he remarked that her costume began too late, and ended too soon, and with more particular reference to his *Mazeppa*, he calculated her toilet in the first act at thousands, and in the third, where she is lashed to the wild steed of the desert, at $4\frac{3}{4}$d.

The Spanish Dancers also made their *début* at the Haymarket about forty years since, and I, as a mere spectator, was very agreeably impressed by their graceful and restrained action, shewing the compatibility of this class of art with decorum.

Buckstone was very deaf, and his son, who lived under the same roof with him in Brompton Square, inherited the infirmity. Such as were familiar with the men will appreciate the oddity of the two Buckstones conversing and shouting at each other, each in turn with his hand to his ear to catch what the other said. The younger Buckstone had at one time an engagement under his father at the Haymarket.

I was once taken by my father to Richmond Lodge, Putney, where Mrs. Fitzwilliam lived under Buckstone's protection. It was a low-pitched bungalow house, lying back from the road, just before you came to the *Arab Boy*; it has now been pulled down to make room for a row of modern buildings of the common stereotyped character.

The very first time I was behind the scenes at any theatre was at the performance for Jerrold's benefit at the Olympic, when I saw Mrs. Fitzwilliam and Madame Vestris. I went behind once or twice during Byron's management of the Prince of Wales's; but I found the practice rather disillusionizing. There was, of course, a wonderful contrast between what Madame Vestris had been, and what she became in old age. Byron went to see her toward the last at the house called Holcrofts at Fulham, and found her darning Charles Mathews's stockings.

They were both mournfully extravagant creatures, and had run through a fortune—or two. The second Mrs. Mathews, whom I met at Doughty Street, tried hard to induce her husband to economize. The very last time I saw him was in Sotheran's shop in the Strand. He was as jaunty as could be, with his cigar in his mouth and the old gay swagger; it cannot have been long before his death.

A near neighbour of my uncle Reynell, while he was in Brompton Vale, was Edward Wright, the eminent Adelphi comedian, whose name used to be so much coupled with that of Paul Bedford. The Wrights and Reynells became very intimate, and the friendship even survived the lifetime of Wright himself. He afterward removed to Merton Villa at Chelsea, and I have often seen him standing at the corner, in the King's Road, waiting for the omnibus. During a length of years he was paramount at the Adelphi, and excelled in farce and melodrama. Bedford and he generally played together, and Wright saved money, which partly disappeared in bricks and mortar (his besetting sin) and partly through legal channels.

Wright belonged to the school of Liston, Robson, Tooie, and Buckstone, but was unlike them all. He was a genuine personality, and could hold the Adelphi audience in the hollow of his hand, so to speak. He had only to shew half his droll face, and the house was convulsed. Bedford and he, Céleste and Webster, went far to make the Adelphi what it was in the days of the *Wreck Ashore* and the *Green Bushes*.

Wallack is not much remembered by the playgoers of our day; but in the once favourite melodrama of *Don César de Bazan*, when he supported the chief part, he was thought unsurpassed. I have seen him more than once at the Haymarket in that piece, and vividly retain the song, accompanied by the guitar, where the disguised brigand reveals himself to the terrified heroine.

They at present produce pantomimes year by year at the houses with names which are little more than clothes-pegs. *Puss in Boots, Cinderella, Aladdin, Robinson Crusoe, Ali Baba,* are mere *noms de guerre.* There is scarcely any of the true comic element left; they are pieces of spectacular incongruity, setting at defiance all known or accepted facts. But these meretricious shows seem to appeal successfully to uncritical sightseers. The earliest thing of the kind I can call to mind was at Covent Garden. It was *Robinson Crusoe,* where the curtain rose to a view of the ship, occupying the whole of the stage, and the hero the only person seen. The serious piece of the evening was Balfe's *Bohemian Girl.*

Many of these theatrical celebrities were, we thus see, associated with Old Brompton, Kensington, or Chelsea, and it was an every-day occurrence to meet some of them walking to town in the forenoon on their way to rehearsal, or in the sixpenny omnibus proceeding to the business of the evening. Penny fares and morning performances were yet to come. I am also speaking of a period when theatres were few, and when Sadler's Wells was very little frequented by West-Enders, while the Theatre Royal, Shoreditch, might have as well been in Tasmania. But the Adelphi, Surrey, and Astley's were great houses for certain specialities.

I accompanied my father as a boy to see at St. James's Theatre two very dissimilar entertainments, the French Plays, where Lablache, Lemaitre, Achard, Cartigny, and other artists, made their first appearance before a London audience, and the *Ethiopian Serenaders*, the prototype of *Christy's Minstrels.*

Comparatively limited, however, as the theatres were in number, some of them were often let, *faute de mieux*, for conjuring and other miscellaneous purposes. M. Philippe, at the St. James's, was the first conjurer I ever saw.

When we were in Brompton, either at Alfred or Prospect Place, the Kenneys lived in South Street, Alexander Square. The name and fame of Kenney are at the present moment chiefly identified with his *Sweethearts and Wives.* He had married the widow of Holcroft, and was a dramatist almost *jure uxoris*. When I saw him he was sadly afflicted, and the household was broken up by his death. All the members of the family, including Mrs. Kenney, were delightful associates, and accomplished men and women.

James, the eldest son, was in the Post-Office, and was a short, dark man, very pleasant and full of anecdote, like his mother, but strangely choleric. He had lodgings in an upper story in the Strand at one time, and owing to some squabble over the tea-table threw a quartern loaf out of the window on to the hat of a passer-by. His younger brother, Charles, was a mercurial, hilarious fellow, who carried the *garçon* into middle life. He used to prepare librettos for the operas, and pretty indifferent they were.

All the Kenneys shone in a particular sort of conversation ; they had mixed in very good society, and in their company there was very slight risk of not being entertained. They were all rather prone to hyperbole, and the odd part was that each would put you on your guard as to the propensity of the rest in this direction.

One of Mrs. Kenney's daughters by Holcroft married the Baron de Merger, of Plessis Barbe, near Tours, and her brother was settled at Tours itself as a civil engineer. I spent some time at the Mergers' in 1855 or thereabout, and I laid the opening scene of the ballad of the *Baron's Daughter* at the point where the bridge spans the Loire by the city.

De Merger's father had been in the service of the great Napoléon, and had been invited by him to become one of his aides-de-camp, but he declined. His son used to tell me how the Emperor never met the elder Merger without saying to him : ' Ah, M. Merger, why would you not become my aide-de-camp ?'

My host spoke very fair English. I suppose that it was hot, thirsty weather when I was at the château, but I have in my remembrance the Baron's disinterested counsel to me on sanitary grounds never to swallow down too much claret, but to moisten the lips and throat with it. I had contracted the tertian ague during a previous visit to the Netherlands, and had a recurrence of it here. De Merger cured me with a tasteless coffee-coloured tisane, in which the leading ingredient was the inner bark of the elm.

De Merger was in politics a Rouge, and belonged to a very advanced political club at Tours, to which he took me one evening, and where I was somewhat uneasy, lest the police should pay us a visit. It was the dawn of the Third Empire. In fact, he himself was rather alarmed one day when a small detachment of cavalry galloped over the bridge of the moat, and drew up in front of the house. He imagined that the soldiers might have instructions to arrest him as a malcontent. It turned out, however, that they had merely come to solicit a *boire*.

It was while I was in the South of France that I first made an acquaintance with the illustrated French literature of the Dumas type and period. It was early in the fifties. Perhaps the most interesting and remarkable books were *Monte Cristo* and Henri Mürger's *Scènes de la Vie Bohème*, 1851, the former, of course, still well remembered, but Mürger's admirable book only a few years ago made familiar to the modern English reader in a translation issued by the late Henry Vizetelly.

The nearest approach to it that we have is Mr. Du Maurier's *Trilby*, where his own student life and that of some of his friends are evidently portrayed. I think that I could fill in the names. Trilby herself is an idealized model, and the English writer's *altogether* appears to be a translation—and not a very good one—of the French 'ensemble,' the expression used when a woman poses for the whole figure.

A daughter of Mrs. Kenney by her final husband

married rather late in life Cox, proprietor of the British Gallery in Pall Mall. This person was very intimate with Joseph Gillott, the Birmingham pen-manufacturer, whose collection of paintings he assisted to form. I believe that *Joe*, as Cox called him, was largely instrumental in building up the other's fortune. The contents of the British Gallery were estimated by the owner at £100,000 ; but when a day of adversity arrived, and the property was sold, the public modified these figures to a very serious extent.

There was another household of which we saw some little about this time—that of Mr. Saxe Bannister, who wrote the *Life of Paterson*, founder of the Bank of England. Bannister had been Attorney-General in one of our colonies, and was a man with a grievance which, with Paterson and teetotalism, absorbed his whole thought and conversation, and constituted, I believe, no inconsiderable part of his estate. It was Paterson who originated the Council of Trade and Plantations, the prototype of the Board of Agriculture, which Arthur Young, its other promoter, not improbably conceived to be a novelty in our administrative system.

I may also mention the widow of Astor, of the

Tottenham Court Road, the pianoforte-maker. She lived, I have heard, in Brompton Crescent. One of her daughters was the second wife of Mr. George Reynell, my maternal great-uncle. The American millionaire, John Jacob Astor, was a younger brother of this one, who fitted him out when he went to America to *make*, not *seek*, his fortune, which was largely due to successful investments in land in or near New York. Of this his sister-in-law assured Mr. Reynell, when he once called on her at Brompton. John Jacob Astor used to send his nephews and nieces in England every year handsome presents. Considering his vast wealth, they were poor. Mrs. George Reynell had only about £300 a year of private income.

CHAPTER VIII.

Kensington—A relic of St. Mary Abbot's—Norland House and its spring—Former solitariness of the neighbourhood—General Fox—Carl Engel—The Bowmans—Fulham—Walham Green and the vicinity — Primæval forest—State of the roads between Fulham and the adjacent places—C—— Cottage—Captain Webb, the highwayman—Specimens of our *causeries* at C—— Cottage—Anecdotes related by both of us of our professional and other acquaintances—Lock—Sir Matthew Thompson—Brunel —- Cockburn —George and Robert Stephenson — Thomas Brassey—Lord Grimthorpe—Some of my tales.

My walks when I lived at Kensington (1862 to 1881) as a householder on my own account, extended over the whole region within a dozen miles or so, and of course took in places in the immediate vicinity. It may be worth noting, in reference to St. Mary Abbot's, of which the grounds once probably extended to Addison Road, that during my residence in the immediate neighbourhood an ancient silver crucifix was dug up in one of the gardens on the eastern side of the road; the relic was by possibility the property of one of the members of the Abbey.

One of the earliest attempts to build on the high-road to Uxbridge was on the site of Norland House, for many years occupied by the Drummonds. It was a very large structure, standing back from the thoroughfare, and was celebrated for a spring, called the Norland Spring, within the walls. This still exists in a house in Norland Terrace. But at the time that the original mansion stood, the whole neighbourhood was perfectly countrified, and very desolate. There were only a few dwellings dotted here and there. The builder had not entered upon the ground. No one had dreamed of Addison Road and its surroundings. My uncle Reynell recollected the spot when there was scarcely a house there. I remember it a private thoroughfare with a bar at the northern extremity, and not a break or turning from end to end. General Charles Fox, brother of Lord Holland, lived in a house on the Uxbridge Road in large grounds taken out of Holland Park. He had married Lady Mary Fitz-clarence, one of the daughters of William IV. by Mrs. Jordan; and he was a noted coin-collector, particularly of the Greek series. After his death his cabinet was sold to the German Government for £23,000. Fox was a familiar figure in Addison Road about 1860.

Next door to us at Addison Road lived Carl Engel, the eminent musical antiquary and expert. He had married a sister of the late Sir William Bowman the oculist. Bowman's daughter was a somewhat studious maiden, and I used to see her occasionally at Engel's. I remember that she spoke to me of Chaucer's *Canterbury Tales* as a book of which she had heard, and which she would like to read. I lent it to her without reflection, and it was returned to me with compliments and many thanks too soon to admit the possibility of the girl having read it. She had shown it to mamma. What would Chaucer have thought of the works of fiction which were not, I presume, judged unfit for Miss Bowman's perusal, and which were either vapid or meretricious? Her brother, whom I also saw at Engel's, the latter always alluded to as 'the good bo-oy'—the present Sir Paget Bowman, I apprehend. After his first wife's death Engel engaged himself to a second lady, but on the eve of the marriage hanged himself in a bedroom cupboard.

Fulham, like Brompton, was a quiet country hamlet, apportioned between labourers' cottages; mansions of long standing and historical interest, such as Moore Park and Fulham Park (both obliterated), and Holcrofts, where Charles Mathews latterly resided—of course in style (also a thing of the past); wide acres of arable and pasture; the village itself; and the old-fashioned moated Palace, where the vernal glory of the scene on an April day is worth the whole episcopal bench.

Walham and Parson's Greens, again, and Eelbrook Common, mark the site of an extensive primeval forest of which the vestiges were discovered in forming the line of railway from Earl's Court, and which was long sparingly covered with buildings. This forest doubtless stretched from the river-banks over the whole adjacent country; the subsoil below the alluvial formation was described to me as resembling black soap; and its effect on vegetation was electrical.

What a retrospect the imagination fills up behind one of the sluggish rivulet meandering through the dark unbroken wold to the Thames, and of Master Piers of Fulham, that angler ages before Walton, and Master Geoffrey Chaucer enjoying together a spring morning's fishing or fowling, where now——

The greater portion of the common at Walham Green has been ruthlessly absorbed; the erection of a church was, as usual, the first act of spoliation.

It may be taken for granted that all the by-paths and lanes connecting Fulham with Hammersmith and Kensington were, half a century since, alike lonely and insecure. The roads on the outskirts in this as in other directions were infested by highwaymen of various pretensions. In old C—— Cottage, opposite the Bishop's Palace, while it remained what its name imports, lived during some time a *Captain* Webb, whose business called him away after dusk. He used to saddle his horse every evening, and sally forth in quest of booty. He was of the race of Turpin and Macheath. He haunted doubtless some locality at a measurable distance from his headquarters. There was an ample choice : Putney and Wimbledon, Hounslow and Bagshot, and much of the route between these points and home.

The evenings at C—— Cottage, Fulham—not Captain's Webb's, but a gentler entertainer's, who had a share in the promotion of the North-Western, Midland, and other railways—have formed within the last twenty years the opportunity of collecting numerous notices of bygone and forgotten facts about persons and places, with which the owner as my by a long way senior was more or less intimately conversant. He was educated at Burlington House, Fulham, which has been already mentioned. His earliest recollection is being taken on somebody's shoulder to see the procession at the coronation of George IV.

My friend met with a cooper in Fulham who had been Webb's servant at C—— Cottage as a youth, and who remembered waiting on the company whom his master occasionally invited to dinner. In these cases the party usually broke up about midnight, but, instead of going home, dispersed on their respective beats in quest of plunder. It was like a meet before the hunt. Webb lies in Fulham church-yard.

The principal market-gardeners and florists in Fulham were Osborn and the Bagleys. The latter had two extensive plots of ground at Sand's End. One of them was a great tomato-grower. Osborn faced Elysium Villas, now meriting that name no longer.

A. told me that he dined with Lock the engineer the evening that the line from Vauxhall to Waterloo was opened. It cost upwards of £800,000, on which he understood that Lock took 5 per cent.

The most expensive piece of work on which he himself was ever engaged was the Wolverhampton and Walsall, the extent being only six and a half miles, and the cost £650,000.

He was mentioning on the same occasion that,

when he was in full professional swing, if a £10,000 job had been brought to him, he would have given £100 to have it taken away again, as these small contracts often involved an actual loss.

The late Sir Matthew Thompson used to say to him: 'When I am at Guisley, I am the squire; when I am at Derby, I am chairman of the Midland Railway; and when I am at Bradford, I am a common brewer.'

A. said that it was through Brunel asking him to recommend a counsel for a great case which was then impending in Parliament that the late Chief Justice Cockburn obtained his first important brief. Cockburn was then, curiously enough, in the Queen's Bench—not as a judge, but as a debtor for £150, and Brunel had to get him out before his services were available.

My friend often saw him after that, and furnished him with technical information, which enabled Cockburn to surprise witnesses by the amount of knowledge which he appeared to possess of the *minutiæ* of engineering work. The old judge would call at A.'s office either on his way to the Court or on his return.

When Cockburn went down to Leicester as a commissioner to inquire into the management of the Corporation, he spent a good deal of his time at Mother Slack's, and if he was wanted, it was the surest place to find him. It used to be alleged that he drew up his report there. In his earlier professional life a lady (not always the same) was often to be observed walking up and down outside Westminster Hall waiting for the learned counsel. No one probably could have related such a varied series of *bonnes-fortunes*. To the country, which paid him so well for his services, he proved himself grateful by distributing his sinistral representatives of both sexes pretty freely, when there was a berth at his disposal or the conditional holder of one, as the case might be. You took the place perhaps—the place and the lady, perhaps. Cockburn was a familiar figure in the thoroughfares which he had to traverse from the Court to his house : a small man, negligent in his attire, and with his neckerchief as frequently as not hind part before. But he was a great lawyer ; some of his successors on the Bench have proved themselves his inferiors in capacity, and his equals, or nearly so, in less desirable respects.

Cockburn was very grateful to those who had served him in early life. He was, like the present Mr. Justice Hawkins, one of the party which accompanied A. in his shooting excursions.

George Stephenson, even in his time, said that, give him a clear and good road without *fishings*, and he would make a train run a hundred miles an hour. He had a poor opinion of canals, and declared that they would all become in the end dry ditches. A. observed to me, when I referred to the railway journey between Manchester and Warrington over Chat Moss, that the most striking thing was to stand on the line a quarter of an hour before a train came up, and feel the vibration arise and gradually increase, as if the whole spongy mass had one pulse and one centre of motion.

It was from Robert Stephenson that my friend acquired the habit of leaving his throat open and not wearing *a comforter*, which, as Stephenson said, tended to render you susceptible to cold, especially when, as in those days, and in both their cases, you had to travel so constantly at all hours of the day and night.

Not long before Thomas Brassey's death, while he was staying at Hastings, he sent for John Stephenson, who had rendered him valuable service in his undertakings as an assistant. When he arrived, the old contractor was very kind in his manner and kept him for some time in conversation ; and when at last he left, Brassey pressed something into his hand. It was a cheque for £5,000.

John Flabell, the contractor from the Black Country, was selected to do the tunnelling on the Brighton line, and had some 350 men under him. These rough fellows rather scandalized the then quiet district, and the local parson begged Flabell to try and keep them in better order. ' And can't you get them to come to church ?' Flabell on the next Saturday pay-day bribed the navvies with a promise of a pint each if they came to church next day in their best ; and they not only came accordingly, but filled the building before the rest of the congregation arrived. Flabell and his lady were there, too. The other worshippers presented themselves, saw no room, and went away in a fume. Presently a loud tap was heard on one of the windows, and a voice outside shouted : ' Gaffer, gaffer ; can't get in. *Don't forget the pint !*

The printed evidence taken in railway bills before Parliamentary committees occasionally offers rather amusing features, and it is necessarily little known. Lord Grimthorpe as Mr. Beckett-Denison was a very noted figure in these matters and scenes in the old days. His cross-examination of Sir Frederick Bramwell, whose name is so much associated with public business, arbitrations, and so forth, in one instance, when Bramwell opposed the promoters of a new northern line, was inimitable for its dexterity. From posing as a personage of immense practical experience in that class of enterprise, he was by a series of cleverly-marshalled questions whittled down at last to the solitary superintendence of the West Bromwich Gas Works; and when Beckett - Denison had forced from his adversary this admission, he said to him with exasperating suavity: 'I think, Sir Frederick, we need not detain you any longer.' Of course, I am relating an incident which is now only historical.

Hawksley the engineer, being under examination in some case by Lord Grimthorpe, was very decided in his replies, and Grimthorpe observed to him: 'You appear, Mr. Hawksley, to have formed very definite opinions about most things.' The other assenting, Beckett-Denison added: 'And pray tell us, are there any points on which you have not arrived at a conclusion?' 'Why, yes,' returned Hawksley; 'I can think of three.' 'What are they?' Beckett-Denison inquired. 'Wills, clocks, and bells,' said Hawksley, referring to the other's three failures. Had he lived to the present day, he might have added to the list.

A. and myself knew in common the two Rennies

Sir John and his brother George. The original Rennie died in 1821. He was an eminent book-collector, and his library was sold some years after his death. His son, Sir John, reserved the first and third folios of Shakespear—1623-63. I have a very lively remembrance of accompanying the second Rennie (Sir John, not George) to Antwerp when I was a youth, and his impatience to disembark, which nearly led to my immersion in the Scheldt. It was just then thought that I might try my hand at engineering, and I did for eight months.

Anyone who only knows Antwerp as it is to-day can have a very imperfect idea of what it was when I landed there with Rennie in 1852.

If I was under no other obligations to the Rennies, I owed to them this— that I planted my foot on that historical ground, that my eye fell on Antwerp, before a thousand gables and a labyrinth of steep, tortuous, dark streets or water-lanes were clean swept away to meet the demands of commerce, more tyrannous than Spaniard or Austrian.

Before I knew Antwerp well, I asked a Belgian the way one day to the Cathedral. I inquired for *la Cathédrale*. He regarded me with an opaque stare. I repeated the question. He shook his head. Presently a light began to break on his honest countenance, and he lifted a finger significantly. 'Ah!' he cried, 'Monsieur cherche la Cathé-DRALE!'

In the *Galerie du Roi*, at Brussels, I was once accosted by a person who spoke good English, and demanded if he could serve me in his capacity as *cicerone* to one of the places of resort for a certain purpose in the City. He said that his fee was five francs. 'Well,' I answered, 'and do you depend on this employment?' 'No,' said he. 'What do you do, then, in the day?' 'Why,' said he, 'I shew gentlemen and ladies over St. Gudule.' This ran on all fours with the female pluralist, who, C. mentioned, in an island not a thousand miles from Southampton was reputed to be the only suspicious character, but who on Sundays acted as pew-opener at her parish church.

I related to A. a singular little episode which occurred while I was in the Netherlands under the Rennies. I often spent from Saturday to Monday under the hospitable roof of an English friend at Yerseke, a few miles from Bath. We played at whist one Saturday evening, and suddenly a card was missed. We searched for it everywhere in vain till by chance someone descried it stuck fast in my slipper. No effort or ingenuity of mine could have placed it there.

Henry Wright, my host, who afterward married a daughter of the second Duke of Wellington and became secretary to the Duke of Sutherland, was a low-built man about five-and-twenty, and was extraordinarily supple and agile. I have seen him clear eighteen feet on the level with a very short run, and when we were alone at Yerseke he would in the not very spacious drawing-room go to one end, and spring over the loo-table with a fresh pair of long wax candles in the centre of it without extinguishing the lights.

I used to travel from Bath to Yerseke in a top - heavy antediluvian coach, passing through several villages on the way. In one, on either side of the road, was an avenue of pear-trees, with the ripe fruit hanging from the branches. When I told A. of this, he concurred with me in thinking that if it had been in England the public would have picked the pears to prove their social and political equality.

My lodgings at Bath faced the chapel. I recounted to A. a petty incident which I witnessed one day as I looked out of my window. A small procession, headed by a man and a woman, came up and entered the chapel. I asked my landlady what they were going to do. To be married. Well, they had lived together twenty years, these two Hollanders, just to see how they suited each other before they passed the probationary stage.

Among my associates on the polders, which Rennie engaged to enclose and reclaim, were Mr. Winder and Heer Müller, the last a most gentlemanly and agreeable Hollander, who spoke broken English, with a very pretty and very French wife. I was once with him on the river (that is, the Scheldt) in a boat, and seeing how inveterately he smoked, I naturally asked him whether he was very fond of it. 'Yes,' was his answer, 'for it do make me dink.' At a dinner given by Winder to the Dutch officers of the small garrison at Bath, he, in responding to the toast of his absent wife's health, declared that he loved her better than his life; but he put *life* in the wrong gender. The two old women with whom I lodged in this place remembered the visit of Napoléon and Maria Louisa there more than forty years before.

Sub rosá, I fell in love at Bath (which they pronounce *Bats*), or rather just outside it, with a maiden of the country called Antje Dronkers, whose papa pursued some local industry; but we were both persons *unius linguæ*, and this kept the flame low. I do not recollect any tears.

But I told A. that I did recollect crying, because I had sent to my father for a little pecuniary aid, my salary being modest, and he had remitted *half a crown*, which was all he could afford, he wrote. I felt ashamed of myself that I should not have been more thoughtful than to ask for the money, and I tried to earn forgiveness some time afterward, when I had saved enough, by purchasing a scent-bottle, which I took to the captain of one of the steam-boats plying between London and Antwerp, *and asked him to deliver it to my mother* at Chelsea, which he did.

I put it to A. whether such reminiscences were not prouder and sweeter than fame or wealth, and he said that he thought so. He was much my senior, but his mother was constantly on his lips.

A , as a former large employer of labour, appreciated my relation of a small experience, when I was last in Rouen. I saw a man sauntering, as I was, up a street, pipe in mouth, and took him for a fellow-traveller. He turned out to be a Londoner, who had come there *in search of work*, and wanted to know if I could recommend him.

CHAPTER IX.

Fulham *causeries* (*continued*)—Earnshaw the chronometer-maker
—Tom Sayers the pugilist—Watch-house in Marylebone Lane
—Glyn the banker—Laura Bell—Skittles—The Leicestershire
set—The Bell at Leicester—Captain Haymes—Story of a
Bishop at Harrogate—An adventure at York—George Tom-
line—Some account of him and his father—The Paston
Letters—Barrington the pickpocket—A curious shop in
Seven Dials.

OF Thomas Earnshaw, the famous chronometer-
maker in Bloomsbury (the second of the name),
my friend was full of anecdotes. He possesses
a chronometer, which Earnshaw gave him. The
latter, a small man with a disproportionately large
head, and not remarkable for the elegance either
of his dress or his diction, was a violent democrat
and something of a freethinker. He did not prosper
very much with the clerical authorities in his parish.
When the collector called for an Easter offering,
he feigned a difficulty in comprehending his meaning. 'Easter offering? What is that, sir?' 'Why,
Mr. Earnshaw, what they give every year to the

rector. It is usual, sir.' 'Is it, sir? Well, here is sixpence to buy a length of rope for his reverence to hang himself.' He once took part in a political open-air meeting in Clerkenwell, and was very fierce and trenchant in his language before he addressed his audience. When he ascended the platform, he was going to commence, when the superintendent of police pulled him by the skirt of his coat, and whispered to him, as a man whom he knew and humoured: 'Mr. Earnshaw, pray come down. If you speak, I must take you.' And Earnshaw melted away among the crowd.

It must have been very funny when little Earnshaw, having been chosen headborough for his parish, called on the rector-archdeacon and apprised him of his nomination by the votes of his fellow-parishioners; and, says he, 'I shall be obliged, Mr. Archdeacon, if you will accompany me to explain to me my outdoor duties, as I am in a difficulty about them, and the law prescribes that in such case I shall apply to you, sir.'

A. is of the Clockmakers' Gild. I told him about the watch which Calvert had mentioned to me (whether truly or not, God knows) as having been made about 1680 for his ancestor Lord Baltimore, proprietor of Maryland, by John Pepys, who, according to my informant, occupied seven months in the work. He offered to shew it to me if I would go up to his house in Camden Town.

We were speaking of Tom Sayers the pugilist. He was a Staffordshire man, and a bricklayer by trade. Brassey employed him to do some of the two-arched bridge at Rugeley on the North Western. He was a pleasant, civil little fellow, nimble on his feet, and standing about five feet six ; but the muscles of his arms were as hard as iron.

The old watch-house in Marylebone Lane, from which the Charlies for that district used to turn out every evening to the number of the days in the year, was referred to. No man knew beforehand to what beat he would be ordered, and the practice was to bring the file to a halt, call a name, and give him his round. This checked collusion and bribery. There was a similar institution on Islington Green, at Knightsbridge, and elsewhere.

Glyn the banker, speaking to A. about the gain to the Bank of England and other similar institutions from the loss of their notes, related a curious instance of the ignorance of seamen in money matters. Before Trafalgar, the crews had been paid in Bank of England notes, the wages having accumulated and specie being scarce ; and many of them, not having the opportunity, perhaps, of spending their earnings in the free manner usual with the profession, carried them down to Portsmouth, but before embarking took the precaution to exchange them for local Bank paper, which, like the Scotchman of former days and his £1 note, they thought better security than that of the National establishment. The Portsea Bank made a good haul over the transaction, as so many of the holders of its paper went to the bottom.

Thistlethwaite, who was a life-tenant of a large property on the Paddington estate, and who married Laura Bell, lived in Grosvenor Square. A singular illustration of the universality of commissions or tips occurred one day. He had told a man to send him round a horse on approval or inspection, and the animal was duly trotted up and down his side of the square, when Captain ——, of the Guards, happened by the merest accident to pass that way. He learned what was going on, and his opinion was asked by T. He was loud in his commendations ; but unluckily T. differed and declined, and the Captain in the Guards lost his percentage.

It was a singular household. Thistlethwaite and his wife, a very pretty little woman, did not see much company, and did not agree very well. Every evening there was a sort of state dinner at eight, and a costly dessert, and only those two, one at one extremity of a long table, and the other at the other. The latest occasion on which they came before the public was in a sort of petty *cause célèbre*, which T. won, arising from Laura's extravagance and a huge bill sent in by a West End firm for dress. Before she married, Laura Bell had a house in Wilton Place, where she received her gentlemen friends, like a modern Aspasia or Phryne. The late Marquis of —— was a noted figure there, and he often came on his white pony. The pony was carried off one day by a preconcerted arrangement, and was not recovered without a handsome reward.

Skittles, who was of a similar type to Laura Bell, was at one time in equal vogue, and used to hold a sort of levée at a West End Restaurant. A noble Lord paid her homage in his younger days, if he did not keep her. I have heard that when his lordship told her that he had spent upon her enough to build the *Great Eastern*, she replied that she had spent upon him enough to float that ship. But poor Skittles came to grief, and died in very bad circumstances indeed.

We spoke of the British earthworks so widely spread over England, and sometimes buried in underwood. I had just returned from Elsted in Sussex. Outside the Fitzhall estate there, I told A., I noticed some remains of this sort. They lie unheeded, being so common. I added that, as I was climbing up Trundle Hill by Goodwood with Mr. Piggott, of Fitzhall, he informed me that from the summit one could see almost all the kingdoms of the earth. ' And are you,' I inquired, ' the gentleman who shews them ?'

I mentioned to A. a trait of the unphilosophical and guileless simplicity of childhood. My son, when he was a very little fellow, was with me in a field in Wales, and we observed a cow gazing at a dog, after the manner of her kind. The boy looked up at me, and said with a dry gravity : ' Might be its mother.'

The late Mr. Thomas Miles, land-agent of Keyham, near Leicester, who probably knew more of the concerns of the families for miles round than any individual of his time, used to tell A. that Jones, the parson at Ashby, would have a cloth laid over the drawing-room carpet on Sundays between services, and have a couple of cocks in 'to give them wind.' This was about 1830.

Mr. Miles, who was born at the close of the last century, was one of those rare characters who seem to possess in one sense neither progenitors nor descendants. He left no actual representative to fill his place. In his professional capacity he naturally enjoyed a good deal of the confidence of his clients, but Miles was regarded by all those who employed him as a personal friend. He was the never-failing resource when anyone was in trouble or in straits, and many a delicate piece of business outside his immediate or strict functions it fell to his lot, in the course of a prolonged life, to discharge.

A remarkably fine Stilton cheese received from Leicester one Christmas (1889-90) led to a conversation on the subject. Stilton cheese, A. said, had been made at Leicester, Coldnewton, and other places near ever since he remembered. They got their name from the circumstance that their peculiar character was first noticed by the frequenters of the Angel at Stilton, which is some thirty-five miles from Leicester, and they became known as Stilton cheeses. But they were never made there. Of late years, since the practice of

sending the milk away to London and other great
centres set in, they have lost their reputation,
and a cheese of the old type, full of *butter*, is an
absolute rarity. You have, in fact, to get it built
expressly for you.

Among the Leicestershire set in the forties was
Captain Haymes, formerly of the Guards, and a
Waterloo man. He lived to be ninety-four, and
hunted within six months of his death. He lived
at Great Glen, near Leicester, had a select circle
of intimates, a good cellar of port, and a knife
and fork for any of the set at three p.m.—the
then usual hour for dinner in the middle classes
both in town and country. Haymes and his guests
drank water with their dinner, and port after, and
each man had his bin and his bottle. The butler
knew everybody's taste. Haymes deprecated too
much talk over the wine. He would say, if there
was a tendency to conversation in excess of what
he judged desirable: 'Gentlemen, I hope you like
your wine? Drink it, then. Don't talk, or you'll
get drunk.'

But Hanbury the brewer used to hold that no
man should be pronounced drunk if he could lie
in bed without being held there.

Haymes and Mrs. Packe-Reading owned between

them nearly the whole of the parish. The latter
conceived the notion of establishing schools for the
children, and sent Mr. Miles to Haymes to invite
him to join her. 'What!' said the Waterloo man,
'schools — education! Damn education! There
was my old soldier who could neither read nor
write, and he attended to his business as my
body - servant. Now I have a fellow who is a
scholar forsooth; why, he spends most of his time
in reading the paper and my letters.'

Miss Reading, who married Charles William
Packe, M.P. for the southern division of Lincolnshire, kept her maiden name. Her husband took
the property with the proviso that there should
be no jointures or dowers made; and as she had
a separate estate, it was arranged in that way.

Michael Bass the brewer told Packe that when
the Bank holiday had been instituted, the first
year's brewings of his firm alone increased by
£90,000, and had never receded.

Leicester itself in the early times was, as we
all know, an important coaching and hunting centre,
and I believe that the *Bell* was one of the leading
houses. A. remembered it before the place had
declined through the railways. Yet I stayed there
with him a few years since only on our way from

Harrogate, and we found a capital cellar of port—
or the remains of one, at least—left by Boyer the
landlord, who had been *chef* at Badminton. They
let us have an excellent bottle of '47 for 10s.,
which in London would have cost a guinea or
more. This is a class of possibility which shrinks
day by day.

Speaking of Harrogate, there was a Bishop at
one of the hotels. His lordship desired to insert
his address on a letter, and was dubious on a
point of orthography. 'Waiter, is there a *w* in
Harrogate?' 'Well, my lord, they do say as
the—sexton's wife—sometimes, my lord.' 'Answer
my question. sir. Is Harrogate spelled with or
without a *w*?' The prelate's dilemma was so far
excusable, for the Spa owed its name to its contiguity to one of the gates of Knaresborough Forest,
of which the Stray is the last vestige.

A. and I strolled one day into a curiosity shop
in York. We saw nothing ; but the owner invited
us to accompany him to his other store, and we
followed him up a ladder into a chamber above.
The place was a model of disorder and congestion.
My eye caught sight of two large china figures
in the distance. 'What were they ?' 'Chelsea—
old—magnificent.' This owner evidently read in

our looks our desire to enjoy a closer inspection, but the position was impregnable. We seemed as if we might be customers. Isaac looked about him, seized a pair of tongs, balanced his person with much adroitness and agility, and the objects were before us. A. turned to me. I shook my head and muttered *Tournai*. We did not exchange any more words, but while the tongs were absorbed with the restoration of the magnificent old Chelsea to its stronghold, we descended the ladder, professing our acknowledgments, and emerged. I asked A. if he felt more easy outside, and he said that he did.

There was a settlement in the Bradgate estate of the Earl of Stamford requiring the outlay of £1,000 a year on plate, and at last this obligation led to the grates in the reception and other rooms being of silver.

Beriah Botfield, best known from his work on the Cathedral Libraries of England, also produced other books, especially the *Stemmata Bottevilliana*, where he laboured to prove his consanguinity with the Thynnes of Longleat, more to his own satisfaction, I have understood, than that of the late Lord Bath; and he formed a considerable library at Decker Hill, Shifnal, dispersed after his death.

In Brompton Cemetery is a tomb inscribed only with the single word LAURA. There lies interred a lady, to whom Botfield was romantically attached.

It was a settlement in this estate that a pipe of port should be laid down every year ; but when the property passed to Mr. Garnett, a clergyman with a large family and an abstainer, he had the proviso set aside by the Court of Chancery.

A. had always kept a good cellar of wine, and we had frequent conversations on the subject. I found that he was interested when I mentioned that at the sale of Lord Peterborough's collection in Portman Square in 1812, port of 1802 (only ten years old) brought 90s. a dozen ; while claret of the same year was carried to £6 10s. a dozen ; and six bottles of malaga, said to be fifty years old, reached £6 11s., or upward of a guinea each.

I took the occasion to notice that Athenæus, in his *Deipnosophistæ*, lets us understand how the ancient Greeks laid down their wine from three to sixty years, according to its strength and character, just as we do.

The coal-field in the Forest of Dean is one of the latest geological deposits or formations of the kind, said A. to me. In some of the coal which used to be got thence there are traces of the fir-bark almost visible to the naked eye, but readily distinguishable under the microscope.

Sir Roderick Murchison held that coal existed everywhere. Yes, the possibilities of it, given sufficient pressure. But a good deal never becomes more than lignite, and that is probably what the Dover seam is.

When the Earl of Lichfield's property was sold at Shuckborough, George Robins was employed as the auctioneer, and, from his usual fashion of delivering an impressive preliminary address, something uncommon was expected on this occasion. But George ascended the rostrum and said : ' My name is George Robins. Porter, bring the first lot.'

After the death of Mr. George Tomline in 1889, the portion of the famous Paston Correspondence, which appears to have been lent out of the Royal collection in the last century, and which Mr. Gairdner was unable to trace, was discovered among the papers at Orwell Park, near Ipswich. Considering the circumstances connected with the matter, it is strange that Mr. Gairdner should not have thought of making an inquiry in that quarter ; but his edition is not at all satisfactory, and I now hope to see a new and complete one. From what one knows of

George Tomline himself, I do not imagine that he had any notion personally that he possessed these manuscripts. He had no taste for literature.

Comparatively trifling incidents are so soon forgotten nowadays, that it may be hardly recollected that it was Tomline who for years kept up a controversy with the Government as to the right of every British subject to have his bullion coined into money at the Mint on demand.

Tomline's father, Dr. George Prettyman, had taken the name of Tomline on succession to the property of Tomline, the Bristol sugar-baker. The latter, it is traditionally said, made the acquaintance of the prelate in a perfectly accidental manner through seeing him in his park, where Tomline was, as a stranger and a visitor to the locality, strolling about. The Bishop at first sent someone to warn the trespasser off, then, learning at the inn where he stayed who he was, invited him to breakfast the next morning, and finally put him up at the palace. Tomline left him all his money — about a million, something like half of which his son lost in the Felixstow railway scheme.

The unreserved portion of the effects of Tomline was sold lately at Christie's and on the premises. Mr. Miles of Keyham remembered well his father,

the Bishop of Winchester, who had been tutor to
the younger Pitt. Through this connection Dr.
Tomline succeeded in obtaining a footing in nearly
all the Enclosure Acts, and particularly in Charn-
wood Forest and at Banbury. On his mother's side,
George Tomline was allied to the Bagot-Lanes,
descendants of the Lane who befriended Charles II.
after the Battle of Worcester; and it was from this
source that the Ribey Grove estate, comprising a
large property in Great Grimsby, was derived.

The Orwell Park estate, twenty-four miles long
by seven miles wide, was all in a ring-fence, except
a small triangular piece owned by a lawyer. This
Tomline never succeeded in securing, and it vexed
him, because it broke the continuity of his shooting.
He used to say that he would have covered it with
five-pound notes to get rid of the proprietor.

A fashionably attired gentleman called on a
London mechanician with a sketch of an instrument
which he desired to be made for him. The shop-
keeper examined the drawing with some curiosity,
and at last undertook to execute the order, but
observed that it would cost fifteen guineas. His
customer did not object, however, so long as the
work was done to his satisfaction, and went away,
promising to call at an appointed time. He came

accordingly, approved of the work, and put down the money, which the other deposited in his purse. Before the party left the shop, the mechanician took the liberty of demanding, as the instrument was of such a peculiar character, what its utility was. 'I will tell you, sir,' quoth his customer, leaning across the counter to him; 'the fact is, it is a contrivance *for picking pockets.*' The man was so disconcerted that he lost all presence of mind, and before he could collect himself, Barrington (for it was he) had left the premises, carrying with him the apparatus and the purse. Barrington was a regular frequenter of Ranelagh Gardens, which he found a highly lucrative hunting-ground.

Bull-baiting was still carried on in the Midlands and in the North down to the second half of the nineteenth century; and the women enjoyed the sport as keenly as the men. At Leigh, near Preston, according to a story told me by a Leigh man, a fellow, in a room with his wife and a dog trained to this exercise, laid his head on the table; the dog rushed at his nose, the husband cried out from the pain, and would have got up; but says the woman, 'Lie still, man, he must draw blood, or he will be just ruined.'

A., all the years I have known him, has taken the

Times newspaper. The unique and long unassailable *prestige* enjoyed by Mr. Walter's undertaking is a phenomenon unlike anything else in journalistic literature. It was almost a fetich. Without being so constituted, the organ possessed an official authority. Its statements were judicial. A good deal of this superstition (for superstition it was) proceeded from the consummate tact of the management. The *Editor of the Times* was impersonal; no one was supposed to know who he was; the public had as distinct a notion of his individuality as of the Cumæan Sibyl or the Grand Lama of Thibet. Now all is changed. Yet A. is of the old school; and he clings to his *Times*, and will do so *usque ad finem*. When you have disposed of his other pleas for it, he brings up his last reserve—it is printed on better paper. The field is to him!

A. referred to Buckingham in Seven Dials, who supplied the rope for executions, and mentioned that there used to be in the window a specimen with a notice—' Any length cut.' It was a peculiar twist, and specially manufactured for the purpose.

CHAPTER X.

Hammersmith—Turnham Green—Linden House—Its association with a *cause célèbre*—Dr. Griffiths and his distinguished friends—Origin of his fortune—Thomas Griffiths Wainewright, the poisoner—Putney—Ladies' Schools—The Trimmers—Fairfax House—Madame Daranda's—Alterations in the High Street—Remains of an ancient building—The rivulet down the street—Tokenhouse Yard—Morris and his father—Anecdote of them relative to the occupation of Paris in 1815—Edward Gibbon's birthplace—Roehampton—Wandsworth—The 'Black Sea'. Beauties of the neighbourhood—Wimbledon Common Its historical interest and importance—Barnes—Explanation of the discovery of Roman coins there.

THE state of the village of Hammersmith is slightly indicated by a very rough woodcut on the title of a tract of 1641, shewing a few low-pitched cottages by the side of the highroad, such as lately existed beyond the site of the new St. Paul's School. Few places near London have so thoroughly lost within the last two generations their old aspect and attraction, and are more hopelessly abandoned to the forms of modern suburban life. The engraving to which I have referred represents the flight of the Vicar of

Christ Church, Newgate Street, from his Parliamentary enemies, and there is the inscription on it : ' *The Way to Hammersmith.*'

We hear very little indeed of this hamlet (for it was nothing more) in history and literature. There was a very curious case of alleged diabolical possession connected with it, in which the principal actor was Susanna, wife of John Fowles. The particulars are printed in a contemporary pamphlet (1698).

Many years subsequently to my settlement in the neighbourhood Hammersmith preserved a fair share of its original appearance and seclusion, and could boast many historical residences, foremost among which was Brandenburg House, removed about 1827 to make room for the new bridge.

I trust that my distinguished friend, Mr. G. L. Gomme, F.S.A., may find leisure to publish his father's and his own Collections toward a new History of this parish.

Turnham Green was another of the spots which I periodically visited in my desultory rambles in the neighbourhood of Kensington during the twenty years which I passed in that once pleasant suburb. In the earlier part of my sojourn there Turnham

Green had not lost by any means so much of its original character and aspect as it has since, and most of the fine old houses in grounds were still standing.

Among them, foremost in more than one point of interest, was Linden House, on the left side of the highroad as you approach the Green. This 'capital' mansion, which was demolished in 1879, was for many years the residence of Dr. Ralph Griffiths, proprietor of the *Monthly Review*, and he died here in 1803. Griffiths had been acquainted with many of the famous men of his time, including Johnson and Goldsmith ; and he was on intimate terms with Wedgwood, whose partner Bentley was his neighbour at one time. The Doctor, of whom I gave many years since all the particulars within my reach, played his trump card by buying of Cleland the manuscript of *Fanny Hill*, and employing a second hand to improve the book, which is said to have been worth £20,000 to him.

I visited the house shortly prior to its removal, and as I passed along the spacious passage leading from the grand old-fashioned doorway to the hall, ascending on the way two or three short flights of steps, it awakened an interesting reflection—

how often that very ground had been trodden before me by the literary and artistic ornaments of the preceding century.

But nearer my own time it had a very different association and quite another sort of tenant in that consummate scoundrel, Thomas Griffiths Wainewright, the *Janus Weathercock* of the *London Magazine*, and the intimate on equal terms at one period of his life of well-nigh the whole world of letters and art.

Wainewright was on his mother's side the grandson of Dr. Griffiths, and by administering strychnine to the only son of his benefactor became heir to such portion of the property as was represented by the house and its effects. I was the first to trace the consanguinity between these two men with so little in common, and to furnish, so far as I could, the whole sad and terrible story of Wainewright's career down to his apprehension by one of the Bow Street runners at the Tavistock in Covent Garden in 1837. I likewise identified him under two other previously unsuspected *noms de plume*.

PUTNEY has always been noted for its schools, and some of the earliest Ladies' Colleges in England were established there.   Evelyn refers to that kept by Mistress Bathsua Makins, who before the Troubles had been governess to the Princess Henrietta, one of the daughters of Charles I. ; and Herrick, in his *Hesperides*, 1648, commemorates Mistress Mary Portman as " The School and pearl of Putney."   She died in 1671.

Mrs. Trimmer kept a ladies' school here, and her family had establishments for young gentlemen through at least two generations at the large house where Colonel Chambers, Garibaldi's Englishman, afterward lived.   This school was founded by Mr. Carmalt, whose name survives in the block of houses erected on the site.

By the way, at Wimbledon, some time since, Dr. Birch kept a seminary for youths.   Had Thackeray's eye fallen on the brass plate outside?

A very early and curious glimpse of Putney occurs in a few of his letters in 1519, to his Government, of the Venetian Envoy to the Court of Henry VIII., Sebastian Giustinian, who retired hither, while the plague was prevailing in London.

In one of Lilburne's tracts, printed in 1649, he speaks of the future Protector and his son-in-law, Ireton, holding an earnest conversation in a garden-house at Putney ; but he does not specify whether it was Fairfax House or some other, and the writer on the next page brings before us Ireton standing before the fireside at his quarters in Kingston, so that he had probably come over to consult the Lord General. And after the interview we hear that he mounted his horse, and departed hurriedly on his return. The little village (for it was no more) was for the time the centre of England.

The two capital mansions were, at all events, Fairfax House and the one formerly occupied by Madame Daranda, of which the site was subsequently converted into a terrace, now swept away. It has been said that at the sale of the Daranda effects title-deeds to certain property in Putney were acquired, or were, at least, brought to light. This and Fairfax House were the places where the Parliamentary leaders met during the Civil War, and where they were quartered.

There used to be Pike Lane near the church. It was the spot where the soldiers piled their weapons during their stay here.

I possess an etching by Arthur Ball of the supposed nunnery (ultimately converted into shops) which immediately faced the church just by the Surrey end of the old bridge.

At present what was down to 1860 a village is a sorrowful desolation of bricks and mortar, touching Wandsworth on one hand and Barnes on the other. The whole of the High Street appears to be made ground : the levels must formerly have been far lower ; for in carrying out long since some public works, at the corner facing the entrance gates to Lime Grove, the foundations of an extensive red-brick building were discovered below the surface, and a rivulet flowed from the top of the street to the river on the right-hand side within memory. A second stream divided Putney from Wandsworth just by the modern railway bridge and East Putney station. It has long been converted into a closed sewer. The 'spacious house with gardens and lands,' to use the historian's own expression, which was the birthplace of the illustrious Gibbon, I suppose to have faced the dead wall of Lime Grove, the seat of the St. Aubyn family down to about 1858, and extended back to the present site of St. John's Church, which was in comparatively recent times a meadow. It is customary to identify the residence of Gibbon's father with Lime Grove itself; but this I apprehend to be erroneous. The description of the place scarcely answers to the latter, which was a mansion in an extensive park, stretching up Putney Hill in one direction, and along the Upper Richmond Road toward Wandsworth in another.

All trace of either building has disappeared, as well as that of the home of the Portens, his maternal relatives, where he spent a portion of his childhood, unless, which is not improbable, it is substantially the same as the residence immediately adjoining the church and churchyard, as Gibbon himself describes it in his *Autobiography*, long occupied by Mrs. Major.

The only *personages* whom we have at present in Putney seem to be the author of *Atalanta in Calydon*, and his friend and companion, Mr. Theodore Watts-Dunton. It is unnecessary to say that a fund of gossip and anecdote has already accumulated round the former.

It is an illustration of altered conditions that, when the South-Western Railway opened its station here, it was feared that the traffic would only be a summer one. Time was when the shooting of the George I. wooden bridge, with its irregular square openings for traffic and its picturesque Dutch toll-house, was accounted by oarsmen a notable feat, as it demanded a quick eye and a knowledge of the current.

I have never seen any explanation of the name still attached to a minor turning out of the High Street—*Tokenhouse Yard*. Here, no doubt, were struck—or at least issued—the tokens of the seventeenth century (1657-68) enumerated by Williamson, and some of them especially relevant to the local ferry.

A singular character lived at Putney many years—a Mr. Morris. He had been a tailor, like his father before him. He was with Poole and Buckmaster before he set up for himself on Ludgate Hill. Morris was an astronomer, a musician, a mechanic, and a botanist, and, indeed, seemed to possess some knowledge of everything. He had been a great reader.

His father was at one time in the army, and served at Waterloo. He was afterward orderly serjeant to the Duke of Wellington, and was with him at Paris during the occupation in 1815. One of young Morris's earliest reminiscences was going with his father one day to the Palace with despatches for the Duke, and being patted on the head by Louis XVIII., who held out his hand for him to kiss. But he would not, he told me, because he disliked Frenchmen, who, he had heard, ate frog.

I think that the ordinary authorities are silent on the point; but Lamb, in a letter to Patmore, mentions that the legs are the only edible part of this creature, and that they are of a rabbity flavour. If a cat takes possession of one in a garden, it eats the legs and leaves the rest.

My uncle Reynell, who lived here from 1855 to 1892, told me that he had seen the late Mr. W. H. Smith, M.P., First Lord of the Treasury, at the bookstall personally inspecting the accounts, and satisfying himself that everything was in order.

The original hamlet of ROEHAMPTON, on the western side of Putney Heath, on rather low ground, consisted of the King's Head, a wooden structure, and forty or fifty cottages and shops of timber and thatch. There was only a single narrow, steep street, with a quaint side-alley or so. It is at present *greatly improved.* Does the name import a fairly remote epoch, before Wimbledon Park was enclosed, or the various encroachments on the Heath had commenced, when the deer roamed at pleasure over the whole adjoining area, and the village was a mere group of keepers' and labourers' huts ?

Wandsworth Common, on the other side of Putney, was in my time a magnificent expanse, and preserved its dimensions down to about 1875, when much fell a prey to Railway, Builder, Church, and *Patriotic* Institution. Those who are as old as myself, or older, must remember the lovely spot known as the *Black Sea*, which was equally used for bathing and angling. It was a large sheet of water over-canopied with ancient trees.

The entrance from Putney into Wandsworth was twenty years ago a pleasingly rural and characteristic bit, resonant with the music of Nature. You had not to go as far as Nightingale Lane, Tooting, to hear that songster. Not only in Turnham Green, Chiswick, Bedford Park, Fulham, and Barnes, were it and the cuckoo regular visitors in their respective seasons, but at the point where Putney merges in Wandsworth, so long as the vicinity was open and quiet. Both on the right and left hand of the road formerly lay stretches of garden and pasture, and on the former side the footway rose two or three feet above the road, and was bordered by fine old trees. The carriage-way had been even then widened from the original dimensions, when the whole extent from the village was a lane, the dead wall of Lime Grove, Sir John St. Aubyn's, occupying the greater part of the southern side. Altogether, Wandsworth has so far been less denaturalized than its more westerly neighbour. The lane at the top of Putney Hill leading into Wandsworth used to be called Cutathwart, vulgarly Cut-throat, Lane.

Beyond Roehampton, to the south and west, extends WIMBLEDON COMMON, of which the more thickly wooded portion on the Kingston side forms one of the most interesting spots in the vicinity of the Metropolis, as it is, to a large extent, in its primitive condition, and may be once more enjoyed, when the shooting-butts are happily abandoned, by the pedestrian without danger and molestation, provided that the golf-players are kept within reasonable bounds. There is very slight doubt that the point known as Cæsar's Camp was the site of British earthworks, and that the entire ground represents the scene of conflicts between the Britons and the Romans, and a fortified position of the former, when they retired from the more immediate precincts of the river.

BARNES may be regarded as the last important suburban survival, with its own common, the extensive grounds of Barn Elms, and an expanse behind of 3,000 or 4,000 acres of heath, parkland, and demesne, including that unique feature, Putney Park Lane and its immediate environs. Barnes has lived to see the successive degradation of Putney, Wandsworth, Richmond, Hammersmith, Fulham, Chiswick, Turnham Green, Acton, and Ealing.

In the *Antiquary* for July, 1885, I collected all

the available information of a local or manorial nature. One of the quern stones is still to be seen at the garden entrance to a house on Mill Hill. The common was once the home of many rare descriptions of fern and aquatic plants ; and in the marshy part near the cemetery the latter still flourish to some extent, and attract certain uncommon *genera* of the moth. Altogether, the entomology of this narrow area is still fairly extensive and interesting. Dr. Diamond told me that the common was once famous for a particular species of fly, of which he mentioned the name ; but it has escaped my memory.

Prior to the advent of the railway and the builder, it was a sequestered spot. I have bathed as a boy in the large sheet of water on the southern side near the present station ; and I remember a foot-race which Sir Robert Hamilton and myself had at the cross-roads when we were at the War Office together, but his longer legs made me a very bad second. My uncle Foulkes was intimate with Mr. Scarth, owner of a large estate at Barnes, now divided. He lived at Mill Hill, and had an Arab boy as one of his servants. He had brought him home from his travels in the East, and eventually set him up in a public-house at Putney, still called after him.

Northcote the painter once met Hazlitt with the

remark, ' There's been such a beau-ti-ful murder, sir.' There must be some inborn principle in our moral nature which renders these things attractive, and holds them fast in the memory. Those which I never forgot are the cases of James Greenacre, in Putney Park Lane, immediately adjacent to Barnes, in 1837; of Mr. De la Rue, murdered at Highgate, by Hocker, in 1845; and of Mr. O'Connor, the victim of the Mannings, in 1849. My father was personally acquainted with O'Connor, who was a reporter on one of the papers. Not far from St. Helier, Jersey, you have the small house pointed out where the Mannings lived prior to their settlement in London.

In Barnes churchyard is a yew-tree, planted, as appears from the register, in 1653 (possibly to inaugurate the Protectorate). When I last saw it, it did not present an aspect of great antiquity. Here was buried in 1672 Abiezer Cobb *alias* Higham, a fanatic in the days of Cromwell; he was a native of Warwick, and was at one time post-master of Merton College, Oxford.

Lysons, writing nearly a century ago, loosely estimates the common at about 150 acres; but its extent was formerly greater. On the southern side the Charity estate and the South-Western Railway premises, and on the northern the cemetery, have been taken out of it, and encroachments have formerly been made everywhere. It originally stretched from the Richmond Road on the south, to the borders of Mortlake on the west, to the village of Barnes on the north, and the boundary ditch between Barnes and Putney eastward. Of course, it has fallen, in common with other open spaces, a prey to indifference, ignorance, and dishonesty (the most ancient trespass dating back to the Plantagenet times). The pound, which stood near Mill Hill, no longer exists; it forms the scene of a well-known metrical *jeu d'esprit*, in which Quin and Foote are the actors. The mill was valued at fifteen shillings a year 800 years ago.

Between this and Roehampton, in relaying the drains, many years since, between the Jesuits' College and the Convent, the workmen came upon a considerable number of children's skeletons, of which the history was unknown.

It may be convenient to mention that the occasional discovery of Roman coins on the shore at Barnes is supposed to be due to the utilization of the soil removed in laying the foundations of the modern London Bridge up the river, where it served to make up the towing-path at the point named.

THE FOURTH GENERATION

PART II.

CHAPTER I.

The Royal Family—The library given by George IV. to the nation—The Duke of Sussex—The Queen—The 'Jubilee' coinage—Our obligations to Her Majesty—Orders of Merit for civilians—Penalty of a long reign—The Queen thinks a book too dear--The offer of Her Majesty to pay income-tax —A curious disillusionizing glimpse—The Royal Family as people of business—The Prince Consort—The Albert Memorial—A few particulars and anecdotes—Princess Beatrice at Darmstadt—The Battenbergs and Batenborgs— The Duke of Cambridge—The Kaiser—*Le Grand Monarque* —Caroline Bonaparte—Louis XVIII.—Nicholas of Russia and his son—Sir Roderick Murchison—Napoleon III. and my father—The Emperor's alleged parentage.

THE late Lord Romilly used to say that the great book-collector, Richard Heber, was once dining with George IV. soon after the accession of the latter, and the Russian Ambassador was also at table. The King was speaking to the Ambassador about the library his father had collected, and was saying that he did not care much about it. He added that he thought he should not mind letting it go, and the Russian Envoy intimated that his Imperial master, he felt assured, would be only too glad to become the purchaser. The King seemed to like the notion; but nothing more was said just then. Heber left the table, to hasten to the Premier's, told him what had passed, said that it would be a disgrace to the country if the books went, and so on, and Lord Liverpool waited on His Majesty and gave him to understand that it would not do, but that if he would present them to the nation, he (Liverpool) would use his influence to get a vote in the Commons to pay the King's debts.

This view of the circumstance attending the gift to the public in 1823 of the Royal Library formed by George III. is in direct conflict with that commonly received, and will read curiously by the side of the glowing eulogiums on the munificence and literary zeal of His Majesty, both as Prince and King, which meet our eye in various contemporary publications.

Miss Clara Maceroni said that at a party, where she met the Duke of Sussex, the King's brother, His Royal Highness was asked to sing, and when he had finished there was cordial applause. He whispered to someone near him: 'It was well enough for a Duke.' This was the collector of Bibles and miscellaneous literature sold in 1827. The taste for books certainly appears to have been hereditary in the older members of the Hanoverian line; and we trace it back to other branches, beside that of Lüneburg. Now Books have gone out of favour, and Horses and Cards have their turn. The Kaiser Napoléon-Nelson's toys, soldiers and ships, are perhaps to be preferred. The Duke belonged to the Second St. James's Royal Arch Lodge of Masons, which is entitled to wear a crown in its badge. I have given some account in my *Livery Companies of London* of the probable origin of this movement.

I have only once seen the Queen. It was on Constitution Hill, when Her Majesty was driving in a carriage and pair with one or two others; the Prince was not with her. In response to my respectful salutation, Her Majesty bowed to me; for not a soul save myself was in sight. This was in the days when the old Duke of Wellington was to be met with in Piccadilly sometimes, leading his horse at the edge of the kerb.

How many hundreds of thousands must be in the position of never having seen our present Sovereign, and of being acquainted with her features only through the coinage. They may well wonder whether all the pieces of money represent the same personage.

The most singular circumstance connected with what is improperly termed the Jubilee money—for the type was settled without reference to that anniversary—is that, although it is by a German artist, it is not even by a good one. Her Majesty's Government, perhaps, would not pay the price for a first-class design, like that for the beautiful commemorative thaler of Maria Theresa, produced in 1888 under the auspices of the Numismatic Society of Vienna.

It really constitutes an interesting consideration, that the majority of the subjects of the British Crown have never beheld the countenance of the Sovereign, nor heard the tone of her voice. It is an understood thing that there is an august personage at the head of affairs, and the machinery works tolerably well. But what effect the stealthy levelling down may produce, no one is far-sighted enough to forecast. We might go farther and fare worse; and perhaps sufficient influence may be brought to bear on popular sentiment by the united agency of all responsible citizens to stop at such reforms as may be practicable in the existing system without changing its external characteristics.

Her Majesty has unquestionably contributed to impart a higher and purer tone to society, and if there are such things as corruption and immorality (are there?), they have to be a good deal more *sub rosa*. It was quite time in 1837 that a term should be put to the scandalous state of affairs under the four Georges and William IV., which Greville in his *Memoirs*, and Thackeray and Carlyle, and indeed Dickens, in their works, did so much to expose.

We complain of having rulers of foreign origin, yet we never succeeded very well when we had Englishmen over us. Since Bosworth—410 years ago—our Kings and Queens have been Welsh, Scotish, Dutch, or German.

There seems a probability that in the future, if Great Britain chooses to retain the present form of government, the succession will pass to the indirect line, and we shall find ourselves once again with an Anglo-Scotish instead of an Anglo-German dynasty. It seems singular that at a distance of 182 years from the Hanoverian accession the Court should still be so German in sympathy and spirit ; but so it is.

It is the inevitable penalty of a lengthened reign to lose all early, and many later, friends, associates, and servants. The Queen has lived to see one old face disappear after another, and to be surrounded by almost totally different conditions from those in which she was brought up, and it is no slight praise to say that our Sovereign has in large measure adapted herself to the vast change.

It is characteristic of Her Majesty's usual frugality, that when a bookseller sent a stray from the old Royal Library to be submitted to her by the librarian at Windsor, for £150, she wrote on the memorandum : ' A very nice book—but the price !'

How different from her royal grandfather, who was a munificent book-buyer, and, even if the figure had been rather outrageous, would not in his better days have stuck at a few pounds to secure such an article, and he had probably far less means for the purpose than Her Majesty.

The alleged offer of our Sovereign at the outset to pay income-tax was very properly met in the negative. A certain specific sum having been set aside for the Queen's use in her official capacity, it would have been undignified on the part of the nation to have insisted on any deduction. On the contrary, the Prince Consort was said to have left a will, which was never proved, its provisions being kept a secret ; and it seems a question whether, had the point been pressed, it was, under such circumstances, a valid document, the Prince being a subject of the Crown, however exalted his rank.

Is it not apt to strike one as a case where the realities of life infringe on the melodramatic presentment, where one, going through the throne-room at Buckingham Palace, and seeing no one, ventures to approach the seat of majesty, only to discover beneath it a dustpan and a broom ? But it is, after all, yet stranger that we should so constantly forget that kings and queens are human beings like ourselves, who look down upon us from the very elevation conferred on them by us for our own convenience.

The creation, with the Queen's approval, of Orders of Merit of late years, and the admission in some cases of ladies, is, as it appears to me, a very sagacious and opportune movement. Civilians, as well as soldiers and sailors, must be freely decorated and honoured. We shall want a solid barrier against aggressive Socialism ; and the Queen and the Court are apparently aware of it, judging from their somewhat promiscuous affability and their almost affecting solicitude for the health even of the Unpresented.

Our Royal Family are excellent people of business, and from the time of the Great Exhibition of 1851 onward have had the most favourable opportunities of making advantageous investments in every direction, and of almost every class. The late Prince Consort knew how to manage his private affairs with all that attention to detail which is so essential to commercial success—an aptitude derived from his youthful experiences in the Vaterland. Was there not a story of some cheque which a certain artist framed, and hung on the wall, as a souvenir of a transaction with His Royal Highness?

But His Royal Highness shewed his common sense in declining to join the Freemasons, on the ground that he would not swear allegiance to laws of which he had no previous cognizance. The lady, whose newly-admitted husband refused disclosure of the *arcana*, was perhaps not far from the truth when she said that they amounted to nothing more than early duck and green peas—a housekeeper's way of putting it.

My uncle Reynell gave me to understand that the late Duke of Cambridge, father of the ex-Commander-in-Chief, acquired from the Government for £8,000 the Combe Wood property, for which a farmer in the neighbourhood was prepared to give double the money.

My wife came home to our house at Kensington one afternoon, and told me that she had seen the Queen at the Albert Memorial in Hyde Park. She was standing there when Her Majesty drove up and approached the spot. The Queen stopped in front of the Memorial, close by my wife, and the latter heard her say, 'Very nice.' This made me laugh, for it reminded me of what the fellow said about the Marlborough gems. But it was declared at the time that the Memorial was not at first, when brand new, unlike a large piece of gilt gingerbread.

I was crossing Putney Bridge on the evening of December 14, 1861, when I heard the Bell of St. Paul's toll, and I asked the gatekeeper what was the matter. He told me that the Prince Consort was dead.

It was a saying that His Royal Highness set the example of men dispensing with gloves on ordinary occasions.

After the death of the Prince Consort at so early an age, the Queen is said to have suffered from insomnia to such an extent that Her Majesty's health was seriously impaired, and there was even a degree of anxiety on the subject.

There used to be a curious superstition about 'Queen's weather.' It was said that Her Majesty appointed a day for a given ceremony, and the rest was a foregone conclusion. Anyone might securely make his own arrangements; it would be 'Queen's weather.' His Grace the Primate of All England formerly authorized special forms of prayer for rain or drought ; but, as the more candid country parson declared, it depends on the quarter from which the wind blows. We do improve a little, in spite of the Church.

A Swiss gentleman from Zurich, whom I met at a house in the country, gave me an odd account of the fire near Darmstadt, where the Princess Beatrice was staying. She was in bed, about one in the morning, and was so tormented by mosquitoes that she rose, lit a candle, and rang for her maid. The two, in their nightdresses, candle in hand, began to hunt for the small game. When a gnat was seen overhead, one or the other bobbed up to try and catch it in the flame, and at last one of them set fire to the curtains. The whole place was soon in a blaze, and the Princess and her maid ran down to the courtyard for their lives, just as they were. Her Royal Highness lost all her clothes, as well as (I understood) the pearls of the Duchess of Kent, which she had had from the Queen.

The Battenbergs of Hesse - Darmstadt have nothing to do with the great house of Brederode, Barons of Bronkhorst in Gronsfelt and of Batenborg, which belonged to Gelderland, and became, and remained during centuries, one of the most distinguished families in the Low Countries. It was

Hendrik van Brederode of this ancient and illustrious line who personally presented to the Duchess of Parma in 1566, on behalf of the Netherlands, a protest against the establishment there of the Inquisition, and who raised troops at his own expense to resist the Spaniards.

When the Prince of Wales brought his new wife from abroad, and arrived with her in London, it was remarked that the first thing the Princess did was to run into the Bricklayers' Arms.

His Royal Highness the Duke of Cambridge married a Miss Fairbrother, daughter of the theatrical publisher in Catherine Street, Strand, who was the mother of Colonel Fitzgeorge and other children. The Colonel, whom I have met at a boarding-house at Ramsgate, united himself to a Quaker lady, whose parents used to frequent the same watering-place. The Duke's alliance was equally creditable to his courage and judgment. The lady was an excellent and exemplary person, whose memory is sweeter and purer than that of some royal and serene highnesses.

The German Kaiser is understood to ascribe his withered arm to the corrupt blood on his mother's side. It has no doubt been deteriorating through intermarriages and other agencies, and it was not very pure when George I. came over, so that it is no doubt a step in the right direction to have begun to seek alliances outside the charmed circle. But, after all, the alleged taint has only gone back whence it came, to the *Vaterland*.

No Act of Parliament can safeguard even imperial and royal personages from the pernicious consequences of contravening the law of nature.

If Louis XIV. was, as reported, the son of M. le Grand by the Queen, he was very properly called Le Grand Monarque. The word *carrosse* in French was originally feminine. But Louis, when young, having once called for *mon carrosse*, its gender was, from deference to his most Christian majesty, altered thenceforward. Madame de Maintenon succeeded to other ladies, whose influence had been paramount with the King by turn. Some one proposed to call her Madame Maintenant.

It used to be said that the Bourbons never forgot and never learned anything. Is not this equally true of the Stuarts?

An English gentleman who was in Paris in 1848, when the remains of the First Napoléon arrived there from St. Helena, saw the coffin, which was on view for a short time at the Invalides, and described it as hardly larger than a child's. The Duke of

Wellington and the Emperor are said to have been of the same height, five feet six inches, and the latter would be wasted by illness before his death. Yet this account seems scarcely credible.

The Napoléon relics at Madame Tussaud's are the most interesting feature in the exhibition, and they will remain so.

There are, of course, persons living who recollect the foundress of this place of entertainment; she died in the forties, and her wax figure, which used to be not far from the entrance in Baker Street, was so realistic that when my father-in-law came up from the country in 1851, and visited Tussaud's, he took it to be the little old lady herself; and next to her, I think, was Cobbett, to whom, the story goes, he offered a pinch of snuff.

I confess that I laid down Masson's *Napoléon et les Femmes* with a very unusual feeling—that I could read it again. It is decidedly a *pièce justificative*, and one not without its sadness.

Caroline Buonaparte sat to Canova for one of his classical models absolutely naked. Being asked whether she did not feel uncomfortable, she replied, ' Why, no ; it was not cold ; there was a fire in the room.' There is a medalet with the three sisters of Napoléon as the Three Graces.

There is an *on dit* about Louis XVIII. which may be true or not. After his restoration, he asked Fouché whether he had ever set spies over him. The Minister of Police under Napoléon admitted that he had. The King asked who it was. Fouché said, 'The Comte de Blacas.' 'How much did he get?' was the farther inquiry. 'Two hundred thousand francs a year.' 'Ah, well,' said Louis, 'he was honest, after all. *I had half.*'

This was the same nobleman whose collections, partly acquired, perhaps, out of the secret-service money, are now in the British Museum.

I have heard it said of Nicholas of Russia that he remarked on one occasion to his son, afterward Alexander II., 'You and I are the only honest men in the Empire,' and that was because it did not pay them to be otherwise. Sir Roderick Murchison, who had, in the course of his geological researches, experienced great assistance from the Czar Nicholas, and been enabled to explore the mineral riches of the Ural range, inverted his glass when, in the Crimean war, he was present at a banquet, and the success of the operations against Russia was proposed as a toast.

While the late Emperor Napoléon III. was residing in London in 1839, my father sent him a copy of the biography of his illustrious relative, and received as a souvenir in return the *Lettres de Napoléon à Joséphine*, 1833, with an inscription on the flyleaf: 'Offert par le P⁷ Napoléon Louis à Monsieur Hazlitt en mémoire de l'ouvrage de son père sur l'empereur Napoléon. Londres, le 18 Mai, 1839.'

His Majesty favoured a certain Dutch Admiral in his phlegmatic temperament; he bore no resemblance to his reputed father, the King of Holland: and until the matter was more or less generally known, his cousin Jerome, who was in the secret, and was in possession of all the facts, used his power as a financial lever. Prince Napoléon used to call the Emperor the kite in the eagle's nest.

CHAPTER II.

Sir Robert Peel in 1817—Mr. Gladstone—My pamphlet on public affairs (1886)—General Gordon—Illustrations of Mr. Gladstone's acquaintance with Ireland and its events—Sir Henry Taylor—General Cunningham—Lord Rosebery—The Primroses of Adelaide, South Australia—A Scotish friend's recollections of them and other early colonists—Draper, the chaplain of the *London*—Instances of longevity—The Tollemaches—Our great families—Mr. Evelyn, of Wootton—A visit to the house—The library—Martin Tupper—Charles Mackay.

THE late Mr. Henderson, who was sixty-three years clerk to the Horners' Company, told me (January 17, 1890) that he was eighty-eight years of age. He had a remarkably full head of hair and a flowing beard, with very little admixture of gray ; but he was much bent, and walked feebly. He mentioned to me that his father took him in 1817 to the House of Commons, and that he often went there afterward. He recollected listening to the speeches of Canning and Peel, of whom the latter struck him at the time as very young in appearance, like a red-headed boy. His father, he said, pointed to Peel, and declared that if he lived he would make a name.

I was told by one of the older officials in Cox and Greenwood's, in Craig's Court, that Sir Robert Peel on one occasion applied at some moment of pressure to Mr. Cox for an advance of £500,000 for a few days for the Government, and that Cox said that he could have a million the next morning if he wanted it.

A reference has been already made to Lord Palmerston in connection with my father's career as a journalist. It was Palmerston who was questioned in the House as to the duties of archdeacons. He had not an idea himself, and asked everybody near him. Not a soul could say. No one was aware that an archdeacon was a sort of ecclesiastical surveyor and appraiser appointed for each county or district. The minister had to inform the honourable member that an archdeacon was a personage who discharged archidiaconal functions.

When a stipendiary magistrate's place fell vacant during Palmerston's Home Secretaryship, he arrived at Downing Street one morning, and was confronted with a pile of letters. 'What the devil are these?' said he to his subordinate. 'Applications for the vacant magistracy.' 'Do they think

I am going to read all these damned things? D'ye know,' addressing the sub, 'anyone who would do?' 'There's Mr. Burrell, my lord—Mr. Burrell of Gray's Inn, a very good man.' 'Well, well,' said Palmerston, 'let him have it, then.' And Burrell had it, and held it many years. He was an intimate friend of Sir John Stoddart and of my father, from whom I had the story.

I first saw Mr. Gladstone at the London Library, St. James's Square, in 1859. I had never seen him before, and likenesses of him were comparatively rare at that time. But I felt sure it was he. I saw him again at his own house in the following year, and after that I never set eyes on him till 1890, when I met him at a book-shop in New Oxford Street. I had meanwhile published, prior to the General Election of 1887, my *Address to the Electors of Mid-Surrey* (Kingston Division), which one of the Conservative party described as 'a parting kick' to the Separatists and Home Rulers. In that interval of thirty years Mr. Gladstone reached the summit of his political glory and the lowest point of his political impotence.

One of the counts in my indictment against him in my pamphlet was the treatment by the Ministry, of which he was the responsible head, of poor, brave Gordon. It was impressive to read in the papers recently that Gordon admitted having carried out many executions, but always, before he gave the order, laid his Bible on his knee, that the Almighty might reverse his judgment if He thought fit, and, quoth Gordon, *He never did.* What sublime fanaticism! What fatuity beyond all redemption—almost beyond credibility! A child's brain joined to a man's heart! This was the very Bible, perchance, which the General's sister gave to the Queen after his death.

Mr. —— told me one day that Mr. Gladstone had been in his shop, and he had told him that if he desired to study the history of Ireland, and had not leisure to work up the subject, he (the bookseller) had a gentleman who would do it for him. But Mr. Gladstone replied that he only wanted knowledge sufficient for *Parliamentary purposes.* This was 'the old Parliamentary hand,' of whom we have all heard more than enough; and who has inflicted greater injury on the country than any individual within my knowledge, and the observation reads with the letter he wrote to a correspondent, advising him to study Irish history, which he had done, so far as his engagements would permit.

If 'the fatal gift of beauty' was the curse of Italy, the fatal gift of words has been the curse of England in the person of a gentleman who was unfit to become a responsible Minister of the Crown.

Sir Henry Taylor used to relate an anecdote of Mr. Stephen, father of Sir James, illustrative of the gratitude of the authorities toward those who exert themselves in the civil service. You may, he said, wear out a finger in writing ; you may wear out a second and a third, and all they will have to remark is, What deformed fingers you have !

The late General Cunningham, one of a trio of accomplished brothers, sons of Allan Cunningham, mentioned that the word *pussy* for a cat came, he believed, from the Persian *pushy*, and was used to distinguish the Persian breed from our own. He also suggested that *hogshead* was a corruption of *ox-hide*, a measure equal to the capacity of an ox's hide. It might therefore somewhat vary according to the prevailing breed in different countries.

Lord Rosebery once said a good thing about Lord Meath and his fondness for securing re-creation-grounds. 'Why, you know,' said he,

' Meath would like to pull down the whole of London, and make it an open space for the use of the inhabitants.'

Mr. Primrose, an uncle of Lord Rosebery, was a brewer at Adelaide, South Australia, and was a near neighbour of my friend the late Mr. Archibald Jaffrey. He lived to a good old age, but was a great tippler, and was very unfortunate in his family, nearly the whole of which predeceased him. When Lord Rosebery visited Adelaide, he called on the Primroses, and went over the brewery, tasting the various ales; and he was very well received. These Primroses first figure in the time of James VI. of Scotland, under whom they laid the foundation of their fortunes.

Lord Rosebery was a special protégé of Mr. Gladstone, and an admitted failure as a political and Parliamentary leader. As a rich man, he was apt to be a valuable ally, and when Mr. Gladstone felt it necessary to retire, he let his lordship slip into his seat, ere long to slip out of it again. I was brought up among Liberals, and with a respect for their principles, till I could not avoid seeing that those principles were merely a passport to office, and that much of the Liberalism consisted in being free with other

people's money in a public sense.   Lord Rosebery's
premiership was not entirely *bonâ fide*, so long
as Mr. Gladstone was in the prompter's box.   It
was a disagreeable blend, of which even his lordship, perhaps, grew a little tired, if not ashamed.

Jaffrey was saying that a visitor to the gallery
at Holyrood, after looking at the portraits of the
Scotish kings on the walls, inquired of the old
woman who shewed the place to him : 'Did you
do these ?'   And, she shaking her head, he added :
'You might have done better.'

Jaffrey was born near Stirling in 1817, and left
his home January 1, 1839, on his way to seek
his fortune in South Australia.   He witnessed at
Liverpool the terrific storm of that month, which
strewed the whole coast with bodies and wreckage,
and the splendid sight, when the calm returned,
of the Mersey filled with craft in full sail pre-
paring to leave for their destinations.   He reminded me of the later one of January, 1866, in
which the *London* was lost in the Bay of Biscay,
Draper, the chaplain, praying to the last in the
midst of the drowning crew and passengers.   At
that moment Draper's son was proceeding to one
of our convict settlements, unknown to him, having
been found guilty of some felony.

The old-fashioned type of pedagogue survived in Scotland in the actual flesh in Sir Walter's day, for Jaffrey gave me a description of Munro, his own schoolmaster at Stirling, with his ballups and his spectacles on the top of his head—two or three pairs sometimes—which impressed me at the time with a persuasion that the cause of learning was even more backward in the North than with us; and this would have been about 1825.

It is a singular circumstance that, from its geological lay, Stirling is affected by nearly every shock of earthquake of a severe character which occurs within a very broad zone.

Jaffrey told me many curious stories about the earlier settlers in South Australia—among others, a brother of George Grote the historian, and a son of Charles Babbage. He was mentioning to me that Sir Henry Ayers, who at one time filled a high position at Adelaide, used to say that David, 'the man after God's own heart,' probably had no hand whatever in the Psalms which pass under his name, unless it was the one where he speaks of walking up to his ankles in the blood of his enemies.

He (that is, Jaffrey) assured me that he was personally acquainted with all the circumstances of the case where a man in a Scotish village, when gold was much scarcer than it is at present, made money by exhibiting at a bawbee a head a sovereign in his possession. He had cleared a fair amount in this way, when someone (there is always a last man) came, and put down his coin. The other, however, said: 'I canna shew ye the piece; but ye can see the paper it was wrop in.'

My old acquaintance died in 1893. It is remarkable enough that his father was born in 1766, so that the two lives covered 127 years. The family at one time owned the property on which the field of Bannockburn is situated. I shall notice two other striking cases of transmission of a name and race through few links, partly arising from late marriages, which, so far as Scotland was concerned, were formerly much more usual.

A son of Captain Groves, R.N., was born in 1829, when his father was sixty years of age. The latter was born in 1769. The Captain used to tell a story *apropos* of the former defective victualling of ships, even those belonging to the service, and how, when his vessel was once weather-bound, they had to catch all the rats aboard, and cook them. They tasted like chicken.

The late Captain Maude, R.N., who died in October, 1886, in his eighty-eighth year, was the son of the first Lord Hawarden, who was born in 1729, and whose father, again, Sir Robert Maude, was born in 1673. Here three generations lasted 213 years.

I have in an antecedent chapter furnished some analogous *data* in relation to our own family.

Lord Tollemache sold his Reynolds and Gainsborough portraits, I understand, to Colnaghi for £60,000, to provide for his second family of nine. He did not wish to send them to Christie's, on account of the publicity, and came to terms with the print-seller, whose first business would be, of course, to notify the fact to everyone likely to be a customer. His lordship bargained for an engraving of each to put in the places of the oils. I believe that his estate in Cheshire is charged with a heavy annual sum for plantations.

A neighbour of mine at Kensington knew one of the Tollemaches in New Zealand, where he had a large property. He told me that this gentleman would take off his shirt and stockings, and wash them himself in a roadside pool.

Another of this race, a tall, ungainly, ill-dressed man of elderly appearance, with a cape which barely covered his elbows, and a weather-beaten umbrella, used to frequent in my brother's time the

Judges' Chambers, and declaim with equal vehemence and zest against the rascality of his brother, with whom he was engaged in some mysterious litigation.   It appeared to be his chief employment.

It is to be lamented, for their own sakes and that of their country, that the British aristocracy is either so poor, or, if otherwise, so sordid.   The recent death of Baron Hirsch put it into my head to consider how much prouder we might be of those who enjoy sundry mediæval designations, no longer articulate or proper to the time, if they could follow a little—to the extent of their power in each case— the example of such a man, or of Count Tolstoi. One can scarcely wonder at Lord R. and Lord C. not being anxious to take their seats in the Upper Chamber.

The great families of the country, titled and untitled, appear to be broadly classifiable into two categories : those which accumulate and hoard their resources, and those which dissipate them ; and it may be difficult to determine which involves the larger amount of injustice and inconvenience.   In a vast artificial community no ideal redistributive arrangement is probably feasible.

A lady, who had been employed as a governess

in some of the great German houses, was describing to me the extraordinary wealth and splendour of some of their establishments, and was saying that in England we have a very imperfect idea of this question, deriving our knowledge from the impecunious foreigners who come over here. My informant instanced to the contrary Count Schönborn, whose family repeatedly filled the archiepiscopal see of Mainz, and who possessed nine residences at least, all maintained in perfect repair, and many of them seldom or never visited by him. Pommersfelder Castle appears to be the principal mansion. The present (1896) Count's grandfather sold some of the Gobelin tapestry and other effects ; but the furniture, books, and pictures are said to be very fine, and the first-named to be in the English taste of the beginning of the century.

A friend at Dorking, whom I was visiting, gave me an account of his visit to Mr. W. J. Evelyn at Wootton. He and a companion found Evelyn alone, and the latter asked them to stay dinner. The somewhat Barmecide repast was laid in the banqueting-hall — a pair of soles, a fowl, and a jelly. They had coffee before dinner, and tea with it, but no wine or beer. The servant-maid brought in the dishes, and left them to help themselves. Evelyn rose when he had finished his fish, and put the empty plate on the sideboard. The others had to do the same. Evelyn grasped his teacup with his hand, instead of taking it by the handle. He spoke very brusquely, and was dressed in a very rough manner. He had been gardening when they arrived.

My friend noticed a good many books in the library, a model of John Evelyn's tomb in Wootton Church, the manuscript of the *Diary*, and some fine old plate of the Diarist's time, including a tall silver cup in the original leathern case.

Evelyn and Martin Tupper were schoolfellows, and Tupper used to be invited to stay at Wootton. Charles Mackay, the poet, who spent his last days, and died, in a small cottage at the foot of Box Hill, was also occasionally asked there. This was so far creditable to Evelyn, as poor Mackay could not possibly be of the slightest utility to him, and did not offer the same sort of interesting personal association as Tupper.

The name of Mackay awakens in my mind the curious reflection that John Timbs and he were two of the men whom my good father, solicitous for my settlement in life, held up to me as great exemplars, and likely to prove influential helpers;

for at one period both lived in good style, and seemed to make literature pay. Timbs died in the Charterhouse.

I have observed that librarians are often selected with a special regard to their ignorance of literature and books, and such was the case here. Evelyn himself has no feeling in this direction, though a fairly good botanist, and so far doing credit to his name ; but he might have pitched on someone who would have helped to recover the numerous volumes which, in Upcott's time, were abstracted from the collection. These are sometimes reported to Evelyn at exorbitant prices ; but he has most frequently missed them altogether, when they might, by a little management, be secured on moderate terms. The list of these strays, which I have drawn up and printed, and which receives periodical additions, begins to be a sadly long one.

The house has, in short, been mercilessly stripped of its ancient treasures, and the present owner is not proud enough, though to the full rich enough, to redeem them when he can, notwithstanding the somewhat heavy penalty payable for his predecessors' gross neglect of the acquisitions and belongings of the historical Evelyn. It was only the other day that the Wootton copy of the first edition of

Spenser's *Faëry Queen* was sold at an auction for £71. It is many years since it left its old home.

My Dorking friend related to me the following. A clergyman there meets a little girl, and, regarding her thoughtfully and solemnly, says, 'Child, do you know who made that vile body of yours?' 'Yes, sir,' replies the child; 'mother made the body, and I made the skirt.'

It was from this gentleman, who had been many years on the medical staff under the Indian Government, that I heard a singular case of infectious disease missing a generation. An Englishman, walking somewhere outside a town in British India, saw a beautiful Hindoo girl bathing in a pool, and was irresistibly smitten by her attractions. The result was a daughter, who married, and who herself had one. The Hindoo's child never betrayed any symptom of carrying in her blood the germ of a particular malady actually communicated by the mother; but the taint betrayed itself in the grand-daughter, to whom it proved fatal, after she had conveyed it to her husband. A tardy retribution, and an unmerited one!

CHAPTER III.

Literary jottings—Shakespear—The Shakespear Papers—Shakespear and Bacon—The *Sonnets*—Yorick—Tennyson—Some
new particulars of him and his father—Longfellow—Brown-
ing--The poet and Lord Coleridge—The Browning Society
—The arrangements for his interment—Amusing anecdote—
The Trinity College MS. of Chaucer—Halliwell's *Shakespeariana*—A curious episode at his daughter's wedding—
Dr. Ingleby—The *Hatless Headman*—G. A. Sala—Alexander
Ireland.

IT seems to me obvious that one main source of the
obscurity of Shakespear's life was the failure of his
contemporaries to understand his greatness. Otherwise they must have committed to writing more
about him. But probably a second reason was the
puritanical element in the family, which would view
at best with indifference any monuments or records
illustrative of the dramatist. In a former section I
have cited a passage from Miss Hazlitt's *American
Diary*, where she speaks of having met at Perth
Amboy a Mr. Shakespear, who resembled the
portraits which she had seen of the great poet.

It is not generally known that, in April, 1616, the

very month of Shakespear's death, there was a great fire at Stratford; but whether any of the papers or books perished there, we do not learn.

Our information about Bacon is meagre enough, although he moved in so much higher a sphere, socially speaking.

Rightly or wrongly, I formulated, in early days, in my own mind an impression that Bacon was a man of short stature, from his disparaging allusion in one of his Essays to tall persons, whose heads he likens to the meanly-furnished upper storeys of lofty houses.

The most curious part of his personal history seems to be that which has no direct connection with it—that is to say, the fact that the two greatest Englishmen should have been contemporaries, and yet have apparently known nothing of each other, which probably led to the silly theory that both were one and the same.

Shakespear, in the line,

'From fairest creatures we desire increase,'

has touched the voluptuous or sensual side of cruelty.

It has constantly struck me, from my intimacy as a bibliographer with the elaborate and explanatory style of Elizabethan title-pages, how remarkable in its simplicity, brevity, and unobtrusiveness, is that to our poet's two earliest productions, which came from the press, let us bear in mind, when he was barely thirty, yet when he was already making his mark. You have to turn over the leaf to discover the author. There are only half a dozen other examples of such reticence in or about the same period within my knowledge. Barnfield, in his *Affectionate Shepherd*, 1594, published when he was a youth of twenty, and the editor of *England's Helicon*, 1600, may have equally borrowed from Shakespear. Barnfield does not even disclose his name in a dedication.

It has long since been mentioned by the present writer that the *Mr. W. H.* of the *Sonnets* was almost undoubtedly not the Earl of Pembroke. We have two sorts of testimony to the contrary, which, taken together, seem to be fairly conclusive. In 1610, Thomas Thorp, the *T. T.* of the *Sonnets*, inscribed to John Florio the first edition of a version of *Epictetus* and *Cebes* in English in terms pedantic and mysterious enough, yet such as the stationer might employ toward a man of letters. In 1616 Thorp brought out an enlarged impression, and dedicated it to William, Earl of Pembroke, in a totally different strain ; for even where Thorp applies the expression, 'True and real upholder of learned endeavours,' to his lordship, he merely quotes what the translator had said. So, in 1610 and 1616, we trace the state of feeling of Thorp toward Florio and Lord Pembroke respectively, and it does not accord with the hypothesis that the person addressed in 1609 by him as *Mr. W. H.* can be the same as the person addressed by him in 1616 as 'The Right Honourable William, Earl of Pembroke.'

In an early manuscript copy of Middleton's *Game at Chess*, formerly in the possession of Mr. C. J. Stewart the bookseller, there is a dedication to *Mr. William Hammond*, evidently a coeval lover and patron of letters ; and how much more likely it is that Thorp, having acquired the *Sonnets* in the form of loose, unconsecutive papers, should have arranged them to the best of his ability, and have connected with them on publication such a name as that of Hammond !

I cannot help cherishing the belief that in Yorick the poet had an eye to Tarlton. He makes Hamlet call him 'The King's Jester,' and say, 'He hath borne me on his back a thousand times.' Tarlton died in 1588, when Shakespear was still a young man.

One of the most prominent of the gentry at ——,

and a justice of peace and quorum, expressed his opinion that I was a clever man. It may be easily imagined how sensible I was of the flattery, when I add that he thought Shakespear a clever man too. But, seriously speaking, cleverness has become an equivocal term.

The obscurity of Shakespear's personal history impels one to seek explanations which are, after all, at best empirical. His unique genius made him stand out so conspicuously from among his literary contemporaries, ' Sicut inter ignes luna minores,' that there was a sort of repellent influence, amounting in the case of a man like Jonson to pique or jealousy, and in still less distinguished persons to awe. The sun draws toward it lesser bodies ; but, then, they are planetary ones of inferior magnitude, in which sensibility is absent. I conjecture that our great poet, a sort of human Sun, lacked *camaraderie*. Who but he, save perhaps Daniel from a clearly different motive, ever withdrew from the scene of his triumphs to end his days in a dull and bigoted country village ? Had he been only such another as Jonson, or Beaumont, or Shirley, we should have known more about him. Shakespear must have secretly felt his own immense transcendency, and at the same time the failure of others to recognise it ;

and to such a cause one may not err in assigning his retirement to Stratford in the prime of life, although there again the sympathy with him was even slighter either among the townspeople or his own circle. Was it not a most self-contained career?

A neighbour told me one day an anecdote of Tennyson. About thirty-five years ago this gentleman was at Somersby, in Lincolnshire, where the poet's father lived, and an old servant of the family, when he went away, said to him, 'You'll be sure, sir, and remember me to Master Alfred.'

Old Dr. Tennyson was rather—well, very irritable. The tale goes that his cook, her dress having caught fire one day, first ran to her master's door, but, being afraid of his temper, went back, and out into the yard, screaming for help. The air fanned the flames, and the woman died of her burns. The Doctor, to prevent the recurrence of such a tragedy, had a butt of water placed outside the kitchen door, so that the cook, if she became ignited again, might jump or be lifted into it, and not trouble him.

Rich men, and even lords, may make verses, though they do not usually cut a very good figure among the freemen of Parnassus. Tennyson was made a peer, because he had first proved himself a man of genius, and had, moreover, written adulatory addresses *ex officio* to the Sovereign.

Emily Davison, daughter of Sir Henry, an Indian functionary of our acquaintance in Brompton days, used to visit a friend of her father's in Onslow Square, and met Tennyson there. The first time she saw him, he was leaning out of the drawing-room window, smoking a pipe with the strongest tobacco, and very roughly dressed, and, the house being in the painter's hands, she took him for one of the workmen — a not unnatural notion for a schoolgirl, as Miss Davison then was.

A pretty little story is told of Longfellow and his love for children, which, as usual, was understood and reciprocated. A little fellow was taken to the poet's house, and found Longfellow in his library. The child looked round the room, and after a while ventured to ask if his host, among his books, had *Jack the Giant-killer*. Longfellow had to own that his collection did not boast it. The boy said nothing, but, paying a second visit, approached Longfellow, holding something in one hand very firmly. He had brought him two cents to buy a copy of the deficient romance, which was to be 'all his own book.'

At one time Robert Browning used to follow the dictates of his own inspiration, and produced poetry, when he had anything worth saying and printing. But latterly I understand that his publishers would jog him on the elbow, and let him know that there was room for a new volume, and the bard would cast about for a subject or a peg to hang a book upon. Messrs. Smith and Elders' cheques are very excellent securities; but they are an indifferent Tenth Muse.

My uncle once went with Robertson, editor of the *Westminster Review*, to wait on Browning at his London residence on the subject of an article for the periodical, and vividly retained an impression of the flowered dressing-gown in which the poet came down to them. There was no idea at that time that he would become a writer of such importance.

Browning having sent to Lord Coleridge one of his new poetical productions, the latter expressed his admiration of what little he was able to understand. Browning observed that if such a reader could comprehend ten per cent. of his work, he ought to be well satisfied.

I agree so far with the late Mr. Reynell, that it was a bizarre kind of proceeding to start a Society to expound the writings of a living author, and I have heard it whispered that the oracle, on being pressed for a solution of some obscure passage in a composition, had sometimes to confess that he could not help the inquirer, though he had no doubt that he knew what he meant when he wrote it. This goes some way to justify Lord Coleridge's criticism.

Browning died without doing more than leave verbal instructions in respect to his funeral or burial-place. He said that, if he died at Paris, he desired to lie by his father there ; if at Florence, by his wife in the old cemetery ; and if at Venice, in some particular church, which I have forgotten— not, I believe, at Lido. The difficulty was, so far as Florence was concerned, that the old cemetery had been closed, and that the municipality could not grant permission for his interment there without some special Ministerial authority ; and the family declined the proposal to exhume his wife, and lay both together in the new ground. It was then that Dean Bradley, who had wavered so long as it was a mere question of compliment, came forward, and assented to his remains being deposited in the Abbey.

I heard from F. an odd story related to him by A. S. of a visit paid to two sporting acquaintances in Buckinghamshire. S. referred to the recent death of Browning, and one of the Nimrods, turning to the other thoughtfully, said, ' Poor Browning ! did he hunt with you ?'

F. has, as I always maintain, one ruling characteristic. He is the most uncommercial man I ever met. It has not been my lot to come across a person so thoroughly superior to pecuniary considerations. On one occasion, when the money could scarcely have been indifferent to him, two literary commissions were thrown in his way: one was worth £120; the other was gratuitous—what they term *honorary*. He preferred the latter. He was mentioning to me the case of the Trinity College manuscript of Chaucer, borrowed by Halliwell-Phillipps from the then librarian without any voucher given, and never returned, as the borrower alleged, after the death of the librarian, that he had restored it to him. It was afterward in a lot which came into the hands of Rodd, the bookseller, either from an auction or by private purchase, and shown to Sir F. Madden, then Keeper of the Manuscripts at the British Museum. Madden recognised the volume, although the Chaucer portion had been taken out and destroyed, and the remaining two parts bound up separately; but he could hardly swear to it in its altered state; it is now in the Museum. Bond told me without reserve, when he was Keeper, that he would not buy any manuscript from Phillipps; and, in fact, I have heard that he did one or two queer things in the printed book department.

When the Birmingham folks declined his *Shakespeariana* at £7,000, an American lady offered to buy them, and present them to the New York Shakespear Society, if they would undertake to preserve them. Halliwell, I understand, was made F.R.S. on the belief that he would draw up the catalogue of the Society's library, which he never did, though he had promised to do it. But it was easier fifty years ago to gain admission.

I have already referred to Phillipps's extraordinary nervousness. He invited me to the wedding of his second daughter to Mr. Hall, and at the breakfast, when the health of the father of the bride was proposed and drunk, I heard a sudden rustle of paper all over the room, and anon perceived that (by a preconcerted arrangement, no doubt) the response was being circulated in the form of a printed slip, owing to Phillipps's constitutional inability to get on his feet and say a few words.

I saw his second wife once or twice at Hollingbury Copse. It was said that her aunt imagined that Phillipps had his eye on *her*, and was surprised and piqued when she found that it was 'my niece' who was the object of pursuit.

Dr. Ingleby, of Valentines, near Ilford, the Shake-spearian scholar, used to drive out about the neighbourhood without his hat, and went by the name of the *Hatless Headman*. When I knew Ingleby, he rented Wanstead from Lord Cowley, and I recall a delightful drive with him in a dogcart through the woods, and the imminent risk I more than once ran of having my head broken by contact with some overhanging bough.

Valentines is a historical mansion, where Archbishop Tillotson formerly resided, and an avenue called his *Walk* still remains. But all the fine old wood-carving by Grinling Gibbons has been replaced by plaster.

The late G. A. Sala was a man of rare industry and capacity. He was a journalist *par excellence*, and his other works were assemblages of articles in book form. But he shewed great power and fluency as a public speaker. I heard him with a good deal of interest and amusement one evening at a dinner at the Mansion House, where he was far away the leading star among the after-dinner orators. He poked some fun at Sir William Smith, of the *Dictionaries*, as to his (Sala's) notion, till he met him there in the flesh, that he was a sort of *nominis umbra*.

Sala was an unimaginative Alexandre Dumas *père*. He was eminently successful, I should imagine, in a pecuniary point of view, yet, like the true Bohemian, died none the richer for that.

The late Mr. Alexander Ireland, of Manchester, who was, I believe, an Edinburgh man, made himself known to me about 1866. He professed to take a warm interest in the writings of my grandfather, and during many years we corresponded together. But, as a person who has alike inherited and accumulated a vast amount of information on all sorts of subjects and people, I have met with passing many of these almost hysterically enthusiastic interviewers, asking one for opinions about British Columbia, Burns, Lamb, Hazlitt, the early English poets, and a legion of other topics; and Ireland was no exception to the rule. These folks gush for a season, while they glean and reconnoitre, then put up their note-books and wish you good-day.

The gentleman just now in question overrated his intimacy with me, as I have already implied, by appropriating without leave or adequate acknowledgment the material collected by me and printed in my 1867 Hazlitt book. I was more sorry than angry, because in the interval I had brought together, unknown to him, a mass of new information, which placed my worthy acquaintance in the unenviable situation described by Macaulay. I cannot altogether refrain from dwelling on the matter, because I am constantly given to understand that the person who thus obliged me *is the only recognised authority on the subject!*

I have involuntarily acted as bush-beater to two in succession—to Mr. Ireland for Hazlitt and to Canon Ainger for Lamb, and need I say how deeply sensible I am of the double honour?

Ireland was engaged to print in confidence the *Vestiges of Creation*, by the late Robert Chambers, published anonymously. The copies were sent up by the typographer to the London houses, and the authorship was for some time kept as a close secret. But, like other secrets, greater and smaller, it was in due course divulged.

When I first visited him at Bowdon, on the Cheshire side of the Irwell, he appeared to be in affluent circumstances through his interest in the *Manchester Examiner* and his general printing business, and he subsequently built a large house in the same suburb to accommodate his library. Of his later history I know very little, except that he sold his books, retired to Southport, and ultimately returned to Bowdon. There was a serious loss of money, I understood, by the editorial mismanagement of the paper, and Ireland and his wife were temporarily in great straits. It was then, I suppose, that Mr. Gladstone gave him £200 out of the Royal Bounty.

He had an old-fashioned way of asking after my wife. He would always say : ' I hope that *Mistress* Hazlitt is well. Mistress Ireland is pretty well, I thank you.' The second Mistress Ireland, who is also no more, was a remarkably intelligent and agreeable woman, the daughter of a gentleman named Nicholson, in Cumberland ; her brother, Henry Alleyne Nicholson, published an interesting monograph on the geology of Cumberland and Westmoreland, 1868.

Ireland had a son and a daughter by his first wife. The son I never met, but I recollect Miss Ireland, who resembled her father in height and general appearance. There was at one time a talk of this lady marrying one of our modern verse-writers.

CHAPTER IV.

Literary acquaintances—The Rev. Thomas Corser—His early knowledge of our family at Wem—Mr. James Crossley—A Milton anecdote—The Rev. Alexander Dyce—My personal contact with him—The Rev. John Mitford—Henry Bradshaw—My obligations to him—His peculiarities—Henry Huth—Sketch of his life—My long and intimate acquaintance with him—His earliest experiences as a collector—His library catalogue—Mrs. Huth—Huth's indifferent health—Circumstances of his death—My conversations with him on various subjects—Herbert Spencer—The Leigh Hunt memorial—Huth's liberality of character and feeling.

My old and excellent acquaintance, the Rev. Thomas Corser, the distinguished book-collector, of Stand, near Manchester, was a native of Whitchurch, and had been a great angler in his earlier days. He interested me, when I saw him at Stand, by telling me that his father was very intimate with Mr. Jenkins, who was Presbyterian minister at Whitchurch, and on very affectionate terms with my great-grandfather at Wem. I went to Stand two or three times, and Corser was always most friendly. The Rectory was a small detached house near the church, and the books were from insufficient space stowed away in bedroom cupboards and even under beds. Corser had to light a candle to look for a Caxton in a cupboard. He could give you a good glass of port, and was not averse to it himself. His library cost, he told me, £9,000, and, although many of the books were given away, realized £20,000. It curiously illustrates the change in the market value of some old books, that Corser kept his second folio Shakespear in the dining-room among the more ordinary works. A five-pound note secured a good copy in his day.

A second leading figure in Manchester literary circles some years since was Mr. James Crossley, a retired solicitor and an enthusiastic book-lover. I saw him repeatedly, when I visited the city, and I ever found him most urbane and communicative. He remembered Piccadilly, Manchester, when two vehicles could not pass each other there. His collection of books was very extensive and multifarious ; but he had certain specialities, particularly the writings of Defoe and of Lancashire and Cheshire authors.

The removal of his library, when he left Piccadilly to reside elsewhere, occupied three weeks, to the amazement and loss of the contractor, who, surveying it cursorily, calculated on achieving the task in as many days, and estimated accordingly.

Crossley was rather a keen hand at a bargain, and was during months engaged in a treaty for a copy of the first edition of *Paradise Lost*. When he had settled on the price, he asked the vendor if he had any more copies ; he would take all he had. The price for a fine copy thirty years ago was a couple of guineas, at which figure I acquired a beautiful one in the original sheep from Tomlins, in Great Russell Street, and when an American agent offered me double, I thought that he was in jest.

The Rev. Alexander Dyce was invariably willing to afford any information to me on literary or bibliographical subjects. When my father was first acquainted with him he lived in Gray's Inn. He was a bachelor. I met him one day at Russell Smith's, in Soho Square, a singularly huge, shambling, awkward, ungainly figure. He had come about an eighteenpenny book he required for use. There was some negotiation as to an abatement of the price, and ultimately he left the shop, book in hand. In a few moments he returned, and asked Smith if, when he had done with it, he would take the volume back at a reasonable reduction. On another occasion when I met Dyce, it was the sale of the library of the Rev. John Mitford in 1860, and he spoke of Mitford's handwriting as a curious mixture of neatness and illegibility—in fact, that the writer had come to him before then to ask him to assist in deciphering it.

There was a creepy story about Mitford and a mysterious affair which took place at his rectory in Suffolk. A dead child was discovered behind a chimney-piece.

This gentleman edited many of the modern poets for Whittingham ; but all that he did, I understand, was to prefix a poorly-worded memoir and a passable sonnet. The texts took care of themselves.

Of the late Mr. Henry Bradshaw, of the University Library, Cambridge. I now regret that I saw so little. Through my old friend, Mr. G. A. Greenhill, of Emmanuel, whom I have known since he was a Bluecoat boy, I had been in communication with Bradshaw some little time before I went up to Cambridge in 1875 to examine personally as many of the rarities there as I could.

I was in the habit of applying to Bradshaw for occasional assistance in regard to unique books at Cambridge, and as he was a very bad correspondent, I employed Greenhill to go to him, and obtain the required information. The curious part was that Bradshaw seated himself at one of the tables with Greenhill, and wrote him a note, which he threw across. When I waited on him myself, however, no man could have been more courteous or more liberal. Incidentally naming to him one day in conversation the Oxendens of Barham, near Canterbury, he gave me to understand that he was related to that family. I think that his sister was Lady Oxenden.

Bradshaw was sadly unpractical and inconsequent. He entered warmly into projects, but scarcely ever pursued the matter any farther. Publishers announced books by him as about to appear, because, judging him by ordinary rules, they concluded that some arrangement, into which he had ostensibly entered, was a settled affair, whereas our excellent friend probably thought no more about it.

Bradshaw had some project for rearranging Sir David Lyndsay's works, as they occur in my *Collections*, according to Furnivall; but I never understood what it was, nor did it come to anything, and when I mentioned the matter to David Laing, he did not seem to see what room or scope there could be for it ; Lyndsay's case stands so differently from Chaucer and the author of *Piers Ploughman*.

The last time we met was in London, not very long prior to his unexpected death, and he informed me that a gentleman at Cambridge had just brought to light a tract which had been mislaid, adding that, as soon as he returned home, he would ask him to transmit me a full account. I knew too well that this was all that I should ever hear of it.

I honestly consider it nevertheless a privilege and an honour to have met Bradshaw, and to have associated with him, for however brief a term. He was so thoroughly genuine and original. It was Furnivall who gave me the account of him which was substantially printed at the time in a memoir. Bradshaw's life was sacrificed to his inveterate neglect to take exercise.

It was somewhat amusing to hear George Bullen speak of him as a man who had been absurdly over-rated in his (Bullen's) opinion.

During my stay at the University upward of twenty years since, I visited most of the libraries, and left very little unnoted. I had at Magdalen a rather interesting conversation with the chamber-fellow of Minors Bright, who was himself away. He furnished me with a few samples of the passages in Pepys's *Diary* which Bright had deemed it necessary to suppress. One I remember was where the Secretary to the Admiralty described his intrigue with a pretty Dutch lady (it was well for his domestic peace that the account was in cryptogram), and another referred to his dilemma at his lodgings, where he was overtaken in the night, and secreted something in the chimney, *faute de cabinet*.

A perfectly fortuitous circumstance introduced me in the winter of 1866 to the late Mr. Henry Huth. I solicited in writing the particulars of a unique volume which he had lately acquired, and he responded by inviting me to his house to inspect it. My conversance with the class of literature in which he ultimately took the greatest amount of interest, and for which his library is remarkable, led to a continuance of our intercourse, and during ten years I saw him regularly, as a rule, on Sunday afternoons when he was in town. My practice was to go to his house about one, lunch with the family, and spend two or three hours afterward in the library with Mr. Huth. Sometimes a guest or two called—Mr. Turner, Mr. Russell, or Mr. Gayangos; but more frequently we were alone.

Mr. Huth was a gentleman, a scholar, and a linguist. He was particularly affable and kind, and no one could be less ostentatious and presuming. He afforded me enormous assistance in the preparation of the later letters of my *Handbook*, and was at all times ready to lend me books, irrespectively of their pecuniary value. I have known what it was to return home from one of my afternoons with him with a hundred-guinea tome under my arm or in my pocket.

He was born in 1815, I believe in Finsbury, where his father, Mr. Frederick Huth, lived at all events when he was a boy. He told me that his brothers and sisters and himself were taken out for exercise in what was then the open ground about. It was still the fashion for men of business in the City to fix themselves tolerably near to their offices, and the Huths removed from Finsbury to Clapton, formerly another favourite resort of City men.

The founder of the firm of F. Huth and Co. was originally a clerk in a mercantile establishment at Hamburg. He went thence to Spain, where he settled and married a Spanish lady; but in 1812, during the disturbances in the Peninsula, he determined to remove to England. It was with great difficulty that he escaped, and shots were fired into the vessel in which he embarked. His aptitude for business gradually gave him a footing in London, and he, from modest beginnings, rose to a share in more ambitious transactions. His son, who characteristically described his father to me as an adventurer, mentioned that folks opened their eyes when a bill drawn upon F. Huth and Co. for £30,000 came into the market, and was duly met. But Frederick Huth was evidently a man of genius.

The house accepted any sort of factorship on a large scale. Huth told me, by way of illustration, that a single transaction in silkworms' eggs from Japan to Italy was worth to them £25,000, or 10 per cent. on a quarter of a million. It is not everybody who can afford to be generous that proves so; but F. Huth and Co., as the firm continues to be called, were in nearly every public subscription in London for a handsome figure—where or what the object was, so long as it was legitimate, it did not signify.

Huth never went back beyond his father, but he shewed me a queer-looking portrait on the staircase at Prince's Gate, which purported to be the effigy of a certain person of his name, whether related to him or not, I am, as he was, uncertain. My former acquaintance married a Viennese, whose brother was a Consul at Hamburg, and a quiet, pleasant fellow enough. Mrs. Huth laid greater stress, poor soul! on her husband's wealth than he did, for of all the men whom I have known he was the most unassuming. As a book-collector, he possessed a tolerable knowledge of the insides of volumes, and he was the master of several languages. It was a saying of his—that no man could be a gentleman who did not understand Latin.

He has said to me more than once that all that he wanted was peace and quietness. In anyone else this would have been affectation; but I think it was the beginning of that nervous debility which so strongly developed itself, and led to his going abroad one year for change and relief. I have known him so overcome by depression that he declared himself to me unable to face the process of looking for a book on the shelves. Halliwell-Phillipps was nearly as hypochondriacal while he lived at Brompton.

Although Huth had the command of a well-appointed stable in town (that at Wykehurst, he told me, was nearly as large as the house), his regular routine was to go to the City in the morning in a four-wheeled cab, and to walk home, taking the booksellers in his way. The carriages were for the ladies.

The earliest dealings of Huth with booksellers were when he was quite a young man, and he used to buy classics of Baldock in Holborn. I do not fancy that he retained any of his juvenile acquisitions. At a later period his brother Louis, to whom he once introduced me, and who lived with his wife (there was no family) in a large house, jocularly termed Windsor Castle, in Sussex, was slightly smitten by bibliomania, and frequented the shop of Payne and Foss. Old Spanish romances were his game, and one day, when the two brothers were there together, Henry diffidently asked the price of one of those excessively rare early folio tales of chivalry. The bookseller replied, Eight; but his questioner did not know whether he meant pounds or shillings. Louis Huth, however, bought it, and subsequently, when he abandoned the pursuit, handed over the volume to the other.

While the Daniel sale was going on in 1864, my friend was at Thames Ditton, and Joseph Lilly used to bring down the day's purchases every evening. Huth gave me a droll account of Lilly's embarrassment, when he asked him on one of these occasions into the room where they were at dessert, and begged him to take a glass of wine. The old bookseller spilled the liquor over the table-cloth and his own clothes, and retreated in the utmost confusion into the servants' hall.

The circumstances of poor Huth's tragic end are perhaps not generally known. One evening in December, 1878, when the other members of the family were from home, he appears to have sat as usual in the little book-room out of the hall, and in rising to have had a slight fit, as there was evidence that, in trying to save himself, he bent the fire-screen. He recovered, however, for the time, and went up by the front-staircase to bed. On the way he experienced a second and more violent seizure, and fell backward, fracturing the skull; and the next morning the servants, not finding him in the breakfast-room, discovered him on the stairs. Life had been long extinct, but there is the possibility that, had his wife and children not been in the country, he might have been saved.

I shall never cease to regret that Huth permitted the catalogue of his library to suffer curtailment, and to fall under the control of a gentleman of great experience and capacity in certain directions, but of no literary training or sympathy. The consequence is that the volumes, which the owner of the collection fondly hoped to render immaculate, are replete alike with grave and with absurd errors, and that, in spite of my earnest representations, much valuable information has been suppressed. Yet it was peculiarly a case in which expense was immaterial, and it did not signify a straw whether the work made five, or six, or ten volumes.

The catalogue does not contain all the Huth books. He did not for some reason wish the Chinese Bible, which someone sold to him in the streets of Mexico, inserted ; and he always told me that there was a copy of one of Southwell's books, which he intended to restore to Stonyhurst College, from which it was a stray, not desiring to keep anything under such circumstances. I do not know what was actually done.

His successor in the possession of the books projects, I understand, a Supplement, including his own acquisitions since his father's death. Of these I have very slight knowledge, except that they comprise an undescribed translation by Harington (not Sir John) of Cornelius Agrippa in Commendation of Matrimony, printed by John Skot in 1528. A Table of *Errata* might be a desirable feature in the proposed Appendix, and it would be a long one. For instance, in one place the Romish Breviary of 1518 is stated to have been printed at the expense of the Count and Countess Frangepane [Frangipani] while they were confined as prisoners of war ' *in the gaol called Dorasel (Torcello, near Venice).*' But *Dorasel* was the Venetian form of Torricella, the state-prison contiguous to the Ducal Palace at Venice itself. This is merely by way of example. The particular item was not catalogued by me.

Huth, as a commercial man, regarded the 'knock-out' in auctions as a moot question. He saw, what many others cannot help seeing, the injustice of one, or two, or more experts attending a public sale of any kind, and virtually giving away the fruit of a life-long study of some subject for the benefit of the vendor's estate ; and it is to be noted that, while a share of the prejudice against the process is due to the class of persons principally concerned in it, an arrangement substantially similar is capable of being made between two gentlemen or two purchasers of acknowledged position, who may say to one another: ' I will leave such a lot to you, if you will leave such another to me '; or, ' Do you buy lot 10, and whatever you give for it I will recoup you, instead of bidding myself, and perhaps, by drawing attention, making it dearer.' The methods of varying the ' knock-out,' in short, are numerous ; and it may seem to many (I think it did so to Huth) that the chief objection is superficial, in two senses—an objection to the idea of vulgar brokers reselling goods in a vulgar pot-house parlour over their liquor, and the objection which a judge or other illiterate person might raise *primâ facie* without any practical conversance with the bearings of the matter.

It is related that at the Mason sale in 1798 the Duke of Roxburgh and Lord Althorp obtained what they severally wanted at moderate prices by one bidding for the two, and then tossing up afterward. This was a type of 'knock-out,' omitting some of the less genteel *agrémens.*

It was Huth who laid down very fairly, as I thought, the principle on which men should be estimated and accepted by society. This is a most important point at the present time, when the classes have become so mixed. He considered that the character of the occupation ought to govern the matter : he remarked that he would not recognise a lucifer-match-maker, a blacking-maker, or a dealer in any other sordid or offensive commodity, whatever his means or surroundings might be.

But this does not appear to me to cover the whole ground, or even to touch the most material element. Something depends, no doubt, on the employment ; but we have also to look at what a man is, and there is then the chronic difficulty that the acquaintance must be personal, as the master of the house is nearly always in these cases far superior to the rest. It asks three generations to make a family, and too often by that time the money has disappeared, and the members are *statu quo ante*—not quite so well off, because they have pretensions which they are too poor to support.

Mr. Huth set aside Sunday afternoons, as I mention, for the visits of his bibliographical acquaintance, and he would make no exceptions to this rule, although I have occasionally called on a week-day in the evening, when I saw so much of him. The late Lord Ashburnham expressed a desire to see the library, but intimated some difficulty or scruple about Sundays, and Mr. Huth told me that there the matter rested. I never heard that his lordship came.

Here I once or twice met Herbert Spencer. He struck me as rather frail and languid. I do not know that any very striking observation escaped from him in my hearing. But I was impressed by his statement of the breakdown of a trial which he had given to vegetarianism, and the loss of brain-power which he had experienced from that sort of diet. F. found the same thing. He came to one's house and dined, like a rabbit, on a cabbage or a lettuce; but he had to return to animal food.

Herbert Spencer stayed three or four years ago at Dorking with Grant Allen, while I was in the same neighbourhood; and I heard that he was then in very failing health and terribly nervous and crotchety. He had conceived an intolerance of remarks of a commonplace and unfruitful character, and had brought with him an apparatus which he could at pleasure slip over his ears, and which spared him the pain of auricular contact with less gifted mortals. Yet how vast a profit some of our greatest writers have derived from the comparative study of inferior minds; and the investigation of graduated intellectual force must be very incomplete without a survey of every form and measure of development. But I conclude that Herbert Spencer adopted this precaution as a valetudinarian in self-defence.

We sometimes talked on religious topics. Huth used to say that he was not himself a church-goer, but that he never interfered with the arrangements of the house in this respect, leaving it open to his children to follow their own inclinations. As so often happens, whatever distinguished him above other persons of great wealth was a life-tenancy; his qualities were personal and not transferable.

When the Leigh Hunt Memorial started, he gave me £5 toward it, and it led to him remarking that he once sent £20 to a son of the author, who pleaded great distress. I felt bound to explain to him that it was probably no such matter, and that the applicant was a person who made use of his name for begging purposes.

He seldom spoke about money, unless it was to ask the price of a book, and that was not often. Even when he employed me to execute literary work, he left the remuneration open. But I recollect that, when I once spoke of someone who had £7.000 a year, he quietly observed that it was a very nice income to have, yet a man could not do much with it.

It was a pleasant little trait which Huth once related to me of his sister, who lived on Wimbledon Common. A very old friend arrived at the house on a visit, and she (I forget her married name, but she was the wife of a partner in the house) was at hand to receive him personally in the hall, and to take his bag, or whatever he carried, from him, of course, to transfer it to a servant. But the attention under the circumstances was what Huth's own wife would have called very ' sweet.'

He was rather ceremonious and reserved; I

ascribed this to his Spanish blood. At first, in his letters, I was *Sir*, then *Dear Sir*. Once I became *My Dear Sir*; but he repented this gushing familiarity, and returned and adhered to the middle form. I was comparatively indifferent to these details. Huth maintained me for over ten years, and enabled me to carry out my bibliographical design. That was his value, and it was a high one.

Huth mentioned to me once at table that the firm kept a certain number of professional works in Moorgate Street, where their place of business was at that time, for reference and consultation. 'Ah!' I was tempted to say, 'that is your *Chitty* library.' But my worthy acquaintance was joke-proof.

He was more exempt than anyone I have met from that narrow partiality for their own property, whatever it may be, which distinguishes the majority of amateurs. He was essentially a man of liberal feeling in all questions; but he offered a powerful contrast to such petty-minded collectors as George Daniel, of Canonbury, who invariably pronounced his own copies of books the *ne plus ultra* of excellence and value.

The prepossession in favour of personal appurtenances, no matter how unimportant they may be, frequently co-exists, however, with the most amiable qualities. The owner of a few defaced coins, some odds and ends of china, a ragged regiment of nondescript books, does not seek to enlarge his knowledge or to refine his taste, even if he has the opportunity. You may tell him where the true examples are to be seen, or you may possess them yourself, and exhibit them to him. It is his mission or cue to admire, not what is worthy of admiration, but what is his. He has passed through life with his eyes shut, and declines to open them to please you or me. The brokers' shops have made his house a shoot for the last half-century ; but he is perfectly satisfied, and is impervious to argument. This is he history of the lamentable assemblages of literary and artistic effects which every season brings to the hammer. The unsophisticated enthusiast is the dealer's and auctioneer's godsend.

Huth and some of his friends projected about 1868 a new literary-paper, and promised me a place upon the staff ; but nothing came of it. *Truth* was once wittily defined to be another and better *World ;* we certainly want another and better *Athenæum*—something, as Huth thought, younger and healthier. Periodicals experience the ailments of old age, like ourselves. I do not see Sir Charles Dilke's paper myself once in ten years, but I understand, from the author of the *Sorrows of Satan* and other reliable authorities, that it does not improve in amiability or generosity.

Macaulay pronounced criticism extinct in this country long before he died ; but it would be desirable to possess, at any rate, an organ free from bias and animus, and capable of informing its readers what the books sent to it for notice really are. There is no necessity, in general, to call into service the almost painful culture of official pluralists ; all that seems to be ordinarily required is a certain measure of educated intelligence and a certain measure of equity. Of course, we want something more than the flippant school-usher and the strait-witted compositor, whose eyes instinctively gravitate to accents and commas, something higher than the *Erratum-*hunter, and more respectable than the party with the vendetta, whose commission, or even whose friend's, to execute a book you may have unluckily intercepted. These prevailing types demonstrate the justice of Macaulay's remark, and explain Mr. Huth's sense of a deficiency in this direction.

I may honestly affirm that I am profoundly indifferent on the subject ; but the publishers may naturally complain that their commercial investments suffer from the present unsatisfactory condition of affairs, while they so importantly contribute to keep the paper on its feet by their advertisements. Might not the proprietor of the *Athenæum*, who is so very liberal in politics, carry the feeling and principle into the conduct of his periodical? Or, as an alternative, might not the Law of Libel be made more stringent and summary?

Reviewing in the press is a process and system of which the general reader of daily and weekly publications has a very limited and imperfect idea. He is apt to misunderstand its nature and significance. A review of a work is simply the opinion of one man about another man's book. The critic may by possibility come to his task with some foreknowledge of the subject, as when a member of the staff of a public institution is employed to notice *ex cathedrâ* a book dealing with his speciality, and rubs down any unfortunate wight who has presumed to encroach on the peculiar domain of these Trades-Unionists— only themselves or their assigns warranted. This signifies, so far as the official range goes, that the normal literary man contributes to pay the salary of the very person who thus narrows his opportunities of employment, and is not unlikely, in addition, to lampoon him in the papers, while the official enjoys the advantage of his prestige in Bloomsbury and elsewhere in granting audiences to publishers eager to have the honour of placing his name on their title-pages, in lieu of ignobly waiting on them. By all means let us have a schedule of themes which may only be handled by the *Illuminati*. Or, shall certain books not be legally current without the old *Permissu Superiorum?*

But, as a rule, it is almost necessarily the case that the critic derives his acquaintance with the topic treated from a more or less cursory perusal of the volume in his hands, and it is not invariably found that he takes such pains as a conscientious judge should do to make himself a master of the bearings and of the author's plan. Of course, the instances are phenomenally rare where a reviewer bestows on his undertaking an adequate amount of labour and thought, to say nothing of his outlay for material to enable him to do justice to his author and to himself. I do not wish to dwell too much on the less usual aspect of the matter, where it is the fashion to say all that is pleasant about the production of a friend, and much that is false and foolish about that of an enemy or rival book-builder, for I verily believe this cruel and cowardly practice to be on the decline among critics of any repute.

There is one thing to be said in favour of the

hypercritical and drastic style which distinguishes a few organs : it keeps authors and editors in their places. They might, after a while, begin to fancy themselves rather clever fellows with a middling knowledge of a subject or so ; but the heel of the censor presses on their neck ever and anon, and they are reminded by him or his assigns that they are damned fools.

I have alluded to my personal want of interest in the notices of my literary efforts. I have also, I fear, been rather backward in replying to challenges in the press. Once it happened that someone wished to know my authority for ascribing a particular tract to a particular writer, and Mr. Huth recommended me to send a reply to the editor. Eventually, when he found me indomitably apathetic on the point, he very kindly set to work and wrote a letter for me, or in my name, I forget which. He was certainly most friendly, and when I borrowed a valuable book now and then, and I suggested that it should be packed up, he, instead of calling a servant, did it himself, for, if there is a thing in which I succeed worse than in writing, it is in making a parcel.

I surprised C. by saying that although I had seen the finest libraries in the country, and they had served me passing well in a bibliographical sense, my

private inclination as a book-lover was in favour of
the humbler gathering which a man makes from
choice of the authors or volumes for which he has
a genuine personal affection. I like the old-fashioned
book-closet, as I do the china-closet. There are two
classes of literature to which one may be partial:
one, which it seems sufficient to borrow at need, and
another, which cannot be spared, lest we should
desire to turn to a passage or to peruse once more a
favourite poem or paper. There is a want of intimacy
between the book and its owner in your great library.
He is the caretaker rather than the master.

CHAPTER V.

Literary acquaintances (*continued*)—The Tyssens—F. W. Cosens
—What he said to me about himself—His taste for Spanish
literature and early English books—His generous contribution
to the Stratford-on-Avon Fund—A strange mistake by a noble
lord—The first book printed at New York—Mr. E. P. Shirley
—Value of pamphlets illustrated—David Laing—His varied
acquirements and disinterested character—A member of the
old Scotish school—His literary performances—What they
cost him and what he gained by them—Sir Walter Scott's
' Dear George '—Relics of Sir Walter—The Britwell Library
— Its origin and fortunes — Samuel Christie-Miller — His
criticisms on the books—Indebtedness of the library to the
Heber sale — Frederic Locker-Lampson — His advantages
as a man of fortune—Comparison of himself with Henry
Huth—His *vers de société*—As a man—As a buyer—Locker's
father and brother—The Mutual Admiration Society.

THREE members of the Tyssen family were distinguished early in the century in different ways.
One brother was a book-collector, a second a numismatist, a third a sportsman. At dinner one evening,
when the three were together, and a friend, an
Admiral R.N., made the fourth, the enthusiast for
coins threw on the table a rare early English silver
penny. ' There!' cried he. ' Congratulate me. I

gave twenty guineas for it.' Of course they did. When he left the room, the sportsman remarked, 'What a fool! Why, he might have got a couple of pointers with the money!' 'Ah!' chimed in the sailor; 'or, better still, the model of a ship.' The bibliophile was generous enough to say nothing. This I had from the son of one of those present.

Concurrently with my knowledge of Mr. Huth, I formed the acquaintance of the late Mr. Frederic William Cosens, the wine-shipper, a self-raised and self-educated man, but a person of the kindest and most amiable character, and of tastes which did him infinite honour. He laboured under many drawbacks. He told me that he was thrown on the world to make his living at fifteen; he had worked hard at his business during the best years of his life; and when he sought me out some five-and-twenty years since, he was only just beginning to relax his attendance on his commercial duties. His relationship with Spain as a wine-importer had naturally led him to contract an interest in the literature of that country, and the circle into which he was drawn at home lent him an inducement to extend his range as a collector to our own early literature, especially Shakesperiana and poetical manuscripts. He was one of the most munificent contributors to the Stratford-on-Avon Fund; and he was of the Forty whom I have commemorated in a preceding section. Huth, as a Spanish scholar, thought rather poorly, I must own, of Cosens's efforts as a translator from Lope de Vega of certain novels cognate in their subject to Shakespear.

Book-collectors are, as a rule, remarkably superficial. I was once at a bookseller's while the present Earl of C—— was looking at the first book printed at New York—the Laws and Acts of the State, which issued from the parent-press of William Bradford in 1693-94, bearing, of course, the same relation to American literature and bibliography as a Caxton does to our own. Yet, incredible as it may appear, his lordship put the precious volume down, with the remark that it did not interest him, *not having been printed in America.* At the foot of the title-page he might have read : '*At New York, Printed and sold by William Bradford, Printer to Their Majesties, King William and Queen Mary,* 1694.' It was the copy which had belonged to Lord Chancellor Somers.

Mr. Charlemagne Tower knew better, and the unique book is at present, by his bequest, in the library of the Pennsylvania Historical Society. From having been since Lord Somers's day in the centre of a volume of tracts, it is in the most beautiful condition imaginable.

It rather surprised me, I confess, to hear the late Mr. Evelyn Philip Shirley, who was greatly interested in all matters relating to early Irish history, say that he did not include tracts in his collection, as it is to that class of record, transmitting to us, as they do, the impressions of contemporaries, and preserving facts not to be found in larger works, that we owe so much information which would have been otherwise lost.

Fox, in his *Book of Martyrs*, especially in the first edition, has inserted the texts of a large number of pamphlets, sometimes *ipsissimis verbis*, but more usually in substance, and in certain cases we are unable, perhaps, to detect his obligations from the disappearance of the originals. Stow did much the same, I think, in his *Chronicle*.

I hold a number of letters on literary or bibliographical topics from David Laing, who was not only an interesting man as a link between the Scotland of Sir Walter Scott and the Scotland which we know, but was quite an Aristarchus in his way, occupying a position, as I have always contended, never attained by any literary person on this side of Tweed. Laing was, in a certain sense, *ambidexter*.

He was equally at home in the old Scotish writers and in the more modern. While he intimately knew, and cordially appreciated, the author of *Waverley*, he vindicated from oblivion and neglect the writings of Knox and of the early *makars*. But I suspect that with us Southrons his sympathy was less profound.

The only occasion on which I had the honour of shaking him by the hand was in the Museum Reading Room. We met by appointment, and I shall never forget the veteran antiquary's change of countenance and accent when I suggested that he should dine with me at Kensington on the next ensuing Sabbath. He might have been the disciple of Knox, as well as his editor. He was of the unco' guid and godly. I heard from him, however, almost down to the last, and often forwarded information to him about books beyond his reach, bearing on some undertaking on which he was engaged. He was the very opposite to a bookmaker. Except Henry Bradshaw, no one of my time ever chewed the cud over an author or a subject as Laing did. His edition of William Dunbar, which had been commenced in 1820, was not published till 1834, nor did the supplement appear till 1865, because he had been hoping to recover certain pieces or facts,

which, after all, he never did ; and his edition of
Robert Henryson, although he was collecting the
material for it *pari passu* with Dunbar, did not see
the light till the Supplement to the latter poet just
mentioned came out. It was in hand between thirty
and forty years.

He used to explain how this arose. He did not
derive any pecuniary advantage from these publications ; his personal means were limited. He had
manifold occupations, and the printing process had
to await a convenient opportunity. He was a pure
littérateur, and a fine old fellow, to boot. I have
known him travel miles at his own expense to verify
some trivial point in person, instead of acquiring the
information at second-hand.

When I was in Edinburgh about 1855, Sir Walter
Scott's ' dear George ' was dead ; but his son, T. G.
Stevenson, kept a bookshop in Prince's Street in a
sort of cellar, to which you descended by a few steps.
His near neighbour, William Paterson, and he had
an odd way of putting visitors, to whom they gave
the confidence, on their guard one against the
other

Sir Walter's inkstand, which he used in his office
at Edinburgh while he discharged the duties of
Sheriff-deputy, came to his assistant or closet-keeper,

Mr. Carmichael, whose daughter Charlotte inherited it, and used to shew it as a curiosity.

Messrs Ballantyne and Co. have at their London house the desk upon which Scott corrected his proofs in his private room at their office.

Mr. William Henry Miller, the founder of the celebrated Britwell Library, was an attorney at Edinburgh, and made his fortune by farming the City sewage, or, at all events, by a share in the enterprise. When 'Measure' Miller, as he was called, from his habit of carrying about an inch-rule to test the relative tallness of copies, began to collect, I do not quite know ; but he was a buyer at the White Knights sale in 1819, where he gave over £60 for the *Book of St. Albans*, printed by Wynkyn de Worde in 1496. An odd story was once afloat that Miller was really a woman ; but how that may have been, I cannot say. He had no family, at any rate, and died without issue in or about 1849, leaving sisters, but bequeathing his property, including the library, to his cousin, Miss Marsh, as I am credibly informed, who left it to a Mr. Samuel Christy, of the firm of hatters in Piccadilly, to whom he or she had taken a liking. This individual took the name of Miller, and altered his original name into *Christie*. He came into a pretty good thing for a hatter, as

Riviere the bookbinder used to remark to me. He had the house at Craigentinny, near Edinburgh; a second at Britwell, near Maidenhead; and a town house in St. James's Place—the same which had once belonged to Samuel Rogers. Christie-Miller was a very commonplace, illiterate man, very proud of his possessions, of which he spoke as if they had been in his family since the Conquest, and laughably distrustful of any and every one. Bradshaw once went to Britwell to see some of the books, and little Miller watched him, as a cat watches a mouse. His own vulgar instincts led him to suspect even a man above suspicion.

He remarked to me one day that he did not quite understand the value and interest of these old books, and he particularly insisted on the incorrectness of the orthography, which was a further betrayal of his extraction.

He more than once rather contemptuously referred to the Huth books, saying that it was impossible for the owner to have secured more than a few here and there of the rarer early English works in poetry and romance; and, of course, had it not been for the Daniel and Corser sales, Huth would have never succeeded in obtaining much, although his large resources and the incessant vigilance of Lilly and other caterers for him did a great deal. It was rather absurd, however, for a *parvenu* like the hatter to pose as a man of the old school, seeing that the library came to him ready-made and by a fluke, and that his knowledge of it was infinitesimal. It may be added that the Britwell Library itself is what we see it mainly through the acquisition by the founder at the Heber sale of the rarest early English books at relatively nominal amounts.

Mr. Frederic Locker-Lampson always struck me as a droll figure. He posed as a friend to men of letters, and subscribed, I believe, to the Literary Fund ; yet he held up his head as if his sole *status* had been his ancient descent and his territorial importance, whereas in reality his main title to notice was what he did in *vers de société*—some very clever and pretty things, but assuredly no poetry. Like Tennyson, he was destitute of humour ; but of course he lacked Tennyson's power.

Mr. Locker-Lampson was comparing his position with that of Huth one day in conversation with me, and pleading on his own behalf that he had at any rate done something—meaning the *London Lyrics*. But Huth was a man of altogether superior calibre and *morale*. The other was a virtuoso, and perhaps a little of the *petit maître*. He was one of the spoiled children of fortune. His metrical trifles shewed you, if you did not know him, that he had a taste for culture and a handsome balance at his banker's. Canon G. very judiciously observed to me that culture might make or mar ; the young men who affect it too frequently carry the hobby to a point where it becomes distasteful or ridiculous. But Locker, as a man of fortune, had no object to gain by enunciating extreme opinions. He held the middle way.

It was one of the most grotesque sights possible to see him, as I did one day, arrive in a high-pitched chariot at Coutts's with some of his belongings. He was perched up on a seat which placed him on a level with the top of an omnibus or a hay-cart, and his expression and air were ludicrously coxombical.

But it was when I had occasion to call at his residence one evening, and he was in full dress, that I was most amused. I had met him in town just before in a stupendous fur-coat, in which he might have passed for a man of fifteen stone ; and in his swallow-tails, with his attenuated frame and his wizen face, you felt as if you could lift him with one hand.

He honoured me by sending me a volume called

Patchwork, published in 1879; but he did not mention that it was on the exact lines of one edited by myself a few years before. He might be supposed not to be aware of it; we moved in such different circles.

Locker also gave me a copy of his *London Lyrics*, with a request that I would send him my written opinion of it. I did so with a certain difficulty, as in a budget of *vers de société*, not of the highest class, one scarcely knew what to say. I have not looked into the book for years: it left on my mind an agreeable impression of a few neatly-turned and graceful stanzas with the same fault which the writer displayed as a collector—an absence of breadth and strength. I remember that Locker characteristically asked me to call for the little volume at a wine-shop in Piccadilly, in which he then had an interest.

Locker, in his parsimonious ways, curiously resembled his relative by marriage, the late Poet Laureate. I met him in the Strand shortly after his accession to the Lampson property through his second wife, and congratulated him. He looked rather grave, and said, 'Ah, yes; but it is terrible to think of the expense I have to incur for repairs.'

It always seemed to me that Locker assumed a false attitude. His claim to consideration was not that he enjoyed so many thousands a year *jure uxoris*, but (as he owned himself) that he was the author of a creditable little book of verses, a lover of old literature, and the possessor of a certain feeling for art. A man of fortune who is also a man of letters is apt to be persuaded by his friends that he is a man of genius. Locker was a second-rate versifier of the Dobson and Calverley school.

He was very manneristic in the way in which he approached you as an applicant for information on literary or bibliographical matters. He assumed an air of bland and almost infantile simplicity, and was apt to draw you out, unless you were on your guard. He once asked me, when I was at his house, to write a note on a flyleaf of a very rare edition of Heywood's *Epigrams*, 1550, which he had bought of John Pearson, calculating that some day my attestation as to the book might make it fetch a few pounds more.

He was a very poor and injudicious buyer. He selected, it is true, for the reputation rather than for the mere rarity, and was so far wise. But he had a fiddling, undecided way of setting about his acquisitions, and the booksellers thought him mean. His collection was formed without any particular method, and its importance has been greatly overrated. Most of his rarest books are miserable copies.

One day, at Chesham Place, Locker was speaking of the habit of stealing books, apropos of something I had told him about a fellow who habitually abstracted a volume whenever he went to Russell Smith's in Soho Square, and, like Lamb in writing about Fauntleroy, he looked at his own hands, and laughingly wondered whether, had he been put to his shifts, he might not have done something of the same sort. His daughter, who afterward married one of Tennyson's sons, was in the room.

By the way, the *modus operandi* of the party above mentioned was remarkable; he stood on the mat by the door out of sheer humility (as it was thought), with his hands behind his back, and while he engaged the bookseller's attention by some query, he managed to insinuate any volume on the shelves in the rear, which happened to be accessible, into his tail-pocket.

An odd adventure which I once had in reference to a rare Elizabethan tract in Locker's hands reminds me that the pursuit of knowledge under difficulties receives its share of illustration from the experiences of the book-hunter. Infinitely diverse are the methods by which I have accomplished the task, piecemeal, of drawing together authentic particulars of the early printed literature of my country for the first time on a systematic and comprehensive principle ; how far I have succeeded I shall leave others to discover and decide ; but I may just suggest a comparison between my *Collections* 1867-96 and the best authorities previously available or extant. At the auction-rooms I have seldom met with much inconvenience ; the leading members of the book-trade have, as a rule, been most helpful ; and the British Museum staff has invariably done its best to promote my objects. But among the minor dealers I have known what it is to witness disappointment, when, instead of an expected and desired customer, it was only a person in search of a title, or some such matter, who had presented himself.

I have just above alluded to Locker. He had agreed, if I would come to Chesham Place, where he then resided, that he would let me see the volume in question ; but when I went, everyone was out, and the book was in charge of a domestic, apparently a kitchenmaid, who apprised me that I might look at it, but that I was on no account to take it away, Mr. Locker said. I archly feigned unawareness of this superfluous communication for the sake of the highly welcome addition to my stores, yet thinking how differently Huth would have behaved. The latter, in truth, possessed qualities rarer and more valuable than the rarest and most valuable book in his fine library.

Altogether Locker was a man of the time, and owed his position to the fact that he was a person of means and a genuine *amateur*. His taste for books he had perhaps inherited from his father, Captain Locker, who seems to have been a collector, and whose *ex libris* I have seen. This was the Edward Locker who published the *Naval Gallery of Greenwich Hospital* and other now not very well recollected works.

Locker was accustomed to say of a certain bookseller who had 'done time,' that when he met him his eyes always mechanically gravitated to his hair.

I shall never forget his gratification, when I once met him in a shop, and shewed him, at his request, while the owner had gone upstairs in quest of something, a copy of a very rare old play, at intercepting it on its way to Mr. Huth, who subsequently found another copy. Locker clapped it in his pocket as if he had purloined it.

Locker was assuredly not prepossessing in his

physical appearance, yet he seems to be entitled to rank among modern lady-killers, and owed his fortune, which so materially seconded his literary and social advancement, as it had done in the case of Disraeli, to two successive marriages.

I have often smiled at the sort of common accord with which the booksellers spoke of him as ' Fred Locker'; it was a piece of affectionate familiarity, almost *camaraderie*, by which he might or might not have been flattered. I cannot be sure whether his rather artificial affability or *bonhomie* was mis-construed by some of those to whom he addressed himself.

He was eminently a gentleman, however, and his manners were even courtly, yet virile. He struck one as a person accustomed to excellent society, as of course he was. Some men are apt to be a little too effeminate—too *ladylike*. There is ——, for example. A couple of girls looking in at a photographer's window, one exclaimed, 'Oh, there's Mr. ——! Isn't he *pretty?*'

Locker's brother, who formerly edited the *Graphic*, paid him full fraternal homage by the sympathetic and obsequious way in which he deployed his eye-glass. I do not know what other literary claims he possessed.

The *Mutual Admiration Society*, to which this class of writer has owed so much, and which, again, thence derives its *raison d'être*, have of late had a merry and triumphant time of it, puffing their friends and themselves on strict debtor and creditor principles, and abusing non-subscribers till, as a natural consequence, they have done their full part in discrediting criticism, even among persons not professedly versed in literary matters, and in prostituting the press, so far as they can, to party and personal objects.

But this unhealthy and mischievous movement has far outgrown the promise of its youth—its limits, as Locker knew it—and the production of a species of literary work, accompanied by so-called artistic embellishments, is at present arranged with the most minute and laborious attention to every detail. The text of a book may be apparently worthless, and the illustrations equally so, but by favour of a sort of critical mesmerism two negatives become an affirmative.

Imprimis, you must buy the book written by one of the set ; the progress toward publication, and the actual day of appearance, will be brought under your notice by a succession of paragraphs, diplomatically distanced, which it is to be hoped you will not find too exciting ; but you must not read the volume till you have gone through the official reviews of it, which will guide you to the beauties, and instruct you how to appreciate them.   Otherwise you may miss the clue.

It was a very different matter when the old writers, as Professor Arber points out, in his Preface to *Tottell's Miscellany*, 1557, 'wrote for their own delectation and for that of their friends : and not for the general public.' The new school has no such disinterested enthusiasm and retiring temper, but is a systematic scheme for hoaxing the readers and buyers of books by means of puffs in the organs of the press, with which it is their first business to connect themselves.   The book itself is a secondary consideration ; it is sufficient for the purchaser or peruser to understand that it is written by the great Mr. ——, whose name and doings he sees so often recorded in the columns of a particular class of paper ; he is not to know that the paragraph is from the same pen as the book, or from that of some *alter ego*, another member of this distinguished co-operative society of Horn and Bellows Blowers, and he must sometimes wonder, when he takes a copy in his hand, whether it is really the article of which so much has been said.

All that seems requisite to complete this ingenious machinery seems to be the hoarding and the sandwich.

Even this sort of history repeats itself. The silly and fulsome descriptions of the home life, the elegant interior, the toilette, the familiar mood, the diet, of these exquisites of the age, recall the *Sentimentalities* of that prince of prigs and coxcombs, Mr. Janus Weathercock, satirized by Hazlitt in the *Dandy School*—alas, in vain! *Tamen usque recurrit.* One sickens of the trash spun out about the Great Impressionists dismounted from their pedestals and consorting with ordinary mortals, like the gods of Olympos.

CHAPTER VI.

Robert Herrick and the Perry-Herricks of Beaumanor Park, Loughborough — My visit to the house — *Cherry Ripe* — Dorothy King — *To keep a true Lent* — Other book-collectors of my time—R. S. Turner —E. H. Lawrence— Story of Ruskin and the Cypriot antiquities of Cesnola— The Freres of Roydon Hall—Their literary associations —A portion of the *Paston Letters* sold with the library — My Cornish acquaintances — Llanhydrock — Mr. and Mrs. Agar-Robartes — Thomas Couch of Bodmin and Jonathan Couch of Polperro—Henry Sewell Stokes, the poet—My conversation with him about Tennyson—The pack-horse road and the British huts near Bodmin—Mr. Aldrich of Iowa, a friend of Jefferson Davis and an autograph-collector, at Barnes.

I PAID a flying visit to Beaumanor Park, near Loughborough, in 1869, to see the Herrick manuscripts, which it was necessary to collate for an edition of the poet undertaken gratuitously by me for the *Library of Old Authors.*

Mr. W. Perry-Herrick, an indirect descendant of the poet, shewed me the stables on this occasion, with some of the curious old-fashioned carriages, which had belonged to members of his family in the present and last century ; and in the house was the truckle-bed on which, according to his account, Richard III. slept the night before Bosworth. You see at Leicester the little bridge over the Stour which occupies the site, and may follow the lines, of that which Richard crossed on horseback on his way to the fatal field, and they shew you the very spot where his foot struck against the side, and refer to the old woman's *prophecy*.

Mr. Perry-Herrick more immediately owed his large fortune to his connection with the Perrys of Wolverhampton, two brothers, who had an interest in the deep coal, and by very penurious habits amassed, it is said, £2,000,000. I do not think that much, if any, of the house built by the poet's uncle remains.

It is a highly touching trait, which a writer in the *Quarterly Review* for 1810 preserves, of an old woman, named Dorothy King, who lived, as her parents had done, at Dean Prior, the poet Herrick's residence and preferment in Devonshire. The Reviewer states that he found, on a visit to the spot, that Mrs. King used to repeat five of Herrick's *Noble Numbers*, including his *Litany*,

which she called her Prayers, and she had no
idea that they had ever been printed, or that
the writer's name was known outside her native
village. She had learned them, as a child, from
her mother.

Only a few days ago I heard a common boy
in the street singing *Cherry Ripe*. Of course, he
had no idea who wrote the verses, nor had he
the whole poem. He had caught it from someone
else. If you had stopped him and said that it
was produced by a clergyman in Devonshire, named
Robert Herrick, two hundred and odd years since,
he would have grinned from ear to ear and been
as wise as before. I passed on.

There is a tradition that Herrick, on his super-
session at the time of the Commonwealth, repeated
to himself his ' Farewell to Dean Bourn ' as he
crossed the brook on his way to return to London.

But I think that the finest thing in all the
Hesperides is to be found among the *Noble
Numbers :*

TO KEEP A TRUE LENT.

   1. Is this a Fast, to keep
       The Larder leane ?
           And cleane
    From fat of Veales, and Sheep ?

2. Is it to quit the dish
          Of Flesh, yet still
                    To fill
    The platter high with Fish?

3. Is it to fast an houre,
          Or rag'd to go,
                    Or show
    A down-cast look, and sowre?

4. No : 'tis a Fast, to dole
          Thy sheaf of wheat,
                    And meat
    Unto the hungry Soule.

5. It is to fast from strife,
          From old debate,
                    And hate ;
    To circumcise thy life.

6. To show a heart grief-rent :
          To sterve thy sin,
                    Not Bin ;
    And that's to keep thy Lent.

R. S. Turner and E. H. Lawrence were, as
collectors, two men of the rarest taste and dis-
crimination, and in their personal appearance two
of the most commonplace. Lawrence had a curious
idiosyncrasy of signing himself F.S.A. even on
his cheques. But no one comprehended better
the difference between a fine article and a poor
one than he did. He was, I believe, a thoroughly
kind-hearted fellow, and from his vocation as a

stockbroker must have accumulated a handsome fortune. The only purchase on his part I never understood was that of a miscellaneous assemblage of Cypriot glass and pottery.

I am prompted to mention here that while the Cypriot antiquities of Cesnola were being packed at Rollin and Feuardent's in Great Russell Street, preparatory to their transfer to the American Government, which bought them entire for £16,000, several distinguished persons interested in art came to see them, among others Ruskin, who made some sketches from these fine objects.

He went down on his knees to examine the details more carefully, but many had been already packed up. 'Ah,' said he, 'I wish I had known of this before. I must go to America to see them when they are on view.' Did he?

The British Museum would have gladly purchased a few ; but, as Cesnola observed, they would have left him with the less valuable bulk.

Turner's death was even more melancholy than Huth's. He had long suffered from morbid depression, and at last threw himself from the top of the well-staircase of a hotel at Brighton. His physical bearing was just as unprepossessing and unaristo-cratic as Lawrence's ; but he had a more polished manner, and spoke correctly. I do not think that he was a scholar, but he knew a great deal about French and Italian books. The former, which cost him about £3,000, fetched £15,000.

Among the sufferers from the acute agricultural depression in East Anglia were the Freres of Roydon Hall, Norfolk. In February, 1896, as I was laying down my pen, Mr. John Tudor Frere, who had previously sold other inherited effects, and had found it necessary to live in the lodge attached to the Hall, parted at Sotheby's rooms with certain of his books, which derived their chief interest from including the collections of Sir John Fenn. The library had been formed by Sheppard Frere, John Frere, and John Hookham Frere, the last a man of some literary and political repute in his day, and a friend of Byron, Coleridge, etc. The prices realized were wholly in excess of the value. I saw three or four members of the family in the auction-room, and I understood that many lots were bought in, and that there is a considerable body of books behind unsold. A portion of the *Paston Letters* (about two-fifths) fetched £400, and ought, with the Tomline volumes elsewhere referred to, to find a home in the British Museum.

Another of my bibliographical expeditions was to

Llanhydrock, near Bodmin, Cornwall, the seat of
the late Mr. Agar-Robartes, M.P., afterward Lord
Robartes. He had married the daughter of Mr.
Carew of Antony. Both Robartes and his wife
were very polite and attentive, and shewed me, or
allowed me to examine, the rare and curious books
in the Long Room there. The house was built by
John, Lord Roberts, first Earl of Radnor, Lord-
Lieutenant of Ireland in the time of Charles II.,
and had his initials and the date of erection carved
on several parts of the premises. I once attended
the little church in the Park, and Robartes himself
read the lessons. There were several old horses
wandering about, their term of service expired ;
for their master never allowed one to be destroyed.

I was permitted to take what notes I pleased of
the old books in the Long Room, and I met with a
few singularly rare items. Mrs. Robartes was good
enough to look out personally for me some volumes
containing manuscript remarks by the first Earl of
Radnor, who died in 1685. My examination of the
library was very cursory, as I was accompanied by
a friend who entertained no literary sympathies ;
and I have recently understood that there are some
undescribed books and tracts overlooked by me,

and that a catalogue of the whole collection may be expected.

Robartes was a very benevolent man, and spent a good deal in charity in the poorer quarters of London, as well as in his native county. His only son Charles, the present Lord Robartes, was a lad when I was last in Cornwall; he had been very simply brought up, and it was said that he thought much of being asked out to tea.

One of our common acquaintances at this time (1875) was Mr. Thomas Couch of Bodmin, the eminent archæologist, whose father, Jonathan Couch of Polperro, wrote the work on British Fishes. The latter derived his information on ichthyology from personal research, and was often to be seen about the precincts of the fishing village, where he lived and died, in primitive attire and barefoot, on his way to the shore and rocks or on his return. Thomas Couch, who assisted me in my edition of Brand's *Popular Antiquities*, compiled a *Glossary of Words used in East Cornwall*, of which a copy, given me by him in 1865, contains large manuscript additions made by me in the course of my Cornish sojourns. He long acted as confidential adviser to Robartes in matters of local charity and distress.

The last time I was at Bodmin, I saw in the

Asylum poor Blight, the accomplished artist, and author of *A Week at the Land's End*; he was hopelessly hypochondriacal.

But one of the most noted characters in those parts, thirty years or so since, was Mr. William Hicks, whose powers as a *raconteur* of Cornish stories have probably never been surpassed. His accurate and droll rendering of the provincial patois and mannerism was irresistible. He was a perfect host in himself at any entertainment. Hicks was intimate with Jackson the water-colour painter, and received him at his house during many years; and Jackson executed quite a series of complimentary pictures for Hicks, who highly prized them. After his death, they were unfortunately removed to a damp house, and I understood that they suffered serious detriment.

The literary circle here in my time also comprised Sir John Maclean, author of a *History of the Deanery of Trigg Minor* and other works; William Jago, a thoughtful and well-informed local antiquary; and Henry Sewell Stokes, the Cornish poet; and there was Blight.

My daughter had written to Mr. Jago's, describing in rather glowing colours an article of dress just acquired; and her young correspondent replied,

'Your hat is a *dream*.' She was probably unacquainted with the fact that this expression is common in French literature.

When I met Stokes, he spoke of Tennyson having been with him, and of their conversation together about the Arthur Poems. Stokes said that T. admitted to him his obligations to the old metrical *Morte Arthur*, and I went so far as to express my opinion that, looking at the antiquity and priority of it, the prototype was the finer production, and it is extraordinary how modern it strikes one as being in comparison with much of the poetry belonging to the same period. This is the common attribute of genius—to make us lose sight of chronological boundaries. It is so with Chaucer. It is so with Shakespear. I would add, it is so largely with the author of *Piers Ploughman*. The essence is of all time ; the outward texture only is antique.

The County Asylum occupies a large plot of ground formerly open and the site of the gallows. The name *Bodmin* is identical with *Bodnam* or *Bodenham;* the original town lay at some distance in the valley.

On the high ground above, three roads run parallel with each other : the pack-horse road, the old coach road, and the modern coach road. Just about here there are some strange low-pitched hovels, which they call British huts.

The pack-horse tracks are of the greatest antiquity. They just remind me of those over the mountains in Cumberland, some distance from Broughton-in-Furness. The keeper of the inn at Broughton, in former days, used to see the packmen from a long way off coming over the hills, and set to work to brew his ale, which was ready against their arrival. They eat the oat-cake in this country, as they do in Nidderdale, instead of bread.

Mr. Aldrich of Iowa, who has been only one of the gentlemen on the other side of the Atlantic to honour me by their correspondence and personal visits, formed the plan of establishing at Webster City, where he lived, a public collection of autographs and manuscripts, and he had met with some considerable success in inducing people, her Britannic Majesty included, to contribute to his object. I gave him some Hazlitt manuscript.

When he last called on me, he had not long since visited Jefferson Davis and his wife, who were very cheerful, with just enough to live upon from the wreck of their fortune. His attainder was never reversed; but he was left unmolested.

CHAPTER VII.

The auction-rooms—Development and machinery of sales by auction—The cataloguer—Influence of sale-catalogues on prices—Origin of my career as a bibliographer—Sotheby's—Account of some of the early sales there—Strange personality of *Mister* Sotheby—The Wolfreston sale in 1856—How it came about.

My bibliographical, numismatic, and other cognate pursuits naturally brought me into contact with those auction-rooms which lend themselves to the dispersion of literary and artistic objects. Of all my haunts in pursuit of information, the famous emporium in Wellington Street has been the most constant and the most productive.

Sales under the hammer originally embraced every description of merchandise within the covers of a single catalogue, just as the fine art auctioneer was a gradual evolution from the house-salesman. A very cursory examination of the catalogues of the last and earliest quarter of the present century will satisfy one that such was the case. As matters now stand, the various kinds of property submitted to competition are not only as a rule carefully classified and separately offered, but certain houses are considered the most advantageous for the realization of particular effects. You are told that you must send pictures and china to Christie's; books, manuscripts, autographs, and coins to Sotheby's; and musical copyrights and literature, and theatrical wardrobes, to Puttick's.

There is some truth in this; but there is a good deal of superstition and prejudice, too, founded on an imperfect conversance with the bearings and inner working of the system. For much depends on an agency to a certain extent independent of the auctioneer. A large proportion of the property sent into the rooms for sale is catalogued by outsiders; there is in many cases no one on the premises qualified to describe correctly and advantageously antiquities, coins, autographs, prints, or even manuscripts and books of other than ordinary character. The expert has to be called in; it does not signify what house it is; the work is his, not the auctioneer's; and the result is mainly in his hands.

If things of value are consigned to Christie's, Sotheby's, Puttick's, or elsewhere, the same course is pursued, and more than probably the same persons are employed. The immediate seller is the medium

for taking the order from the owners, commissioning
the expert, and keeping the account. If he is above
the normal standard, he may have a fair idea beforehand of the nature of the issue, or he may be
acquainted with one class of goods more than with
another. Not seldom his estimate is derived from
the information supplied to him by his agent, the
cataloguer ; and, of course, this is a common incident
in these transactions, as parties so frequently apply
for advances to meet pressing engagements. The
auctioneer is, then, mainly a book-keeper, a financier,
and a salesman. The volume of his business is apt
to be in the ratio of his floating capital, his administrative machinery, and his competence in the
rostrum.

The machinery, as we perceive, is threefold : the
counting-house and establishment, the expert in
the background, and the auctioneer's more or less
influential personality. Where you have these three
conditions fulfilled to a nicety, the success of a house
almost follows as a corollary. But how rarely such
a thing occurs !

And, again, the expert — that very important
factor in this industry—is a Free Lance, whose
services are at the command of every paymaster.
Given a good time, a good cataloguer, and good

property, the counting-house is nearly bound to prove secondary ; and any respectable firm has it in its power to arrange with owners in need of immediate accommodation. Perhaps middle-class or *neutral* effects depend in chief measure on the atmosphere in which they are submitted for sale. You can give away your property, if it is second-rate, at Christie's or Sotheby's without going farther ; you can sell it for the maximum worth on any recognised ground, if certain essential conditions are complied with.

The principle of publishing the results of sales of literary and other high-class property has had the effect of opening the eyes of persons who happen to possess anything of value, and even in the most pressing cases to render careful realization almost as important to the credit of an auctioneer as the payment on account and a prompt settlement are in their way ; and here the expert comes in at every turn. The auctioneer, unless he is a Crichton among auctioneers, may, if he acts on his own judgment, either lose his money by lending too much, or may lose the business by offering too little ; the details of the sale have to be controlled by the cataloguer, and, if he is worthy of his hire, are safest in his hands ; and, after all, the means which are open to any or every house of providing itself with proper financial and executive resources are normal mercantile problems. A well-established and straightforward firm, with an untarnished record and known facilities for converting property into the utmost equivalent cash, may treat the rest as a foregone conclusion.

Many things have occurred since I first became acquainted with Sotheby's. As a mere youth, I had collected for a passing literary purpose an assortment of books which circumstances obliged me to realize when I had done with them. I sent them there. It was my first experience of an auction, and it was a sorrowful one. The volumes, many in handsome new liveries, went for next to nothing. Someone then in Castle Street, now in Piccadilly, bought largely at the sale. It was somewhere about 1858. I thought that I had made up my mind to turn my back on Sotheby's for ever. To buy books and sell them again was clearly a losing game. How little I knew about myself, of what the future would develop, of the direction given to a career by some slight and fortuitous cause!

A copy of Lowndes's *Bibliographer's Manual*, purporting to be a guide to old English books, fell just about the same time in my way. I can hardly tell how it was, but I began to discern and note shortcomings in it. My copy became a repository for marginalia and cuttings. It was as if Sotheby's had baited a hook with that work, guessing that I must bite and be caught; and I did, and was! This is another way of saying that I forgave Sotheby's, and stole back to the old ground.

I found myself once more in Wellington Street, yet with a difference. Some three years had elapsed. A strange new awakening had taken place. I was a bibliographer, with some of the chrysalis still visible. I had begun to make memoranda and copy titles. Neither myself nor anyone else at that juncture was aware that I should carry the hobby further than scores of others who have done the same thing ever since Sotheby's was established, left their mark on a few fly-leaves, and there stopped.

In 1858 the celebrated library of Dr. Philip Bliss was sold here. I did not attend it, but I purchased a lot or so. I had sold my own property rather cheaply. I bought these new items rather dear. I was not discouraged, simply because I was impelled by a secret bent, an innate *lues*, which was steadily and irresistibly disclosing itself. My eyes were turned on other publications treating of our old English authors, and I saw how curiously they resembled the Manual I had and each other in the imperfect justice which they did to the subject. I felt that I could do something better, and I soon began to try.

Of Christie's and Puttick's, and the other emporia where books are knocked down, and occasionally, as in my case, the hopes of their owners with them, I have enjoyed a more limited experience. One point the three haunts which I have been specifying have in common, for as there is no Christie and no Puttick, so there is no Sotheby. It is a *nom de marteau.* Everybody knows Sotheby's. No one would dream of mentioning to you that he was going to Wilkinson's, or had made a purchase at Sotheby, Wilkinson, and Hodge's. These modern excrescences the public repudiates.

The business of the house has enormously expanded; it has identified itself with almost every big affair in books, prints, coins, china, all the days I am able to recall. I have grown up into a slowly-developing knowledge of that eventful and ever-changing scene. I have witnessed all the most important properties which have been submitted to the hammer in those rooms.   I have beheld generations of collectors, generations of booksellers, come and go.   It is not that I am very old, but it has been my fortune to mingle much with my seniors, and I once surprised and amused someone who was speaking to me of Mr. Coventry Patmore by saying : 'Yes, I knew his father and mother, and his grandmother.'   What is more to the immediate purpose, I knew Sotheby's when there was a Sotheby, and was in the room when, in 1864, the tidings came of his death by drowning while on an angling excursion.   I retain his short, slight figure perfectly in my mind.

The last of the Sothebys, besides the works on typographical antiquities and other matters with which his name is honourably connected, compiled a bibliographical account of the Early English Poets, so far as their publications came under the notice of the firm in Wellington Street.   The manuscript was offered to the British Museum by his widow, and Bond consulted me about the purchase, from which I felt bound to dissuade him, as it was an imperfect and jejune performance which my own labours had gone very far to reduce to a *caput mortuum*.

It was precisely when the sale of the grand

Harleian library, of which the catalogue was drawn up for Osborne by Dr. Johnson, was impending, and a larger share of public notice was attracted to these matters, that Samuel Baker started in York Street, Covent Garden. The maiden sale was the collection of books belonging to Thomas Pellet, M.D., which lasted sixteen days, and produced £859 odd.

Of course, very interesting days have been experienced where the financial result was not very striking, as when, in 1799, the firm disposed of the library of the Right Hon. Joseph Addison, 'Author and Secretary of State,' for £533 4s. 4d.; and in 1833 of that of 'the Emperor Napoléon Buonaparte' (*sic*), removed from St. Helena, for £450 9s. (his tortoiseshell walking-stick bringing £38 17s.); and, once more, when the drawings of T. Rowlandson, the caricaturist, were sold in 1818 for £700. Are not those living who would now add a third o, and think the lot not too high? But the portions of the stupendous Heber library dispersed here in 1834, owing to what Dibdin called the *bibliophobia*, nearly ruined the auctioneers. They rallied from the blow, however, and have never suffered any relapse to bad times, whatever account they may be pleased to give of the very piping ones which they have known pretty well ever since '45, when Mr. Benjamin Heywood Bright's important library was entrusted to their care.

I cannot help thinking, however, that whatever credit the existing management may fairly claim, it was the second Sotheby—the *Mister* Sotheby of or about 1816-30—who impressed on the concern his powerful and enduring individuality. He had a long innings, and had excellent opportunities of building up the structure which his son and successor inherited. The latter was the link between the old *régime* and the new. He lived to see many modifications, and to contract an alliance with fresh blood ; and he survives to-day in Wellington Street, hard by Waterloo Bridge, as certainly as Shakespeare does in Stratford-upon-Avon, and elsewhere, carrying on his affairs by proxy, as it were. Others, for the sake of convenience, act on his behalf ; nevertheless, no one should deceive himself. The place is ' Sotheby's ' in 1896 just as it was in 1796.

Two more modern personalities with whom I have come into very frequent contact during my visits to Sotheby's were Mr. John Wilkinson, who died in the commencement of 1894 at a patriarchal age, and Mr. Edward Grose Hodge. Of the latter, who in bygone—half-historical—times occupied a stool in the counting-house as a book-keeper, and was conspicuous by his raven-black locks, I shall say nothing, because I could only reiterate the common feeling about his capacity for business, his gentlemanly address, and his thorough independence of character.

Mr. Wilkinson was the principal seller in my earlier days. His appearance, as it was impressed on my mind when I became an habitual frequenter of the rooms about 1858, was very agreeable, and his manner highly prepossessing ; he was then in the full vigour of life. Halliwell and he were very intimate, and I have dined with him at Halliwell's table. One not very unreasonable idiosyncrasy on his part was his tenacious resistance to the admission of anyone else to a share in the conduct of the sales ; he persisted in keeping his junior partner out so long as he physically could. He liked to lord over the whole show to the very last. I think that the spirit of *monarchy* remains rather strong in Wellington Street.

I understand that the ivory hammer which Mr. George Leigh used during his brief association with the house as a partner had belonged to Langford the auctioneer. It was given by the former to Mr. Benjamin Wheatley, an employé at that time, afterward a partner in another firm ; and it is now in the possession of his son, Mr. H. B. Wheatley.

I can just recall the Wolfreston sale in 1856. I was not actually present, but I heard a good deal about it soon afterward. It was a small collection of early English books and tracts formed under the Tudors and Stuarts ; the copies were often uncut, and as often imperfect or dog's-eared. But there were among them a few startling rarities—some not even till then put on record by the learned in these affairs. The owner would have gladly accepted £30 for the lot, and the day's sale realized £750. Think of that ! Is it nothing to have Sotheby's to our friend ? In spite of disappointments, which will sometimes happen, and flat Saturday afternoons, when sovereigns are constantly knocked down for ten shillings each, this institution is among our public benefactors not the least.

One of the family—the Wolfrestons, not the Sothebys—dined with me years after, and told me how it was. The books had lain in a corner of the library time out of mind unnoticed and unheeded, and it was thought as well to get rid of them. They should have marked the day with a white stone when a friend (he *was* a friend) recommended them to apply to Wellington Street.

CHAPTER VIII.

Persons whom I have met at Sotheby's—A recollection of 1858—
George Daniel of Canonbury—Some account of him and his
books—His visit to Charles Mathews the elder at Highgate
—He tells me a story of Charles Lamb—Samuel Addington
—His extraordinary character as a collector—His method of
buying—Compared with Quaritch—The Sixpenny Solicitor
—Booksellers at Sotheby's—Curious methods of bidding—
The bundle hunter, past and present—His fallen fortunes
—The smaller room at Sotheby's—Anecdote of a Bristol
teapot.

LETTING alone the professional element at Sotheby's,
to which I shall advert in a moment, think of the
names which rise up to one's lips—names of persons
eminent in nearly every vocation and walk of life :
men of genius, of culture, of rank, the student,
the amateur, the spectator!   I have beheld with my
own eyes J. B. Inglis, who had sold a magnificent
library in 1826, before I was born, and lived to
form a second ; George Daniel, David Laing, Henry
Bradshaw, Alexander Dyce, John Forster, J. O.
Halliwell, Sir Stirling Maxwell, Henry Stevens of
Vermont, Sir Thomas Phillipps of Middle Hill,

George Smith, Christie-Miller, R. S. Turner, and Samuel Addington. But Lord Melbourne, Tommy Hill (Paul Pry), Lord Macaulay, M. Libri, Philip Bliss, Bulkeley Bandinel, Lord Crawford, and a host of others, have crossed this threshold. Henry Huth looked in once or twice while the Daniel sale was going on, and you brush elbows at this moment with other notabilities of our own day.

So it has always been ; there is a weird fascination, there is a charm, which draws us all more or less toward the spot where the game of chance (for such it is) is being played, even if we do not enter the lists, or let our own voices become audible. Leigh Hunt used to be fond of telling me how he had attended the Roxburghe sale in 1812, just as a looker-on, out of a sort of speculative curiosity, which it might ask a separate paper to define.

The tap of the hammer against the desk is often awaited with considerable anxiety by those actually competing for the lot before the room.

I had a singular adventure here in 1858. Among a mass of rubbish a unique copy of the Earl of Surrey's English Virgil was put up one day. The bidding for it stopped at £6 12s. 6d. At that sum it was mine. But the hammer did not fall. The auctioneer repeated the amount several times, and kept his eye on the open door. The company did not understand what this strange movement signified. No one topped my offer. All at once, breathless, rushed in Mr. Thorpe, agent for the library at Britwell, asked what lot was up, and what price had been reached. '£6 12s. 6d.,' now said Mr. Wilkinson, unmasking, and I lost my gem, which Mr. Thorpe carried off at £20. How I disliked him!

An occasional visitor to the rooms was George Daniel, of Canonbury, whom I well recollect. I sat next to him at a sale, and when some ordinary bookseller's lot was knocked down in his name, I innocently inquired if he had purchased it. 'No, sir,' he urbanely replied; 'if I were to buy all *that* Mr. Daniel does, I should have an Alexandrian library.' The authentic G. D. was a retired accountant, whose idiosyncrasy consisted of *rares morceaux, bonnes bouches,* uniques—copies of books with a *provenance,* or in jackets made for them by Roger Payne; nay, in the original parchment or paper wrapper, or in a bit of real mutton, which certain men call sheep. He was a person of literary tastes, and had written books in his day. But his chief celebrity was as an acquirer of those of others, provided always that they were old enough or rare enough. An item never passed into his possession without at once *ipso facto* gaining new attributes, almost invariably worded in a holograph memorandum on the fly-leaf.

Daniel was in the market at a fortunate and peculiar juncture, just when prices were depressed, about the time of the great Heber sale. His marvellous gleanings came to the hammer precisely when the quarto Shakespear, the black-letter romance, the unique book of Elizabethan verse, had grown worth ten times their weight in sovereigns. Sir William Tite, J. O. Halliwell, and Henry Huth, were to the front.

It was in 1864. What a wonderful sight it was! No living man had ever witnessed the like. Copies of Shakespear printed from the prompters' manuscripts and published at fourpence, fetched £300 or £400. I remember old Joseph Lilly, when he had secured the famous ballads, which came from the Tollemaches of Helmingham Hall, holding up the folio volume in which they were contained in triumph, as Mr. Huth happened to enter the room.

Poor Daniel! He had no mean estimate of his treasures; what he had was always better than what you had. Books, prints, autographs, it was all the same. I met him one morning in Long Acre.

I had bought a very fine copy of Taylor the Water Poet. 'Oh yes, sir,' he said, 'I saw it; but not quite so fine as mine.' He went up to Highgate to look through Charles Mathews the elder's engravings. They were all duplicates—of course, inferior ones. 'Damn him, sir!' cried Mathews afterward to a friend; 'I should like him to have had a duplicate of my poor leg.'

This was the commercial bias of the ex-accountant.

Another thing which I had direct from Daniel was the occasional habit which Charles Lamb had of paying him a visit, and looking at his old books— looking at them, not touching. 'For,' said Daniel to me, 'you know, sir, I could not have allowed that. Why, Mr. Lamb would turn over the leaves of a volume with his wet finger'—and the narrator represented the operation in the street, so far as he could without a book and with gloved hands— 'and I always kept a particular copy of old ballads for him.'

While Daniel's books were on view at the auction-room, in 1864, one of his family came for the purpose of seeing them, as it appeared that he never shewed his treasures to his children. From the account which a descendant gave me, I judge that the handsome result of the sale did not prove of much benefit to those interested.

Daniel was a virtuoso rather than a connoisseur. He studied the commercial barometer, and knew the right things to buy. Still, as the money expended would have realized at compound interest more than even the extravagant prices paid for his bibliographical rarities in 1864, and as he could not have forecast the issue, some credit is due to him for having preferred to invest his savings as he did in early English books. He purchased in later life very sparingly, and so far did not obey the ordinary instincts of the collector, whose zest is derived from acquiring, not from possessing. He is apt to contemplate the treasures which he has secured with the sated feeling of the author toward the printed transfers from his own mind.

A noted and conspicuous character in the rooms during many years, whenever any remarkable objects were to be submitted to competition, was Mr. Samuel Addington, of St. Martin's Lane. A tall, imposing figure, with an inclination at the last to stoop somewhat, Addington deserves to be regarded in one or two respects as the most extraordinary person who frequented Sotheby's in my earlier recollection. He was, like R. S. Turner and Edwin Lawrence, illiterate, but also, like them, a man of the keenest and truest instinct for what was worth having, and withal of commanding presence.

His collections of Prints, Miniatures, Books, Manuscripts, Coins, were *a-per-se.* I once had occasion to solicit for a literary acquaintance the loan of the miniature of Dr. Donne by Oliver, and Addington shewed me some of his gems, and gems they were. His knowledge of them was mainly *per* Catalogue. When he upset a tray of coins, someone had to go and set it in order again. It was his instinct which was so surprising. His handwriting was rather worse, I think, than mine, and was wanting in character.

I frequently met him at Sotheby's and in the street (he generally walked with his head slightly inclined and his hands crossed behind his back), and have more than once seen him arming Mrs. Noseda, the printseller, to the Royal Academy. She was the only person on whose judgment in her particular line he relied. But Addington also saw a good deal of Wareham, the dealer in antiquities, and, it is said, helped him.

He bought in his time almost everything, and of the finest and choicest, for the cost did not signify.

He lived over his shop in the Lane, and was a bachelor with some £15,000 a year. I think that he dined nearer the Elizabethan hour than most of us do; and when there was something to attract him to Wellington Street, it was his not unfrequent habit to arrive there on the stroke of one p.m., his frugal dessert—an orange—in his hand. If you were on the scent after a prize in the rooms, and Addington had fixed his mind upon the same lot, you were as one whose chance had gone.

He was perhaps the first who set the precedent of giving prices for articles totally beyond record and example. It was his cue, and it is, so to speak, his epitaph. Addington, as a collector, followed somewhat parallel lines to Quaritch as a man of business—he declined to be beaten. As some of us are said to be makers of history, Addington was, and the autocrat of the auction-room still is, a maker of market values and prices current. I hardly believe that his knowledge of books and other curiosities was in any way great. He watched the biddings carefully, ignored all lots which fell at humble prices, but began to prick up his ears when £10 or £20 had been reached. His entrance into the fray was ordinarily prefigured by the relegation of his glasses to the top of his head.

Let me consecrate a few lines to a widely different individual who haunted this purlieu in my youth, the Sixpenny Solicitor. He was a tall, poorly-clad man who wore an appallingly bad hat. I kept his name in my head, as I did the odour which accompanied him in my nostrils, for years. I regret the loss of the one, not that of the other. Someone thinks that it was Adams; perhaps so—but no matter. He used to sit at the table too, but as far as he could from everybody else. He might harbour a consciousness that he was not too welcome; and sixpence was his Alpha and his Omega. Ay, and you would have been surprised at the lots which fell to him. He was one of the surest customers of the firm, for he invariably paid cash, which is a strongly-marked exception to the general rule. Poor fellow! at last I lost sight of him. Of his humble profits much, I fear, went in the purchase of liquor, probably on a par in quality with his habiliments and his hat.

Among the booksellers who have assembled here, and whose acquaintance and sympathy I have enjoyed through many pleasant, if laborious, years, I may enumerate Joseph Lilly, the Boones, Bernard Quaritch, F. S. Ellis, the two Molini, the younger Pickering, James Toovey (of the *Temple of Leather and Literature*, Piccadilly), George Willis, Edward

Stibbs, the two Wallers, the Russell-Smiths, the Walfords, William Reeves, George Bumstead, and the Rimells. I once fell in with Robert Triphook, and conversed with him; but he had retired before my time. The elder Boone had a curious way of bidding; he sat just under the auctioneer, and would tap the heel of Mr. Wilkinson's boot with his pencil.

Bumstead, who executed commissions for George Smith and Sir Stirling Maxwell, usually stood by the side of the rostrum, and, laying his hand on his right cheek, made his thumb turn as on a hinge, each movement signifying an advance. A third was supposed to remain in the field so long as he kept his eye on the seller, or continued to strike his catalogue with his pencil.

These and other *droles* were the strategists, the employers of a secret language. Is it necessary to say that they all conceived themselves unobserved? But, again, there was the opposite extreme—the stentorian throat, generally of some provincial or Continental tyro, which made the room vibrate, and everybody present look round; and an occasional episode, a generation ago, was the shout with which poor Tom Arthur, if he had indulged rather too freely at his mid-day repast before the sale, bade at random for whatever was on the table.

One signal difference between Sotheby's as it now exists, and the house as I was familiar with it in my younger days, lies in the almost ruined hopes of the Bundle-hunter. There was a time when this peculiar pursuit was attended by lucrative results, and partook of that adventurous complexion so dear to the trader, the dream of whose life it is to become rich soon and retire early. Weird tales used to be related of fabulous bargains acquired by keen and persistent study of the Bundle.

Those are living who remember what it was to discover in the heart of one some gem beyond price, some reputed *introuvable*. The very interior was a *terra incognita*, a Pandora's box, a possible Eldorado. A relic of the days of the earlier Tudors or a Wynkyn de Worde, a lost Elizabethan fragment or some piece by Taylor the Water Poet, which the world had long despaired of ever beholding, can it be that such, and many more like these—nay, better —were once not seldom the portions of the wary and diligent harvestman? Ay, indeed ; and not very different was it of old with the composite volume— the heterogeneous assemblage of pieces united by unforeseeing owners or indiscreet bibliopegists (bless them both !) in unholy wedlock ; nor with the folio volume, lettered outside perchance, 'Old Newspapers,' and the resting place of black-letter ballads threescore and upward, which, a beneficent spirit casting a spell on all save *one alone*, no other eye discerned.

Yet now and again the labours of the seeker are still rewarded. Stories have been rife within reasonable years of literary *bijoux* disinterred by the vigilant and sagacious explorer from unpromising, nay, repellent, upper stratifications of ragged, dust-ingrained, penny-box ware. Mark you, the successful expert of the Victorian era has all his work before him. He has to be wary to excess. He has to snatch the right moment for investigating the contents of these 'parcels,' as the phrase is. He must assure himself that no enemy is in ambush. A quick eye, a deft hand, and an impassible demeanour are essential.

Let him not be too sanguine till the hammer is down, and the prize is his; for instances are cited by the knowing in these by-paths of research where the hidden quarry has been secretly noted by more than a single hunter—by a second Argus—and then, while others have beaten the bush, the auctioneer it is who catches the hare; for, however sorrowful it may be to relate it, the baffled game operates exactly in a contrary direction, and the article, instead of dropping for a song, realizes in the heat of exasperated competition a figure which makes the occupant of the rostrum lick his lips, as it is not etiquette for him to betray emotion in any other way.

But the prevailing experience at present is certainly in the direction opposite to that which the nugget-digger desiderates. The auctioneer's staff, doubtless obeying instructions, is most distastefully minute in detailing out the contents of lots and parcels, and in searching beforehand for hidden ore. From the bundle-hunter's seeing-point the game is well-nigh up. Ere long the bladder will be pricked, and he will be like another Othello. When a volume of commonplace tracts fills an entire page, if not two, of a catalogue, it is time for him to break his staff. The latter-day auctioneer, sooth to say, errs on the side of accentuation.

It seems, however, as if the keenest and most jealous competition, the most strongly emphasized printed accounts, and the latest improvements in distributing and circulating catalogues of sales, are unequal to the removal of a curious phenomenon which periodically recurs, and yet on each occasion is declared to be so remarkable that it cannot by possibility happen again : I mean the Frost—the sudden and capricious fall of the temperature in the room, or in the veins of those frequenting it, to zero.

Who shall attempt to explain it ?   Provided always that property of a certain stamp usually protects itself by guaranteeing attendance and opposition, it is not that the character of the sale is unfavourable, or that of the articles offered liable to question, for I have had personal experience of cases where some of the rarest books and best copies went at nominal figures.   The trade 'hung off'; there was a likelier sale elsewhere ; business was quiet and stocks were full ; or it was an occasion where the national library might have filled many gaps, and the authorities were enjoying a nap, or the Trustees had sagaciously interdicted farther expenditure for the time being, because Parliament had not passed the vote, and they were too proud or too cautious to go on credit.   At one time, mediocre copies of more or less common books are found realizing artificially high prices ; at another, old English plays and poetry, and historical tracts of the utmost rarity, are given away.   Lotteries are forbidden by statute, yet this is the greatest lottery of all !

Now it begins, I apprehend, to be better understood that it is not only the property which governs the result, but the atmosphere and the name.   Some years ago, for instance, Mr. Gladstone placed his old china in the hands of Christie's for sale. It was a very second-rate collection, but the reputation of the owner drew a company which was willing to pay for sentiment.

Of the smaller room looking to Wellington Street, and a later addition, where the coin, print, and autograph sales are often held, I do not profess to know much. The earliest boom, by the way, in the numismatic department was the noble collection of Marmaduke Trattle in 1832, which brought nearly £11,000. In later life, when my own attention was directed to one or two studies outside the library, I acquired the habit of looking on now and then while these collateral descriptions of property were changing hands, but I seldom intervened.

On the dispersion of the Edkins collection of Bristol porcelain many years ago, my brother had been asked by Dr. Diamond of Twickenham, who could not be there in person, if he would mind going to £20 for a certain teapot. The trust was accepted, and the holder of this heavy commission (as it seemed to him to be) imagined himself the central figure in a thrilling episode— the hero, in fact, of the day. When the item came on, a gentleman stepped forward and said to the auctioneer : 'If it will save the time of the company, sir, I will say £105 just to start you !'

CHAPTER IX.

One or two coin-collectors—Lord Ashburnham—How he lost his first collection—Edward Wigan—Illustration of his enthusiasm—The Blenheim sale—The Marlborough gems—The Althorp Library—The house in Leicester Square—Its history and development—Remarkable sales which have been held by Messrs. Puttick and Simpson—Books—Manuscripts—Autographs—My obligations to the house—The Somers Tracts.

THE late Earl of Ashburnham formed two collections of Greek coins. The first he used to carry about with him in his yacht, and it was taken by pirates. Lord A. saw one of his coins offered for sale in a Greek or Mediterranean town, and it led to a revival of the hobby. His cabinet was not extensive, but included many rare pieces.

Mr. Edward Wigan, of the great hop firm in the Borough, whose cabinets were privately bought by Rollin and Feuardent of Paris after his death, was one of the most ardent collectors we have ever had of Greek and Roman silver and copper coins. But of Greek copper he made a speciality. He bought a good deal of Whelan in the Haymarket, and Mr. F. Whelan, then a boy, recollects his visits to his father's, when the sherry was invariably brought out, and any fresh acquisition discussed. One day a rare type of Greek money lay on Whelan's table, and Wigan was tantalized by the announcement that it was not for immediate sale. He went on talking to Whelan, and every now and then reverting to the coin. At last he took up a slip of paper, and, writing his name at the foot, cried: 'There, fill it up with what figure you like.' He could afford to be liberal. He told F. W. that his share of the profits one half-year was £34,000.

Wigan to a considerable extent derived his taste for coins from General York-Moore, with whom he grew very intimate, and in whose company he was often to be seen—too often, some say; for the General was convivial to a fault.

The Duke of Marlborough, I believe, imagined that the proceeds of the sale of the Blenheim library would be handed over to him; but the trustees insisted on the fund being applied to the improvement of the estate, and a round sum went in a contract with Fentums for new grates for Blenheim. While the auction was going on in Leicester Square, a firm of solicitors at Manchester was kept informed from day to day of the result.

The gentleman who gave a large sum for the Marlborough gems, without knowing much about them, once allowed the Rev. S. S. Lewis, of Corpus, Cambridge, to shew the collection to a friend of his. But the owner chose to be present, and after observing silence for some time, while Lewis was doing the honours, he ventured to interpolate at a pause in the proceedings a humble piece of criticism. Taking up one of the treasures, he said to the visitor: 'That's *nice!*' '*Nice!* Mr. ——,' exclaimed Lewis; '"nice" is a word to apply to a jam-tart, not to an ancient gem.'

Lewis himself left an important collection of coins and other antiquities to Corpus. I was told that he had laid out £500 a year on this fancy or pursuit during more than twenty years. Among much that was mediocre in point of preservation (for Lewis did not specially study what is called *state*), there were many fine things which he had acquired during his travels in Greece and elsewhere. Someone related to me an odd trait in him, when a young lady who had died testified her regard for Lewis by leaving him £5,000. He went into an ordinary shop with the cheque, and asked my informant if he would oblige him with change. He had a brother, whom I never saw, but who had, I was told, a funny way, if he met you and you made an observation which struck him, of saying : ' Ah ! very curious,' pulling out a memorandum-book ; ' would you mind me jotting that down ?'

Lord Spencer told me in 1868, when I paid a visit to Althorp to take notes of some of the books so far unseen by me, many years prior to the dispersion of the Blenheim-Sunderland library, that the latter books were so neglected that birds had built their nests behind the shelves.

Hearing recently that the Spencer collection had gone to Manchester, and recalling the look of Althorp as it was when the library remained there, I asked someone in town what had been done to fill up the gaps ; and I was told that the large billiard room with the gallery had been *clean swept away*, and that the empty shelves were replenished with all sorts of commonplace stuff gathered from the shops. What a fall ! They sold Wimbledon to save the books, and they have sold the books to save themselves. What would Dibdin's Spencer say, if he could behold Althorp almost a sepulchre ? Let the pictures and china go, and the house might as well be levelled with the ground.

There are many not willing to acknowledge themselves very old who remember the porticoed entrance in Piccadilly, a little westward from St. James's Church, where lay the place of business of Messrs. Puttick and Simpson. It is only about a dozen years since the building stood there ; but the sale-room itself had been already demolished, necessitating the removal elsewhere ; and every trace of it and the other buildings which occupied the site has disappeared. Nor had the names which I now give been identified with the locality much more than a decade. But it was old ground, and they succeeded to an established and respectable inheritance. In 1794 this spot held the Great Room of Mr. Stewart, who continued here alone till 1825-26, when Mr. Benjamin Wheatley, a member of the staff at Sotheby's, and Mr. Adlard, a son of the printer of that name, purchased the business with the understanding that the old name should stand for a time, the house being styled Stewart, Wheatley and Adlard. It was in the days of the nominal triumvirate that the famous library of the Rev. Theodore Williams was sold here.

Mr. Stewart did not long survive his arrangement with Messrs. Wheatley and Adlard, the two latter being found carrying on the concern in 1830, and in

1837 Mr. Wheatley died. The latter was a man of superior attainments, and sold many fine collections, including part of the Heber library. The interest seems to have passed into the hands of Messrs. John and James Fletcher shortly afterward, but a son of Mr. Wheatley was admitted for the sake of the familiar name ; the style of the firm for a short time was Fletcher and Wheatley, but in 1843 ' Mr. Fletcher ' occurs on the catalogues, and he inserts, as a novel feature, a notice to executors, assignees, and others, stating that he is prepared to make advances to the extent of three-fourths of the value of goods actually in his hands. Of course, the value was what Mr. Fletcher computed it to be, and, to go back for a moment to 1837, we observe at the end of a catalogue of dramatic poetry an announcement of other sales in prospect, in one of which there was to be a fine portrait of the second Marquis of Bute by Gainsborough.

It was while the late Mr. B. R. Wheatley belonged to the firm, and prior to his father's death, that the auction-room was converted on one occasion into a theatre for the production of Goldsmith's *She Stoops to Conquer* by amateurs, Mr. Wheatley himself, then quite a lad, with a strong taste and talent for theatricals, taking the part of Tony Lumpkin.

We lose sight of Mr. Fletcher in 1846, in which year he sold a further portion of the stock of Mr. John Bohn, and come face to face with the now long-familiar names of Puttick and Simpson, the former, who had been a clerk to Mr. Fletcher, taking Mr. Simpson into partnership. This change took place between April and July, 1846, and in all their earlier catalogues the new firm describe themselves as successors to Mr. Fletcher. Mr. Puttick was an active man of business, and from this point we have to date the commencement of a period of distinct progress and improvement.

To enumerate even the more important auctions which have been held in the Great Room, 191, Piccadilly, and since the removal to 47, Leicester Square, in 1858, would occupy more space than I can spare. Taking, so far as literary property is concerned, 1846 as my point of departure, I may give a few items:

The Donnadieu Books and Manuscripts, £3,923; the Libri Collection, £8,929: Books and Manuscripts of Dawson Turner, £9,453 19s.; Books and Manuscripts of Edward Crowninshield, of Boston, N.E., £4,826 6s.; Books and Manuscripts of Sir Edward Dering, £7,259 16s.; the Emperor Maximilian's Mexican Library (1869), £3,985 12s. 6d.; Books from William Penn's Library, £1,350; Books of Sir Edward Nicholas, Secretary to Charles I. (1877). £977 16s.; the Sunderland Library (1881-83) £60,000; the Gosford Library (1884), £11,318 5s. 6d.; the Hartley Library (1885-87), £16,530.

But the list is inexhaustible.

Then, in the department of Autograph Letters, there is a continuous record from 1848, if we exclude such as form part of prior miscellaneous sales. Many of us recollect the Ollier Collection—not so long ago—when a sonnet, and a published one, too, in the handwriting of Keats, realized here £8 15s.

Numerous catalogues before us shew that Mr. Redford in his ' Art Sales,' as well as Mr. Tuer in his Bartolozzi volume, does imperfect justice to the pictures and prints which have found new owners under the hammer here and in Piccadilly right away from 1806. A suggestive clause presents itself in the Conditions of Sale attached to this class of property so far back as 1812, when intending buyers of paintings are apprised by Mr. Stewart that ' to prevent inconveniences that frequently attend long and open accounts, the remainder of the purchase-money is to be absolutely paid on or before delivery.'

The prices obtained were, in the old days, fairly high ; but even *chef Douvres* (as Mr. Stewart was pleased to write it) did not invariably answer the expectations of the parties interested. Do we not still find the same thing occasionally?

The series of priced catalogues from 1805 (the earliest in the possession of Messrs. Puttick and

Simpson) to the present time is a strange sort of homily on the fortunes of families, the progress of learning, and the caprices of taste.

To the *littérateur* and bibliographer, through all the long vista of years, these classic rooms, associated with Sir Joshua Reynolds and his friends, and with the Western Literary Institution, have afforded many and many a precious gem and fascinating discovery.

It would be ungrateful to the house in Leicester Square if I were not to confess that it has yielded me in my time many a pleasant discovery and many an excellent bargain. Was it not there that I bought the classic Somers Tracts in thirty folio volumes, with the 'Laws of New York,' 1693—the first book printed there, I take it- and several other unique Americana among them? Did I not attend the great Surrenden sale there, when the Dering books were offered, and have to my next neighbour at the table no less a man than John Forster, Esquire? How vividly I call to mind pointing out to him the rarity and interest of an uncut copy on large paper of Archbishop Laud's 'Speech in the Star Chamber,' 1637, and his magnificent affability in rendering me thanks!

The contributors to the press, as a rule, depend on

the priced catalogue of a sale for their guidance in selecting the items for the paragraph which they draw up for the organ by which they happen to be employed.   They seldom possess much independent experience.   They let their eyes run down the columns, and note the highest prices, the disadvantage being that they are apt to miss the rarities which go, perchance, below their value, no less than to cite without comment the lots which on some special account fetch artificial figures.

CHAPTER X.

The British Museum—My recollection of the old building and Reading Room—Members of the staff whom I have known—Panizzi and the New General Catalogue—Sir Henry Ellis—George Bullen—Grenville Collection—Mr. Grenville and my father—The frequenters of the Reading Room—Mr. Gladstone's views about the Museum staff—Proposed insulation of the national collections—Publishers—Different schools or types—George Routledge—Henry George Bohn—George Willis—A literary adventure—Some other booksellers—The Leadenhall and Cornhill schools of painting—The *édition de luxe*—The Illustrated Copy.

THE present Principal Librarian and Keeper of the Printed Books at the British Museum are respectively the fifth and fourth holders of the office whom I have known. After the retirement of Sir Henry Ellis in 1856, the influence of Lord Brougham procured the appointment of Antonio Panizzi, who had succeeded in ingratiating himself with that once powerful statesman and Minister. He also courted old Mr. Grenville.

Jones, who followed Panizzi, owed his fortune to the latter ; but Dr. Bond was selected partly

on the alternate principle, and partly from the
absence of anyone at the moment from the other
Departments willing or competent to take the post.
Dr. Newton had the first offer, and declined.   Bond
was by far the best and most liberal man whom
we have had ; but Sir E. M. Thompson, who was
brought up under him in the Manuscript Department, was the most judicious choice which the
Trustees could have made when Bond resigned.

When I first frequented the Museum, the old
Reading Room was, of course, still in use.   Mr.
Watts was keeper of the Printed Books.   At that
time the national library was very weak in early
English literature, and Watts took comparatively
little interest in it, having made no special study
of the subject.   Under the advice of one or another,
certain gaps had been filled up as opportunities
presented themselves, and at the Bright sale in
1845 more particularly the Museum authorities
secured many valuable items.   Within the last
thirty years, however, under the auspices of Mr.
Rye, Mr. Bullen, and Mr. Garnett, the acquisitions
in this direction have been continuous and immense.
Even phenomenal prices have been given for exceptionally interesting and important articles, and
had it not been for the keenness of private compe-

tition, the national collection would at this moment be marvellously complete. But the annual grant for the library is moderate; and while the English or American amateur can afford to outbid the Trustees, the latter can afford on their part to wait. They are, as I have more than once remarked, the heirs of all men.

Yet it is more than ridiculous to expend £22,000,000 on the Navy, because that step strengthens the Government in the popular estimation, and to make a pretence of economy in another direction, of which the general knowledge is less clear, by paring down the allowance for books and manuscripts a thousand or so. It is not that Ministers care for the Navy more than the Museum; but the Navy means Votes, and the other does not.

At the same time, the steady absorption of our early literature by the British Museum, and of ancient books generally by that and other public libraries in Europe and America, with the tendency to destroy volumes belonging to the theological and scientific series, for which the demand has ceased, must have the ultimate effect of narrowing the opportunities for forming important private cabinets, and of gradually diminishing the bulk of old printed matter in existence ; and with what is actually valueless much which was highly deserving of preservation has not only perished in the past, but perishes from ignorance or accident year by year.

Take one case out of thousands. An old gentleman in Suffolk was discovered by his cousin, my informant, not long since, making a bonfire of some old books, including a copy of Burton's *Anatomy of Melancholy*, 1621. On being challenged for his reason for committing this act of vandalism, the owner remarked that he had been looking into the Burton, and did not think it was a fit book for the girls—his four daughters, of whom the most juvenile was about fifty.

Here was one of the makers of rare books ! The same wise gentleman had included in the holocaust a manuscript Diary kept by his father during sixty years.

The *magnum opus* of Panizzi was, I believe, the New General Catalogue of the Printed Books. On this scheme and his editorial work on the lives and writings of Dante, Ariosto, and Boiardo, his fame rests. I prefer to limit myself to a passing criticism on that section of the Panizzi undertaking of which my bibliographical labours and researches have led me to take special cognizance, and I must affirm that the arrangement of the entries is most embarrassing and most troublesome. Items, instead of being placed under obvious heads, are reached with more or less sacrifice of time by cross-references to other volumes of the Catalogue and other letters of the alphabet, necessarily occupying the time of workers and consulters.

Some of the present staff of officials are fully sensible of the injudicious character of the plan pursued, and seem to be of my opinion, that the whole fabric ought to be reconstructed in the public interest. The pedantic and nonsensical practice of mixing up I and J and U and V, and of ranging certain classes of books under *Academies*, must ultimately be given up.

The fifth article of the Protest made by the late Mr. Bolton Corney against the appointment of Panizzi to the head of the Museum in 1856 runs thus : ' Because the said Antonio Panizzi, on account of the failure of his engagements with regard to the Catalogue of printed books, and the fictions and absurdities of the only fragment thereof hitherto published, appears to have deserved reprehension rather than promotion.'

When my father lived in Great Russell Street

in 1846, the Museum was still enclosed within a
dead wall, and was guarded by sentinels.

It was from Sir Henry Ellis that I obtained my
first reader's ticket. My next step was to lose it,
and during about twenty years I held none, nor
was ever challenged. Then came the dynamite
scare, and one day I was stopped at the door
of the Library. 'You know me?' I said. 'Yes,
sir.' 'How singular!' 'Well, you see, sir, it is
our orders. If you were the Archbishop of
Canterbury, sir——' This appeal I was powerless
to resist, and I went round the other way.

I never saw Ellis; but I had to communicate
with him in 1869 on a literary matter in which he
had a voice. So far back as 1813 he had edited
Brand's *Popular Antiquities;* and without taking
into account the legal bearing of his phenomenal
survivorship till I had printed off, and was ready
to issue, my new recension, I found myself in the
dilemma of having to secure his assent prior to
publication. Ellis peremptorily refused; but twelve
days after he died, and, although the copyright did
not *ipso facto* determine, I launched my scheme
neck or naught. The letter to me, written in his
ninety-second year, was probably the last which the
old gentleman ever despatched.

My father found himself in a similar dilemma, when he inserted in the *Romancist*, in 1840, a tale called the *Children of the Abbey*, written generations before ; but he was less fortunate than myself. The authoress emerged, to his consternation, from her hiding-place, and had to be ' squared.' God knows if she might not do the same thing now, if anyone had the hardihood to try the experiment !

The late Mr. George Bullen is my authority for stating that at Paris they have among the archives both the original *Edict of Nantes* and the original Revocation. Panizzi told Bullen that ' he never knew a Protestant turn Papist unless he was a damned fool, or a Papist turn Protestant unless he was a damned rogue.'

Bullen was civilly elbowed out of the Keepership of the Printed Books, as Reid was out of that of the Prints. He had applied to F. for a testimonial to support his candidature for Bond's place as principal librarian ; but F. excused himself. At the same time, it is due alike to Bullen and Reid, and I may add Vaux, to testify that they always displayed toward myself, as a student and inquirer, the utmost amount of friendly sympathy and interest.

Bullen had, however, a tiresome and tantalizing way of disparaging the commercial value (of which he, in fact, knew little or nothing) of any rare book submitted to his approval, and then making a great splutter about the remarkable acquisition which the Museum had obtained through his discernment. From his want of knowledge, the national library missed many *desiderata*. His predecessor Rye was a stronger man, and relied on his own judgment ; whereas Bullen made the circuit of the building, if something was offered, in quest of opinions upon it. *For what was he there?* He was paid for *his* opinion ; and he had none.

The weakest proceeding under his Keepership was the compilation of the three-volume catalogue of Early English Literature, which might, without detriment on the one hand, and with positive advantage on the other, have been, in the first place, digested into one ; but the book abounds with errors of every description, nor is it easy to see of what use, save as a work of strictly local reference, a new and improved edition would be, since the whole of the most valuable material is more fully, if not more accurately, described elsewhere.

I recollect, as an old frequenter of the place, the curious episodes of Vaux and Madden ; but I desist from entering into them, as they are of no general interest.

A reminiscence of the Museum, as agreeable as it is permanent, is the gracious reply by Mr. Watts, when he was superintendent of the Reading Room, to my explanation that I was Mr. Hazlitt's son. ' Mr. Hazlitt *yourself*,' Mr. Watts was kind enough to say. The words made me feel that I was really an individual.

The Grenville collection at the Museum is, of course, infinitely precious ; but the owner unfortunately displayed too little caution in examining the copies of books which he bought, and many of which have proved imperfect. I recollect that, when my father resided at Old Brompton in the early forties in Mr. Grenville's lifetime, he occasionally obtained the loan of some volume for a passing literary purpose, and that the old servant who brought it to our house flattered his master, as we thought, by his resemblance to him in his general manner and bearing.

How many a worthy soul with a mysterious *pied à terre*—God knows where or what—finds shelter and warmth beneath the ample and friendly dome of the new Reading Room ! What many of them do, how they live, may be within the knowledge of some ; all that I can affirm is that, within my experience, a succession of them, which seems interminable, has come and gone, and has vexed the souls of hapless officials, to whom Job the prophetic was, in point of patience, a baby.

The Superintendent must perforce be genial and obliging to all comers. It is in his diploma. The public has been exceedingly fortunate here. Mr. Watts, Mr. Bullen, Mr. Garnett, Mr. Fortescue, and Mr. Wilson, have left in succession nothing to be desired in the way of courtesy and good temper. I once watched a lady-reader, who had manifestly made some subject her absorbing study, while she catechized Mr. Garnett, and I have to avow that even he at last came to the end of his resources. But he had a thousand topics at his fingers' ends, the lady, perhaps, only that one.

I am not going for an instant to allege that Mr. Garnett is addicted to favouritism ; but if any gentleman calls to see him, and finds that he has an American lady with him, his best plan is to say that he will look in again that day week. Our lady-cousins from the other side are certainly desperate button-holers.

Such odd figures, occasionally with cloaks of imposing amplitude—such bizarre costumes ! Gentlemen of foreign extraction and ancient lineage— maybe, counts in the land of their birth ; elderly persons of the softer sex in motley toilettes, in whom the softness has become barely recognisable, with whom one almost associates the notion of a snuffbox ; damsels in spectacles, who, if they do time-work, spend unconscionably too large a share of the day in mild flirtations with picturesquely pallid and *négligé* young men, which relieve the pervading silence with a sort of *sotto-voce* buzz. If one had the means of forming these and the rest to be found in the Rotunda any given morning into a procession, what spectacle stranger ?—and if one could get at the story of the Thousand and One Readers, it might have its instructive and amusing side. Ah me ! it would have its mournful and tragic.

I have now and then used the Medal and Print rooms, and have always met with the utmost consideration. The late Keeper of the Prints told me a curious anecdote about the *Temptation* by Dürer. The Museum example was very fine ; but a gentleman called one day, asked to see it, and said that he had a better one, he thought. Would they like to look at his ? Of course, Mr. Reid was incredulous, and replied that they would. The owner brought it shortly after ; it completely eclipsed the one in the national collection, and Mr. Edwards presented it. They never heard a word more about him, except that that was his name.

Dr. Gray, of the Natural History Section, received Du Chaillu, the African explorer, on his visit to London and the Museum, and, there being some scepticism at the time as to the truth of the writer's account of the gorilla, and Gray seeming to share the prevailing doubts, Du Chaillu expressed his disapprobation by spitting in his face. It was a brother of Gray who was engaged as an assistant by Sir Richard Phillips, and who is the boy attending the author on the vignette of the title-page of Phillips's *Morning's Walk from London to Kew*, 1817. Gray's brother had also a taste for natural history and botany. He was subsequently secretary at Crockford's.

The shabbiest tricks are played by persons frequenting the Reading Room, as no one will be surprised to hear who has studied the physiognomy and costume of many of those admitted. Bullen shewed me one day a volume of one of the Quarterlies with several pages cut out by a student, who had presumably a commission to copy the matter. Another time both copies of Halliwell's *Dictionary of Old Plays* had been simultaneously stolen. Even the leaden weights disappeared. A detective was placed at a reading-desk to reconnoitre; he lost his great-coat, which he had laid on the back of his chair; and the thief was not detected till a second spy was stationed in the roof to watch for him.

Mr. Gladstone used to hold that the employments here were of such an exceptionally agreeable and compensating character that gentlemen should be readily found willing to fulfil them on the most reasonable terms—a proposition which might be equally applicable to the staff of a pastrycook or a dealer in sweetmeats. The result—not a very satisfactory or proud one—is seen in the notorious resort to outside work for publishers, periodicals, and auctioneers. Certain members of the staff, in fact, go so far as to look upon given topics as their freehold, and resent personally, or through their friends on the press, the interference of unofficial workers, as if some provinces of research were a sort of literary Tom Tiddler's Ground. This seems to be an injustice and an anomaly calling for rectification.

The scheme for insulating the building as a means of security against fire, and of obtaining additional space by the demolition of all the surrounding houses, is all very well; but a still more immediate danger is the residential principle and privilege, which involve a peculiar risk, owing to the exemption of the officials in their homes from the eye of any night-watcher; and at the South Kensington establishment it is even worse, as certain members of the staff have open fires in their private rooms, and smoke there, as they do in some of the Oxford and Cambridge college libraries. There will be a terrible catastrophe one day, and has not Parliament given £200,000 to remove, as we were told, the mischief? In 1865 there was a fire in the Binding Department, but the loss was happily less serious than it might have been.

There are schools of Publishers as there are of Art and Cookery. We get the old-established respectable houses, which deal only with certain classes of books and people, and correspond with you on quarto paper. There are the specialists, who limit themselves to subjects or topics. There are the opportunists, who seek to profit by every ephemeral taste and fancy which takes the public captive. There are the book-drapers, who treat literature like any other dry goods, and sell it in gross, as if it were cheese or sugar. They will deliver you a hundredweight of Dickens, or shoot down into your shop-cellar half a ton of 'assorted' sixpenny ware.

Someone was speaking to me of a publisher who suffered imprisonment for issuing immoral French books in an English dress, and was reminding me of the applicability of Macaulay's criticism on the spasmodic virtue of the British public and authorities; for almost before the prisoner's term had expired, another house brought out the same things without comment. It is not what is done, but the doer and the manner of doing.

'One man may steal a horse, and another may not look over the hedge.' A person is prosecuted and imprisoned, no doubt deservedly, for publishing objectionable books. The auctioneers issue catalogues giving full and appetizing titles of others ten times as bad, and offer them for public inspection and sale with impunity.

There comes into my hands opportunely for recommendation as a model and *beau idéal* of what I mean, a 'Catalogue of Valuable and Rare Books and Manuscripts, Consisting of Duplicates from the Library of the Right Hon. the Earl of Crawford, and A Selection from the French Library of the Right Hon. Lord Ashburton.' The singular and unusual part is that one does not know where the first Right Honourable ends, and the second Right Honourable begins. Mayhap, one has bought up the other ; but however that may be, the foreign element is a fairly representative one as regards the most licentious literature of all periods, with notes drawing attention to the character of the lot in many instances, where there might be a doubt in the mind of the bidder.

It is a great mistake to suppose that improper literature is mostly sold in such places as Holywell Street. The West End is the actual centre. The residual stock of the late Mr. —— was said at the time to have been secured *en bloc* for a foreign market ; *mais on ne sait pas toujours.* I was told (to be sure, not by a person of unimpeachable veracity) that those items in a celebrated Yorkshire library which were too bad for the auctioneers were not thrown into the moat, as generally believed, but secured by him by a *coup de main*, of which he was justly proud.

Two men whom I should select as, in their respective lines, models of integrity in the publishing way are Mr. William Reeves and the late Mr. John Russell-Smith ; but the latter was less liberal than Reeves. Certain houses, of course, carry loyally out any undertaking into which they may enter, and their word is as good as their bond. But there are others with which it is an absolute courtship of misery to deal, even if you hold them in the clauses of an agreement as in a vice.

The late George Routledge was a very frank and unpretending North-Countryman, though latterly rather fond of letting one know that he was a justice of the peace. The last time I saw him was at his place of business at the back of Ludgate Hill. He mentioned to me that he had been served with a notice of action by a lady for some remark about her in a book recently published by him, but which he had not examined, or even seen, prior to issue; and he also told me that he had just had an indignant letter from some clergyman for reprinting Voltaire's *Candide* in Professor Morley's cheap series. I took the occasion to inquire where the Professor saw the affinity between *Candide* and Johnson's *Rasselas*, which he had put together in a volume on that account.

When I first remember Routledge, he was in Soho Square, where Chidley had been before him, and where Russell-Smith succeeded him. My old acquaintance, Mr. Henry Pyne, late Assistant Tithe Commissioner, used to refer sometimes to him, for Routledge had been at first, by the interest of the Member for Carlisle, a clerk in that office, and occasionally his first wife would bring him his dinner in a pocket handkerchief.

I was in lodgings in Buckingham Street, Strand,

in 1862, when I was informed that a gentleman wished to see me. I went down, and found Routledge on the stairs. He had come personally to ask me to prepare a second edition of a small fugitive volume, which he had published in 1858, on British Columbia, and which I had with my excellent father's help compiled in the first *furor* of the emigration movement in two or three weeks.

The firm of Chapman and Hall, like many others, traded, to a certain extent, for many years under a *nom de guerre*, one of the partners being non-existent. Somebody once asked Frederick Chapman of whom the house really consisted. 'I'm Chapman,' he replied, 'and that's *Hall.*'

Some memorabilia about the late Henry George Bohn are already in print. Many others might, no doubt, be collected.

I was told that at a wine sale Bohn insisted on tasting all the samples, and became incapable of looking after himself; they had to carry him down and put him into a cab. He found the next morning that he had bought two hundred dozen.

He was very fond of boasting about being invited to great folks' houses. He told a *confrère* one day that it was a very singular thing that at Lord ———'s there was no fish. 'Ah,' rejoined the other wickedly, 'perhaps they ate it all upstairs.'

It was an edifying spectacle to watch Henry Bohn and his brother John verbally sparring across the table at Sotheby's. I was not present when E. is reported to have openly told Bohn that some statement was the biggest lie which he had ever uttered, and that it must by consequence be a big one.

As regarded the relations between Bohn and his sisters, he used to insist that he had made them handsome proposals, which they rejected. They came into Russell-Smith's, in Soho Square, when I was there one day, to beg him to give them sixpence.

The predecessor of John Bohn as principal cataloguer at Sotheby's was Bryant, of Wardour Street, who supplied Dr. Bliss and other collectors of a bygone generation with some of their treasures, and who had a hand in the new edition of Lowndes. Bryant, who died in 1864, once made this very judicious observation to me—that there were many books which occurred very seldom, and when they did, were worth very little.

The edition of Lowndes which bears the name of H. G. Bohn as the overseer was, in fact, done,

so far as it was done at all, by Bryant, with the
occasional assistance of others. Bohn, when anyone
came to him with a complaint of mistakes in the
book, used always to exclaim, ' Oh, it was that ass
Bryant ' ; but if you went to Bohn, and mentioned
that some particular article was improved, he would
say, ' Ah, yes, I did that myself.'

J. W. Parker, the publisher, speaking of books
which paid, asked F. what book he supposed had
proved most remunerative to him. On F. shaking
his head, Parker said, ' Why, I gave my daughter
£25, thirty-six years ago, to compile a little selection of hymns and psalms, and last year it brought in
£200 profit, and it has never been worthless to me.'

There are here and there instances where a firm,
enjoying an independent fortune, consults its own
pleasure or caprice in its selection of authors and its
espousal of schemes, sometimes quite irrespectively
of the financial question ; it is Maecenas in the
counting-house ; and modern *littérateurs*, even if
they are not Horaces, might be apt to find a better
account in paying their addresses to such than to
noble lords or royal highnesses, who have nowadays, as a rule, very different fish to fry.

If ever there should come a time when publisher
and author act in loyal and mutually satisfactory

co-operation, it would be the Golden Age indeed—
the lion lying down with the lamb, although which
is the lion and which is the lamb in this case I
forbear to pronounce.

‘ Repairs neatly executed ’ might be a good title
for a paper on the well-known literary contingency,
where a famous author, such as ——, or ——, or
——, is just the least weak in his information, his
grammar, and his points, and where some obscure
person in the background is engaged by the publisher with his privity and at his cost to make the
otherwise *chef d'œuvre* exactly suitable for public
use and view. The odd part comes when the
famous author carries about his volume, as a sample
of his cunning and style, and perhaps receives a
commission to execute a second masterpiece.

It can only yield astonishment to general readers
to hear that there have long been individuals whose
most lucrative employment consists in ‘ finishing,’ to
use bookbinders' parlance, works which have been
‘ forwarded ’ by the author. The name of the
former seldom appears, and it is often the case—
always, where it happens that anyone has much
credit to lose—that it is to the reviser's advantage
that he should preserve a strict *incognito*. For
here the exceptions, where a manuscript emerges

from this process a source of gratifying surprise to the parties concerned, are so rare, that they prove the rule indeed. Every season witnesses the sale of hundredweights of written matter by auction or otherwise, which has been carefully prepared by the departed author with a view to publication by Murray or Longman, and which is at last *en route* to that *Alma Mater* of Scriblerus, the omnivorous paper-mill.

George Willis the bookseller, who recently passed away at an advanced age, and who is associated in the mind of the more modern collector with the late firm of Willis and Sotheran, was an Essex man. My father told me that he recollected him as a stall-keeper in Prince's Street, Coventry Street, and his wife attended to the stall while he went in quest of stock. He used to say that his main idea was to buy for a shilling and sell for eighteen-pence—very good interest, but only six-pence. Mrs. Willis has been seen at her husband's stall with an umbrella over her head.

I believe that he subsequently occupied the corner shop where Noah Huett was in my time—originally small premises, which Huett enlarged. Then he went to the Piazza in Covent Garden, where he failed. But he was a man of persevering character and commercial aptitude, and during the time that he was in partnership with Mr. Sotheran completely recovered his position. Willis and Sotheran's General Catalogue for 1862 long remained a standard work of reference.

I personally remember Willis as a very pleasant, courteous, and intelligent man of business, and his *Current Notes*—a sort of illustrated *Notes and Queries*—is a favourite book with many. He joined his sons in the card-making way, and, as I heard, lost a good deal of the money which he had taken out of the concern in the Strand.

I owed to Willis a rather curious experience. He introduced me, about 1865, to a member of the Society of Friends, a former neighbour of his at Reigate, and an eminent photographer, who, having executed a series of views in Egypt, desired to publish the work *with a poetical letter-press in the old spelling*. I agreed to revise this for him, and after some delay the first instalment arrived, was put as far as possible into form in a couple of hours, and was despatched home. Hearing no more for some time, I dropped the poetical photographer a civil reminder, and was then apprised that he had abandoned the project. But he kept his engagement with me. It was £25 not very hardly earned.

I have sometimes speculated whether he would have printed the text in Gothic letter. Good, as Jerrold once said of a weak play shown to him, was not the word for his literary offspring.

Baldock in Holborn I have already introduced. Not far from him were the places of business of Petheram and Newman. The former had an assistant named John Hotten, a Cornish man, better known as John *Camden* Hotten, who, before he set up in business in London, spent some time in the United States at Petheram's suggestion. Newman was a strictly upright man, and dealt in topography. He found in his later days, when his health failed, a valuable friend in Leonard Hartley the collector, at whose house in Hastings he died.

A rather good story was once told about Newman. There was a sale at Sotheby's just in his way, rich in the very class of books which he wanted for Hartley and other clients. He was not an habitual attendant at the auctions, but on this occasion he was there in person, and bade for every lot. A whisper circulated that it was a *rig*, that it was Newman's property. 'Let him have his stuff back again,' said his *confrères*. But it turned out that they were mistaken ; and some of them had to go round to him the next day and give him his own price for what they required, or find that the items were bought on commission for common acquaintances.

Mr. F. S. Ellis used to say that the meaning of the term *confrère* in the book trade was a man who would cut your throat, if he could do it with impunity.

Another person of whom I bought a few curious books was Elkins. He had an odd little shop at the top of Lombard Street, about the size of a rabbit-hutch, into which, as into a spider's web, he was wont to inveigle the unwary. Let it pass. He did me no great harm. He laid his net, I conceive, for the City groundlings, who are still affectionately nursed by Jew and Gentile, planting on the route from railway terminus to counting-house triumphs of pictorial art. Occasionally these interesting characters reside on a line, and enter into conversation with their fellow-passengers, who are quite casually apprised that certain masterpieces of the Leadenhall or Cornhill school are to be seen at such and such an address. But the old book-shop has migrated westward.

The book-buyer is not exempt from the danger which besets all other classes of enthusiasts for what strikes the fancy as rare or curious, or both. It is by no means invariably the case that an inexperienced collector can safely place himself in the hands of an occupier of ordinary business premises ; he will probably have to pay for his education before he can trust to his own judgment ; but the back-parlour, where property is *introduced* to gentlemen of means by enterprising merchants, whose affairs are entirely conducted by correspondence, is the rock to be avoided. It is a type of the confidence-trick.

E. H. was laughing at that almost effete phantasma, the *édition de luxe;* and he said that he thought, if the craze had gone much farther, it would have been necessary for an intending purchaser, before his book came home, to hire a paddock. The only kind of work suitable for such treatment is what may be termed literary *bijouterie.*

Another unwholesome development is the Illustrated Copy. This first arose from the Grangerite movement, and, the trade having accumulated a vast number of portraits and views, every book which contained copious references to persons and places became a convenient and remunerative shoot for these productions, intrinsically and independently unsaleable. The conception has been worn well-nigh threadbare, but there must be up and down the world cartloads of this species of manufacture, since it was found to be so profitable, and appealed to so many who were not critical judges of prints or drawings.

There is not one book of this character in ten thousand which is unimpeachable throughout. To obtain certain material it is necessary to wait perhaps months, perhaps years ; and the commercial illustrator cannot afford to lock up his capital too long. It is only in those excessively rare cases where a private connoisseur of fortune engages in the undertaking that a creditable result accrues. But, from the increasing scarcity of fine early prints in the right state, the pursuit has become almost hopelessly difficult. Even the few examples purchased by the late Mr. Huth struck me as very unequal and unsatisfying.

I have arrived at the conclusion of my somewhat peculiar and somewhat difficult undertaking, of which the scope and dimensions exceed by much my original estimate. But there was a strong temptation throughout, under the different sections into which I have divided the work, to bring forward as I proceeded, details only occurring to my memory by association or accident ; and I sincerely and respectfully hope that these may not too often strike my readers either as trivial or obnoxious. It becomes rather hard, when one has to deal with a vast number of names, and with infinite matters of fact, opinion, and taste, to draw the line with absolute precision, and to avoid in all cases personalities affecting the departed, or expressions of feeling which may prove unpalatable to a few still among us. There has not been on my part any desire to give wilful or wanton umbrage to anyone. I think that my references to living contemporaries, as well as to those whom we have lost, are, as a rule, neither unjust nor intemperate ; and my farewell wish is, that my volumes may, on the whole, be treated as a not unacceptable addition to the class to which they belong.

THE END.

BILLING AND SONS, PRINTERS, GUILDFORD.